Capitalism's
Eye

Capitalism's
Eye

KEVIN HETHERINGTON

Cultural Spaces of the Commodity

Routledge
Taylor & Francis Group
New York   London

Published in 2007.

Reprinted by permission of the publisher from THE ARCADES PROJECT by Walter Benjamin, translated by Howard Eiland and Kevin McLaughlin, pp. 7, 9, 10,13,14,19,20,25,26,212,405,406,407,409,415,463,669. Cambridge, MA: The Belknap Press of Harvard University Press, Copyright (c)1999 by the President and Fellows of Harvard College. Originally published as Das Passagen-Werk, edited by Rolf Teidman, Copyright (c)1982 by Suhrkamp Verlag.

Routledge
Taylor & Francis Group
270 Madison Avenue
New York, NY 10016

Routledge
Taylor & Francis Group
2 Park Square
Milton Park, Abingdon
Oxon OX14 4RN

© 2008 by Taylor & Francis Group, LLC
Routledge is an imprint of Taylor & Francis Group, an Informa business

Printed in the United States of America on acid-free paper
10 9 8 7 6 5 4 3 2 1

International Standard Book Number-13: 978-0-415-93341-4 (Softcover) 978-0-415-93340-7 (Hardcover)

Library of Congress Cataloging-in-Publication Data

Hetherington, Kevin.
    Capitalism's eye : cultural spaces of the commodity / Kevin Hetherington.
        p. cm. -- (Cultural spaces)
    ISBN 978-0-415-93341-4 (pbk.) -- ISBN 978-0-415-93340-7 (cloth)
    1. Consumption (Economics)--United States--History. 2. Consumption (Economics)--Europe--History. 3. Consumer behavior--United States. 4. Consumer behavior--Europe. 5. Senses and sensation. I. Title.

HC110.C6H48 2007   1006556388
330.12'2--dc22   2006102735

Visit the Taylor & Francis Web site at
http://www.taylorandfrancis.com

and the Routledge Web site at
http://www.routledge.com

For Linda

the Haussmannization of Paris, has been seen as the beginnings of a society of the spectacle/fetishism that is believed to describe the character of contemporary consumer societies (see Clark 1984; Harvey 1985; Richards 1991). My question is to ask whether that is indeed the case.

The following three chapters look more closely at the development of this idea of spectacle out of theories of commodity fetishism that has recently become hegemonic within studies of consumer culture. The chapters do not present the arguments in chronological order. In Chapter 2 I look at the development of the concept of spectacle in Guy Debord's now famous formulation that is most in use today and find it to be wanting. However, rather than seeking to put him to death, I acknowledge that his use of the practice of détournement has something to teach us in our approach to critique. In Chapter 3 I go back to Marx and look more closely at what he says about the phantasmagoric character of commodity fetishism. I am particularly interested in looking at some of the assumptions that he makes about subjectivity in his analysis—what I call his production view of the subject (see also Munro 1996). Likewise, Chapter 4 traces the use of the term phantasmagoria through the work of Lukacs and Adorno and finds it to be wanting before turning to Benjamin's more ambiguous and, I would argue, more fruitful approach to the whole question of fetishism, which begins to open up for us the possibility of developing an understanding of a consumption rather than production view of subjectivity.

There are three further "old grounds" that I then turn to, cultural space in which we might explore this consumption view of the subject and its relationship to the fetishistic and phantasmagoric. In Chapter 5 I look at the departments store as a space of acquisition of commodities and develop this idea of a consumption view of the subject through the figure of the flâneuse. Her paradoxical and uncertain position within that paradoxical space is what brings her and not the better-known male counterpart, the figure of the flâneur, to the fore. Similarly, Chapter 6 on the domestic interior and its concerns with interiority and the use of commodities, notably their neutralization as unstable things from the market in a seemingly stable space of moral certainty, focuses on the figure of the housewife as a blank and paradoxical figure for the consuming subject around whom the conditions of uncertainty associated with capitalism are stabilized and placed within a moral order of displaced meanings (see McCracken 1988). Finally, I look at the issue of disposal of commodities in the space of the museum. While the collector is a figure for the consuming subject in this space, it is the status of the object and its paradoxical position as both artifact/commodity that interests me most here and tells us something about the relationship between the experiences of the human subject, consumer culture, and history.

Across all of these chapters my argument develops to suggest that we should consider the consuming subject as someone who *takes possession* of the commodity within these spaces of the fetishism of the commodity. This is a theme touched on briefly in Benjamin's *The Arcades Project* in relation to the collector (1999b, 9) and is one that I seek to develop more generally here. Most theories of commodity fetishism/phantasmagoria/spectacle see us possessed by the commodity. That may to some extent be the case, but what it does not recognize is our own activity in appropriating the figure of the fetish within our own consumer subjectivity and practices. To treat this being possessed/taking possession as a more complex and paradoxical situation gives us a different outlook on consumer culture, providing us with, if you like, a reason for going over old ground and showing it to be, if not ungrounded, then at least more folded and complex than we might once have thought.

In the process of researching and writing this book I would like to thank the following people with whom I have discussed ideas, responded to criticisms, kindly been given new insights, presented draft chapters, received generous comments, and sought advice: John Law, Rolland Munro, Anne Cronin, John Urry, Dick Pels, Gordon Fyfe, Beatriz Jaguaribe, Maria Isabel Mendes D'Almeida, Enrique Larreta, Frederick Vandenberghe, Bob Jessop, Tony Bennett, Jackie Stacey, Sharon Zukin, John Holm, and Glen McIver. I would like to thank members of the Material Culture and Consumption Group at Lancaster University for their comments on presentations of various chapters, my colleagues at the Open University, and also those at conferences and seminars who heard me give versions of some of these chapters and made helpful comments. All the usual disclaimers about me being solely responsible for this work apply. I would like to single out Dave McBride for thanks for commissioning the work and for his patience, perseverance, and encouragement during its delayed production and delivery. Many thanks also go to Steven Rutter, Anne Horowitz, and Michael Davidson at Routledge for seeing the book through the production process. Above all, I would like to thank Linda for all her love, support, and encouragement during the writing of this book. It is dedicated to her.

Chapter 7 draws on material that has been published previously:

The section on *Modernity, Museums and the Viewed Object* is a revised version of material that first appeared in 'From Blindness to Blindness: Museums, Heterogeneity and the Subject.' in John Law and John hassard (eds) (1999) *Actor-Network Theory and After*, Oxford: Blackwell/The Sociological Review. pp. 51–73. I am grateful to The Sociological Review for permission to re-print it here.

The Section on *Commodities, Disposal and the Museum* is a revised version of material that first appeared in 'Second-handedness: Consumption, Disposal and Absent Presence' *Environment and Planning D: Society and Space* 22: 157–173. I am grateful to the publishers Pion for permission to re-print it here.

Chapter One
Relations of Production under Glass

You have most of you probably heard of the careful and economical critic, who proposed to reduce the extravagance of the wish of the impatient separated lovers, that the gods would annihilate space and time; and who remarked that it would answer the end desired if one of the two were annihilated. By annihilating the space which separates different nations, we produce a spectacle in which is also annihilated the time which separates one stage of a nation's progress from another.

William Whewell, Master of Trinity College, Inaugural Lecture to the Council of the Society of Arts, November 26, 1851, page 6

I find that I am "used up" by the Exhibition. I don't say there is nothing in it: there is too much. I have only been twice, so many things bewilder one. I have a natural horror of sights, and the fusion of so many sights in one, has not decreased it. I am not sure that I have seen anything but the fountain and the amazon.

Charles Dickens, diary entry, July 25, 1851[1]

THE CRYSTAL PALACE

Over six million people visited the Great Exhibition in 1851, or, to use the exact Victorian statistics collected at the time, 6,063,986 people (Timbs 1851, 341). It was held in Hyde Park in central London from May to October in that year in Joseph Paxton's Crystal Palace. Intended as a temporary structure in glass and iron, and constructed from Paxton's proverbial back-of-an-envelope sketch (actually drawn on blotting paper) by the Birmingham-based company Fox and Henderson, the building has since become iconic of nineteenth-century architectural design and the beginnings of modern consumer culture (see Giedion 1941; Chadwick 1961;

Benjamin 1973a, 1999a; Berman 1982; Sennett 1987; Richards 1991; McKean 1994; A. Miller 1995). With the modernity of its iron frame resplendent in plate glass—a product only introduced in the 1830s and made economical by the repeal of the glass tax in 1845—and with almost a million exhibits of the machinery and decorative arts of the day on display inside, here, surely, was a nascent example of a *society of the spectacle*—a mode of representing social relations through a fetishized visual naturalizing of the capitalist mode of production (Debord 1977; Richards 1991). Certainly it was a spectacle. There can be no doubt about that. But how we understand spectacle and what the implications of that term might be for our broader understanding of the emergence of a modern consumer culture during the nineteenth century shouldn't be taken for granted at the outset by simply invoking the word *spectacle*.[2] Rather, it needs to be put to the question.

If the building itself has remained iconic of that time, the reception given to what was exhibited inside has largely been much less favorable. The many machines on display, no doubt important in their day, have long since been confined to the stack of engineering history. But the spectre of mid-nineteenth-century decorative arts still has the capacity to haunt those with any aesthetic sensitivity. While there have in recent years been attempts to re-evaluate Victorian design and decorative arts in a more positive light, the overly ornate contents (kitsch at times; see Olalquiaga 1999, 30ff) have remained a subject of derision largely because of their apparent poor design qualities and seemingly confused aesthetic principles. The criticism was made at the time and was only to increase during the twentieth century (see notably Pevsner 1936, 1951). Seen variously as a debasement of the truth to materials by machinofacture; a masking of the revealed construction found in quality craft-made products; stylistically derivative, eclectic, or insufficiently modern, the material cultural contents of the Great Exhibition have been criticized as illustrating all that is bad about Victorian design values.[3] In a sense, "great building, lousy contents" has been the judgment of history on the Great Exhibition.

Nonetheless, the exhibition captivated the imagination of the British population through those summer months and became the model for the many Universal Expositions held across the world for at least half a century thereafter (Greenhalgh 1988). Only the Eiffel Tower, another supposedly temporary structure, from the Paris 1889 Exposition and the Paris Exposition of 1900 with its Art Nouveau aesthetic, comes anywhere near to rivaling it in terms of cultural influence and iconic significance.[4] In Britain, its cultural importance remained long after the Crystal Palace, relocated to Sydenham in south London after the exhibition, burned down in 1936. Such was its status that the hundredth anniversary of the event was marked by a major exhibition in its honor, the Festival of Britain, which attempted to use it to re-invoke the optimism in national achievement and Empire of that earlier event at a time when Britain, in a period of postwar austerity and uncertainty of its status as a nation, was undergoing reconstruction.[5]

The overall number of visitors is a staggering one for the time, equivalent to one-third of the British population, indicative not only of the public interest in such a spectacle but also of the effectiveness of the media hype surrounding the event—notably expressed though the media of illustrated journals and newspapers as well as through local meetings held all over the country in the lead-up to its opening. Of overwhelming significance to the success of the exhibition was the facility provided by the railway as a means of getting both people and the exhibits themselves to the exhibition at a reasonable price.[6] The Great Exhibition was a hugely successful enterprise in the Victorian ideas of public mobility and public access (Schivelbusch 1986; Davis 1999; Auerbach 1999; Leapman 2001).[7]

Of course, quite a number of those visitors came from overseas too. Some of the more notable ones (from home as well as abroad) published accounts of their experiences and recollections (see, for instance, Berlyn 1851; Greeley 1851; Redding 1851; Thompson 1852). Many, particularly the better off and well educated, like Charles Dickens (himself a member of a committee set up to look into how working-class people might be attracted to the exhibition), visited the exhibition more than once. Repeat visits were a common feature among the aristocracy and the middle classes in general. Indeed, it became a key event in the season of that year, along with the Derby and many fashionable parties and balls. Queen Victoria visited it on numerous occasions and was delighted by what she saw as her husband Prince Albert's achievement in promoting the project sometimes against the wishes of a grudging nation.

At the outset, prices for admission were high: by invitation only on the day of the royal opening (although the captain of a junk moored on the Thames did manage to get in uninvited and was wrongly presented to the queen as the Chinese ambassador); then £1 on the second and third days to give the aristocracy an unimpeded view; dropping to 5s (shillings) on the fourth day; then 2s 6d (pence) on Fridays and 5s on Saturdays thereafter. Beginning on May 22 the famous "shilling days" were introduced (Monday to Thursday), the low price intended to attract the working-class visitor (see Stephenson 1851, 50; Timbs 1851; see also Short 1966; Leapman 2001). These were extremely popular and the number of visitors steadily rose throughout the summer, in large part because of the railways and the cheap admission price, with the last week being the busiest week of all when almost half a million attended (Timbs 1851, 341). This concern with access extended further than to the working class. Special attention was also given to those with disabilities, notably disabled soldiers, who were admitted in their carriages on Saturday mornings, a higher price day, but when the crowds were smaller (Thompson 1852, 577).

To accommodate the public, the company of Schweppes was given the contract to provide refreshments for visitors once inside the exhibition (no alcohol available, only ginger beer and lemonade as well as tea, coffee, sandwiches, ices, and buns), though people often brought their own. Many complained about the high prices charged and about the poor quality of the food available and chose to picnic in the surrounding Hyde Park instead (Leapman 2001). Restroom facilities were available, and, for a small charge, one could deposit one's umbrella in the cloakroom for the duration of a visit. Indeed, £881 16s 10d of the total takings of £505,107 5s 7d came though this source; a total figure well in excess of the £170,743 total exhibition costs (Timbs 1851, 342).

The streets surrounding the exhibition were filled with crowds, carriages, and omnibuses for the duration of the exhibition. Many visitors, often in groups from towns and villages across the country, arrived by train, often on excursions arranged by the Leicester-based company Thomas Cook (set up in 1841), who largely made their reputation as a travel agency off the back of this event (Brendon 1991, 55ff). Many of these tours must have had something of a parochial feel about them, of an old world entering, tentatively and for the first time, the modern age. Most seem to have been led by the parish priest, a symbol of the old pastoral order. There are reports of these somewhat bewildered and awestruck parties seen wandering through the exhibition on what, for many, may well have been their first visit to the metropolis (Leapman 2001). Often the group would have saved money all year through a locally established subscription society in order to raise funds to pay for their excursion; a return train ticket from York to London third class, for instance, cost 5s.[8]

Very few were disappointed with what they saw: the machinery sections and domestic appliances were a particular attraction for working-class visitors—many were agricultural workers or factory employees just beginning to see the mechanization of work around them for the first time (Short 1966). The middle classes, predictably perhaps, were more interested in the vast array of decorative arts and sculpture on display, with the anticipated improving effects of this art on moral character often noted.[9] Yet despite the popularity of the event, the trope of bewilderment at such an abundance of things and its spatial ordering logic remained prominent as a response.

The exhibition was full of things, full of the material culture of industrial capitalism. Decorative arts, sculpture, machines, appliances, gadgets… and visitors did not quite know what to make of it all (Richards 1991). Enthralled by the spectacle, they found it all a little overwhelming to take in. As American visitor Horace Greeley, himself one of the knowledgeable jurors for the exhibition, put it:

> I believe I have thus far been among the most industrious visitors, and yet I have not yet even glanced at one half the articles exhibited, while I have only glanced at most of those I have seen. (1851, 32–33)

He goes on, observing other visitors' distracted reception of what they saw:

> Of a million who come to gaze, only a hundred thousand may come with any clear idea of profiting by the show. (1851, 116)

The intention for the exhibition was clear enough—a comparative international survey of industrial production at that time, allowing one nation to compare itself with another and with a sense of competition, progress, and a spirit of free trade emerging out of that spectacle. The British organizers assumed that in most classes of artifact they, as the most advanced industrial nation, would be seen to be the best, except, perhaps, in some areas of high taste and fine art where it was acknowledged that France still led the way in fashion (although it was noted that America was fast catching up in terms of more everyday, useful items, which caused some consternation and anxiety among the British organizers and which sometimes led, in the popular literature, to the castigation of U.S. industry on the grounds that it was a product of a nation that had relied on slavery for its growth). Where the British were deemed not to be the best, they felt the opportunity was there to learn and to improve. This sense of improvement relates to character—civilizational, national, and also individual—as well as to design and production techniques. Exposing people to the improvements of industry, it was hoped, might have a civilizing and improving effect on them, whether they be national leaders, manufacturers, designers, members of the educated middle class, or factory hands (on the governance role of nineteenth-century museums in this respect, see Bennett 1995; on the cultural significance of character to nineteenth-century society, see Susman 2003).

Improvement is a term central to nineteenth-century discourse about the opportunities afforded to nation-states by industrialization and was clearly apparent in the ethos that lay behind the exhibition as well as in the organization of its displays.[10] *To improve* was to mean *to become better over time*. This notion of improvement, and its associations with the idea of progress, now seems to us as so self-evident and natural that it is barely worth a comment but it is important to recognize that improvement was not always understood in this way. A century earlier the term meant something else; it was part of a different discourse—one more concerned with spatial than with temporal development (Hetherington 2001). The change to this later discourse emerges in different contexts from around 1740, but it was still developing in 1851 and this had important implications for the Great Exhibition.

In the late seventeenth and early eighteenth centuries, at the time when writers such as Daniel Defoe (1971) and Celia Fiennes (1949) set out on their travels to survey the manufacturing practices and productivity of Britain, improvement—a commonly used term—was typically seen as part of a discourse about space rather than about time. Economic and industrial surveys up until about 1740 were largely undertaken to look at how things could be improved upon in comparison with other places but without a direct sense of temporal progress being involved. The discourse was spatial in how it understood improvement.[11] The model was something like this: field A was better at producing wheat than field B, so, B should be improved to be more like A. One improved the land by doing work to it (often by draining it). Machinery and later the division of labour were also enrolled as potential sources of improvement to manufacturing in this respect. In effect, one looked at how a place, or an object, could be improved through work. The sense of improvement as a temporal trope, although already a feature of the Protestant discourse on moral character during the seventeenth century, only began to be associated with the idea of society more generally in the later eighteenth century as a key Enlightenment theme, first in the writings on progress by Vico and then more significantly, perhaps, in the work of Adam Ferguson (1966) and also in the writings of the art critic Johan Winckelmann (1972; for a discussion of the history of the idea of progress, see Spadafora 1990).

A key place where it gets articulated is in the large number of industrial surveys undertaken in the late eighteenth century from around 1770. These surveys increasingly began to express a confidence in temporal rather than spatial improvement after about that date (see Hetherington 2001; also Briggs 1959).[12] The industrial exhibitions that were held during the early decades of the nineteenth century were part of this surveying movement, and they culminate in the Great Exhibition (Luckhurst 1951). These are important sites that helped to establish this discourse of societal improvement over time. By 1851 such an idea had become central to the discourse of industrialism—it was a theme that early French sociological writers like Henri Saint-Simon and Auguste Comte (themselves drawing on early nineteenth-century British social reformers like Jeremy Bentham and Robert Owen) were also to stress in their influential understanding of the progressive character of industrial society (Kumar 1978). By the mid-nineteenth century, therefore, improvement had become part of a temporal discourse surrounding the changing character of production, yet its effects were still emerging and consequences were being worked through. As an industrial survey, the Great Exhibition illustrates the consolidation of this discursive shift in material and spatial form. The question such a discourse posed was, "How to display that view of industrial improvement as progress to the public in a way they would understand?"

Certainly the temporal discourse of improvement was explicit and clear in the writing surrounding the exhibition. For example, William Whewell, the master of Trinity College Cambridge, who had been involved with the exhibition, put it clearly in his inaugural lecture to the Society of Arts soon after the event had finished:

> In the useful and ornamental arts nations are always going forwards, from stage to stage. Different nations have reached different stages of progress, and their different stages are seen at once, in the aspect which they have at this moment in the magical glass, which the enchanters of our time have made rise out of the ground like an exhalation. (1851, 6)

However, such ideas were not so clearly expressed in the organization of the exhibition itself. The organizers chose to arrange the space to capture the totality of forms of improvement along classificatory lines rather than through any sense of a linear temporal narrative. In a manner, in part more in keeping with early eighteenth-century thinking, they thought that a simple spatial comparison of how one thing made in country A could be shown alongside a lesser example made in country B would reveal not only how things were being done better in country A but also how A was *temporally* more advanced as a nation than B as a consequence. A complex process of jury-awarded prizes within each class of object was established to try and legitimize this process. But through introducing a degree of time/space complexity into the representation of improvement in the layout, classification, and cataloging, the exhibition was, in effect, engaged in different modes of ordering at the same time. It introduced complexity and paradox where it had sought to convey simplicity and clarity. What is perhaps most significant is the emergence of a new form of consumer spectacle associated with issues of novelty and progress in the midst of this uncertain process of representing progress in production.

Things shimmered with expectant possibility for the organizers of the Great Exhibition even though there was much that was solid and weighty in aesthetics, construction, and design. The modernity of the production techniques was not yet reflected in its own aesthetic—what we have since come to call modernism. The eclecticism, the ornate use of decoration, the kitsch and the sentimental artifacts on display were make-do precursors to modernism, a bricolage attempt to use a mixture of styles from the past to convey a sense of novelty and improvement rather than invent something genuinely novel and original to express this optimism in the future. The designers of the time did not have the language of modernism. The discourse of the modern in the mid-nineteenth century was still disentangling itself from the eighteenth-century notion of the modern as a means for comparison with the ancient and classical rather than a way of looking to create something new in the future. The values of improvement had yet to attain an appropriate aesthetic expression in 1851.

Nonetheless, if Defoe's writing marks the end of an earlier view of improvement through spatial comparison and the Enlightenment introduces the idea of temporal comparison to that of improvement, then nineteenth-century ideas of improvement, reflected in the Great Exhibition, illustrate a confidence in the ideas that effort and hard work (notably industrial work) would inevitably lead to better things in the future than those found in the past (Smiles 1986). They also believed that this would have positive moral outcomes for both individual character and society. The idea that exposing people to the best art that civilization could produce would have a civilizing effect on them was a prominent Victorian theme (Ruskin 1854; Arnold 1960). And for some (although not Ruskin 1854) it was no longer just the auratic art of earlier civilizations that was called on to perform this role, as had been the case in the late eighteenth century (Winckelmann 1972); the organizers believed that modern, industrial civilization should also be able to achieve these ends on its own terms and through its own forms and that this could be revealed by a survey of its mass-produced industrial products.

Whether all this was clear to the visitors to the exhibition is doubtful. Newspaper reports and writings of the time suggest that a sense of amused or entertained bewilderment at all the improvements on display was the most common sentiment among many visitors. Indeed, not everyone had been charitable about the exhibition in the lead-up to its opening. In the two years prior to 1851 there had been numerous controversies surrounding the planned event. The *Times* blew hot and cold on the exhibition idea (Davis 1999), and several MPs in the protectionist camp were staunch opponents throughout of what they saw as a free trade event. The local wealthy residents of the newly developed area of London known as Kensington surrounding the southern end of the park where the Crystal Palace was situated (near Rotten Row) were appalled at the prospect (Leapman 2001). There were worries about cholera spreading in London as a consequence of the crowds and fears about revolutionary agitators and riots; the events of 1848 across Europe were still fresh in the memory, including the Chartists' activities in England during that year (Cole 1884). There were worries also about the roof leaking or falling in on such a strange modern building, and there was much agonizing over what should happen to the ancient elm trees that stood on the proposed site—itself venerated Crown land. In fact, the transept of the building, a design feature that has done much to help make it such an iconic one of consumer spectacle, subsequently was introduced as an afterthought in order to accommodate these trees!

Even after it opened and was deemed a success, people were still unclear about what to make of it. As one of the most astute observers of his age, Dickens (quoted at the beginning of this chapter) appears at first glance to be right about the Great Exhibition. It was indeed full of things, full of clutter, full of inventions, knick-knacks, farm implements, patented machines that would never see work, and works of art that would end up unloved in provincial museum collections across the country seemingly all jumbled up side by side into one panoramic spectacle. Victorian culture and its spaces of consumption in general—not only the Great Exhibition, but also department stores, parlors, and museums—have come to be understood in this way, as sites of abundance and clutter. Part of our task must be to understand some of the implications of all this.

And yet Dickens was less complimentary in his view than many of the other visitors who went there that July day. The newspapers, in general, report a favorable response. He wanted to imagine the exhibition to be more like an art gallery than a popular spectacle. He wanted it to be a singular, Kantian visual space where individual items rather than classes of things could be displayed for solitary and absorbed contemplation—and to be able to appreciate them clearly he believed one had to see them clearly. He went looking for detail and was horrified by the prospect of the amalgamated totality as a sight. He felt bewildered, overwhelmed, *distracted* by what he saw.

Indeed, one of the leading organizers of the exhibition, Sir Henry Cole, writing his memoirs some 30 years later, also felt the need to acknowledge the overwhelming sense of bewilderment and distraction that many visitors came away with from the exhibition (1884, 197). It was not that people were not used to visual entertainment spectacles; indeed, London had been awash with them since the Restoration in the seventeenth century as the main form of popular entertainment (Altick 1978). What was different with this one was the sense of novelty and complexity in trying to turn the idea of progress itself into a spectacle. In other words, how the displays were organized, what the intended narrative messages were, how it positioned the viewing subject, what the audience reception was, and the relationship between production and consumption were ambiguous and unresolved matters in the Crystal Palace. The tension, above all, was between modes of reception: a desire to promote character and moral improvement through absorbed solitary contemplation on the one hand and the achievement of a spectacle with mass audience distraction appeal on the other.

How the exhibition was organized was one of the key problems for many visitors. The model the organizers adopted for ordering the displays was partly informed by established Aristotelian principles concerning form and partly by a concern for national comparison (A. Miller 1995, 52) in order that the governing trope of improvement might be expressed. Objects, therefore, were grouped both by nation and by the classes of (i) raw materials, (ii) machinery and mechanical inventions, (iii) manufactures, and (iv) sculpture and plastic arts in order to demonstrate improvement within each case. While this was all very tidy in principle, in practice, when all of the accepted items for display were listed by the organizing committees (it seems at times as if there were almost as many of these as there were exhibits), there were many items that did not fit this neat order intended to put improvement on display. The organizers felt the need for a sense of clarity if this sense of improvement was to be demonstrated. To achieve that, they felt the need to dispose of the anomalous; the artifact that didn't fit neatly into any category or that which might fit into more than one. They did this by inventing a further 29 subcategories into which to group all of the artifacts and make them knowable to the curious (Richards 1991, 32).

Of course, orders of classification always remain incomplete. But this incompleteness was not seen to be down to a deficiency of specimens as might have been the case in the past but to a deficiency of classes that made up the display. The fascination with class as an ordering principle is a product of the modern episteme in which species, objects, and groups of people are understood to belong within such totalizing and subdivided ordering regimes. It is this ordering system that was reflected in the Great Exhibition. And yet the sense of being confronted by a bewildering scene of abundance with little order or logic was the outcome for many visitors as was acknowledged by the organizers like Cole. Viewing subjects had to respond to a discourse of improvement that was clear in principle but not yet established epistemologically within a naturalized visual ordering regime.

In addition, bewilderment was also expressed by the proliferation of the many guidebooks and catalogues that were available to the visiting public—an acknowledgment, perhaps, that they needed help in understanding all that was on view. For those who could afford £3 3s, there was the vast *Official, Descriptive and Illustrated Catalogue* (1851), today something of a collectors' item. It was published by Spicer Brothers initially in three volumes with a fourth supplementary volume appearing later and a fifth volume, a *Report of the Juries,* on the prizes awarded to exhibits and exhibitors, appearing the following year. It begins with a pullout plan of the Crystal Palace, a short introductory essay on the history of exhibitions leading up to and culminating in the Great Exhibition, and is followed by a chapter on the construction of the Crystal Palace itself. After that, one finds page after endless page, many of them richly illustrated, some with pullout plans and drawings, describing the details of the hundreds of thousands of varied exhibits to be found in the exhibition. No one could have studied all of them in detail in the manner imagined by the editors in the five short months that the exhibition was open to the public. In each case, the detail is accompanied by some information about the exhibitors but with little further commentary (1851). It is an organized, classified catalogue, but one does not see that. What one sees as one is immersed in reading it is an almost endless list of things that overwhelms the reader just as the exhibition itself seemingly overwhelmed the viewer. One becomes immersed in this panorama, unable to see where it ends if one tries to engage with it in the manner intended—almost like trying to read a telephone directory from cover to cover. Serious contemplation and study is all but impossible. The tendency, far more, is to avoid being overwhelmed by it by *browsing through it in a somewhat distracted manner*. It is this that characterizes the way of seeing constituted by the spectacle of the exhibition in practice.

More selective commentaries on the Great Exhibition were offered by other publications such as special issues of the *Art Journal* (1851), *Illustrated London News* (1851), and *Illustrated Exhibitor* (1851), to name a few of the better-known works. Many visitors, however, chose to buy the cheaper abridged one-volume edition of the catalogue for 10s or one of the many shorter unofficial guides and pamphlets to the exhibition that could be purchased from London booksellers in the surrounding streets. While more limited in scope, these publications also followed the totalizing format of the official catalogue, only were briefer and more selective in what they covered, more attuned to the idea of totality as spectacle. Noteworthy, perhaps, was that there was even a handbook to the Official Catalogue to help one find one's way around its many hundreds of pages (Hunt 1851).[13] The emphasis in this was on the star exhibits, or "lions" of the exhibition, encouraging a selective browsing of the many artifacts and a more concentrated study of the auratic few such as the Koh-i-noor diamond.

It took over a year for educated commentators to begin to make any sense of it all, first through the *Report of the Juries,* the prize-awarding committees for each of the many sections into which the exhibition was organized, and then through numerous publications documenting and highlighting the key exhibits that had been on display (see, for instance, Beard et al. 1852). Only then did a sense of the improvements that had been judged to have been made (or lack of them) emerge.

The outcome of this process was one of bewilderment and distraction. In effect, the organizers wanted to put not just things on display but the category of improvement itself. And yet, for many, improvement was not emergent from the display; rather, abundance was. There were, for example, satirical pamphlets published explicitly lampooning the exhibition for its overabundant presentation of useless objects, confused display principles, hyperbole, and cant. One, *Mr Goggleye's Visit to the Exhibition of National Industry Held in London on the 1st April 1851,* the incorrect date (the exhibition itself was opened on May 1) no doubt a reference to an April Fool's Day joke, written by one "Tim Takemin," shows us that not all were awestruck by the exhibition. Industrial society, reflected in these consumer products, was a society of proliferation and abundance; that is what we can now see from a distance of over a century and a half. Improvement could only be seen from an authorial outside—a view from nowhere of the totality. The subject positioned within this panoramic space, "the visitor," "the consumer" could only but make out an overwhelming abundance of things that surrounded them and could only engage with the exhibition in that manner—on the inside through a creative but local, partial, and situated rather than distant and authorial knowledge (on situated knowledge, see Haraway 1991; Cooper and Law 1995). This was not a matter of choice but how they were positioned or interpellated as viewing subjects.

Notwithstanding this distracted reception, 1851 undeniably marks the emergence of a confidence in improvement as progress and a desire to create a spectacle of it. Yet it also demonstrates a degree of uncertainty about how to express materially and aesthetically that idea of a better future through spectacle. The nature of the exhibits themselves also revealed this. Arguably, Paxton achieved it best with his building—it was an instrument truly suited to the representation of a panoramic totality, an instrument of enclosure—but most of the designers of the artifacts exhibited within were not nearly as successful when judged solely on recognized precepts of aesthetics. To utilize machine-made design features as a capability was though to be enough by many of them as a sign of improvement just as it was to many of the exhibition organizers as well.[14] It showed with confidence what could be done if not what should be done. Out of this emerged a lack of interest with the detail of the example, often paying too little attention to the relationship between form and function in an artifact, replacing it more with a concern for what was represented by the example as part of a reflection of a broader totality of an improving industrial society. It is not so much the quality of the craft that had gone into an object that mattered but more an overwhelming sense of possibility that reflected the scope of industrial manufacture. Uniqueness, craft, and singularity were replaced by the ornament of possibility that was facilitated by the machine's capacity for reproducibility. The aim was to allow that to be compared with the products of other nations rather than any notion of the object as an expression of an ideal form suited to a purpose.

Ideal forms were weighted down, therefore, with elaborate machine-produced ornamentation: Gothic, classical, rococo, eclectic, an illustration of what could be achieved by machine technology as an end in itself. But this eclecticism was not, contrary to Pevsner (1951) and other subsequent critics, just a form of aesthetic confusion. Rather, it was a direct expression of a changing experience of visual consumption—from absorbed contemplation of singular artifacts to distracted interest in the accumulation of a mass of (commodified) things that were now on display before the eye of the capitalist subject.

MR. GOGGLEYES MEETS MR. MONEYBAGS: DISTRACTION AND THE COMMODITY

> I am, by the way, morally convinced that Willich and Co. are hatching an ambitious plan for the revolutionisation of England during the exhibition, although it's equally certain that they won't raise a finger.

Friedrich Engels to Karl Marx, *Undated Letter,* **written around May 6, 1851**[15]

If the environs of Hyde Park resembled something of a tourist bazaar during that summer, the exhibition itself was surprisingly coy on the subject of commerce. It was definitely not a straightforward shop window on the world of consumption as has sometimes been imagined. In fact, the idea of the shop window is really inaugurated by the Great Exhibition and only existed in very limited form before, notably in the glass-roofed arcades of Paris and London (Benjamin 1999a). Certainly it wasn't until the Universal Exposition of 1900 in Paris that such a direct connection was made with the world of shopping when price lists were introduced to world fairs for the first time and a direct acknowledgement of the commodity status of the artifacts on display was made explicit (Richards 1991). Certainly that was not there in 1851, much to the annoyance of a rather curmudgeonly Charles Babbage (1851), who proposed the idea that it should be, as did some of the more entrepreneurial exhibitors. And yet this was a space of the commodity all the same—but a *paradoxical* one.

While not a showroom in the strict sense of being like an upmarket shop where one could browse, view, and buy things, it was more like a warehouse, a storeroom of the commodity awaiting recognition as such. The ordering of what was on display was principally expressed in a manner akin to a stocktaking, rather than a showroom, with the catalogue as the recorded accounts. And yet the sense of a visible spectacle of abundance that later characterized the department store and had already been seen in the arcades and commercial bazaars from the 1820s was there nonetheless (Adburgham 1964; Benjamin 1973a, 1999a; Williams 1982; Geist 1985; Cummings and Lewandowska 2000). Certainly one could inquire about prices with the exhibitors after the event and indeed place orders with them (Queen Victoria, for instance, bought quite a number of items), but the organizers were adamant that they would not debase the improving ambitions of the exhibition by allowing anything as low as price labels or any visible display of commercialism other than at the ticket office and in the refreshment area. Indeed, many of the decorative arts exhibits were not intended for sale at all. Manufacturing exhibition pieces, and for those high-status artifacts to then end up either in aristocratic or new money private collections or quite often in the public museums that were being established at the time across Britain, required an element of indifference to the sale of those artifacts and an emphasis on what we now call their de-commodified singularization (Kopytoff 1986) or removal from the marketplace. It was only through that process that such items could achieve exhibition quality status as priceless wonders. But pricelessness is not the same thing as a disavowal of exchange value (Thompson 1979). Rather, it is often a subtle and indirect reinforcement of it.

What we can say is that the commodity was a connoted effect of the exhibition rather than a direct part of its more overt denoted, if confused, narrative of improvement. That narrative was of improvement through *industry* in all senses of the word rather than *trade*. The organizers' understanding of improvement was loftier than any association with mere commerce. They were concerned with putting the products of industrial improvement on display and educating (improving) manufacturers, workers, and the consuming public alike on the best principles of design within an industrializing society rather than in selling things; a principle that could show itself to the rest of the world with pride and not feel culturally diminished by association with the marketplace. Nonetheless, it was clear to many at the time that the exhibition was a free trade–inspired event supported by many businesses that saw trading opportunities and the potential for expanded markets by being associated with the fair precisely for that reason. And, as we have seen, it was very successful as a commercial enterprise in terms of the profits that it made as an event.

Certainly Marx had no doubt about the free trade issue. For him, the world at that time was witnessing the global spread of capitalism, unimpeded by national boundaries, and the exhibition was an acknowledgement of the need for this internationalizing of trade by the more enlightened members of the bourgeoisie. Surprisingly perhaps, he and Engels had little to say about the exhibition in terms of offering an analysis of the actual event. Preoccupied, no doubt, with the political fallout and feuding among revolutionaries after 1848, a few letters between them suggest they probably visited it but even that is not entirely clear and certainly it was not an event that exercised them to any great extent. They already had their analysis ready in advance of it. What they did say, in a review of May–October 1850 in *the Neue Rheinische Zeitung Revue,* was clear enough:

> This exhibition was announced by the English bourgeoisie already in 1849, with the most impressive cold-bloodedness, at a time when the whole Con- tinent was still dreaming of revolution. For this exhibition they have sum- moned all their vassals from France to China to a great examination, in which they are to demonstrate how they have been using their time; and even the omnipotent Tsar of Russia feels obliged to order his subjects to appear in large numbers at this great examination…. This exhibition is a striking proof of the concentrated power with which modern large-scale industry is everywhere demolishing national barriers and increasingly blurring local peculiarities of production, society and national character among all peoples. By putting on show the massed resources of modern industry in a small concentrated space, just at a time when modern bourgeois society is being undermined from all sides, it is also displaying material which have been produced, and are still being produced day after day in these turbulent times, for the construction of a new society. With this exhibition, the bourgeoisie of the world has erected in the modern Rome its Pantheon, where, with self-satisfied pride, it exhibits the gods which it has made for itself. It thus gives a practical proof of the fact that the "impotence and vexation of the citizen" which German ideologists preach about year in year out, is only these gentleman's own impotent failure to under- stand the modern movement, and their own vexation at this impotence. The bourgeoisie is celebrating this, its great festival, at a moment when the collapse of its social order in all its splendour is imminent, a collapse which will demon- strate more forcefully than ever how the forces which it has created have out- grown its control. In a future exhibition the bourgeoisie will perhaps no longer figure as the owners of these productive forces but only as their ciceroni.[16]

The 1840s were a decade of profound transformation in Britain as well as in Europe as a whole.[17] This was the age not only of socialist agitation and revolution but in Britain also of the railways, photography, a unified postal system, industrialization, and machinofacture; a time of mobile social relations and relations of social and physical mobility then at their most novel. The Great Exhibition might best be understood as capturing something of the turbulence of that previous revolutionary decade and its concern to judge the improvements that had been made or needed to be made. It is as ciceroni to the 1840s and the promise of improvement within that revolutionary decade that animated the exhibition organizers more than anything else. We need, therefore, to inquire into the nature of the exhibition as a reflection of capitalist enterprise because to assume that we can simply read it as a spectacle of nascent consumer culture and commodity fetishism it not as obvious as one might imagine (Ranciere and Vauday, 1988; Richards 1991).

In sum, it was more a spectacle of production rather than of consumption. It is indirectly and somewhat paradoxically that consumption figures. It was a display of the products of the factory but one dressed up in the guises of an amalgam of the "dreamhouses" of the shop, the bourgeois interior, and the museum (Benjamin 1999a). The exhibition is best understood, therefore, as an uncertain and often contradictory examination of the changes of the recent productive past, of the turbulence of the social relations of industrialization in the 1840s and their effects in material form in particular. The discourse of improvement is there for sure but not straightforwardly in the sense of "look how much we are progressing," more "let's see how much we have improved—we need to know if we are to advance further." The Great Exhibition was, in effect, an audit, a giant stocktaking of the "improvements" of the 1840s rather than a harbinger of new things already mapped out in advance.

Certainly it changed the nature of expositions and the display of commodified and mass-produced things and had an impact on the principles of spectacle and display in consumer form thereafter. Industrial exhibitions had previously been small national affairs, notably in France, where they had been held since Year 6 (1798). British expositions of earlier times, such as those held by the Society of Arts (Luckhurst 1951) and the Mechanics Institute (Kusamitsu 1980), had either been concerned solely with fine art (excluded from the 1851 exhibition—mainly because of worries over French superiority to British examples in this field) or were more local affairs and a part of the discourse of the industrial survey. The Great Exhibition did not provide a spectacular view of the consumer culture of subsequent decades—it was confused about that—but rather a sanitized view of the relations of production behind the factory system with the interior of the factory sublimated, replaced instead by products that spoke of a vision of interiority—one that was character building.

There were indeed the trappings of the factory system on display: pressing machines, steam engines, ploughs, and spinning jennies were there in great number. There was even a giant lump of coal displayed at one of the entrances. While not the centerpiece in the exhibition, they were not entirely hidden away either. They were a mark of an improving society but it was the artifacts that came out of that society's industrial centers, its luxury artifacts and also its mass-produced decorative arts, as well as the so-called lions of the exhibition, that spoke, at least to the organizers and the juries, most loudly of progress.

There were some, of course, who disagreed. The design reform movement of the later nineteenth century took the Great Exhibition as its critical starting point. For its critics it illustrated all that was wrong and bad about design in the nineteenth century (a view strongly reinforced by the exhibits to be found in the successor but less important exhibition held in London in 1862). The artifacts in the Great Exhibition became not the spur to improvement through machine-designed artifacts but a reaction against this, culminating in anti-machinofacture design reform associated with the South Kensington museum, schools of art and design, and the arts and crafts movement in general over the subsequent half century. John Ruskin (1854) and a young William Morris, for example, were appalled by what they saw in the Great Exhibition and went on to shun the idea of industrial design altogether in favor of a romantic view of the "truth to materials" expressed in handmade craft items and a medieval craft ideal. Critical, too, in some ways, was Sir Henry Cole, one of the principle organizers of the event. Less radical in his criticisms than Ruskin, he went on to found a school for design in Kensington in what later became the Victoria and Albert Museum off the back of the profits made by the Great Exhibition in order to better educate manufacturers and designers into good design and style principles befitting an industrial age of mass production and consumption, something he felt was lacking in many of the exhibits of 1851.

As a stocktaking, therefore, it showed the aesthetic limitations of how to express improvement and change brought about by industrialization, rather than its strengths. This uncertainty, however, might best be understood as an expression of a moment of a broader social de-territorialization rather than simply on aesthetic grounds alone. Where the Great Exhibition succeeded was in reflecting the instability and uncertainty within society of that time. Judged as a moment of emergence, as something new, it was a significant event. In particular, what is most clear in this is the confusion of temporal and spatial narratives of improvement that led to so much trouble in its classificatory regime and its desire for totality of representation. A spectacle of abundance is not the best way to convey a narrative of improvement. The exhibition was a total visual scene rather than a story. It was a panorama. We can say, therefore, that while the organizers set out to achieve the latter (narrative) they ended up creating the former (spectacle) in a new panoramic form. And it is the consequence of that for consumer society that we have had to live with ever since. That spectacle is closely related to the development of a new kind of subject position—the consumer—and a new form of modern experience (Erlebnis)—a bewildered and fragmented one that has become clearer over time and has underpinned the development of the consumer culture that I want to explore in this book (see Simmel 1971b; Benjamin 1973a; Frisby 1985; Koselleck 2004).

A BEWILDERED AND DISTRACTED SUBJECTIVITY

How to see the future and be confident in it was something that the Great Exhibition sought to address. Utilizing spectacle as a way of trying to present industrial society as a totality and making that apparent to all was one of the intentions of this process. To understand the implications in this linking of the idea of spectacle with a panoramic totality, we need to inquire in more detail into the nature of spectacle and to the character of the spectators who went there to look at this

becoming something that is embodied within a material and naturalized world. The subject becomes principally a visual subject and vision becomes subjectivized as a consequence of this process.[20]

We see a similar line of argument in Thomas Richards's (1991) analysis of Victorian commodity culture that he associates strongly with the Great Exhibition. For Richards, this subjectivizing of vision has its articulation with commodity production and consumption. He is concerned with the beginnings of not only how we see things but also how those things and the way of seeing them are commodified in the nineteenth century:

> Out of this disparate array of popular technologies of spectacular representation the Great Exhibition fashioned a new high style suited to commodities, a style that became the basis for Victorian commodity culture. In particular, the exhibition was responsible for synthesising what can be seen as the six major foundations of a semiotics of commodity spectacle: the establishment of an autonomous iconography for the manufactured object; the use of commemoration to place objects in history; the invention of a democratic ideology of consumerism; the transformation of the commodity into language; *the figuration of a consuming subject*; and the invention of the myth of the abundant society. (1991, 58–59, italics added)

We can, perhaps, begin to make sense of the Great Exhibition now if we say that its regime of curiosity was that of the dreamworld of subject-constitution through object-possession in all its bewildering and abundant opportunity (Williams 1982; Benjamin 1999a). It afforded a series of connoted visual effects whose expression in a naturalist form of representation as totality (around the theme of improvement) created a distraction of vision that challenged earlier and more contemplative forms. These effects generated new forms of sense making—a mode of sense making, moreover, that we have come to call, in the context of consumer culture, *fetishistic*.[21] For it is through the fetishization of objects within this panoramic display that the subject appears to *take possession* of the commodity both literally and visually. They do so, above all, as distracted (*bewildered* was the word Dickens used) subjects and it is my intention to develop this argument and explore its implications throughout this book.

CONCLUSION

The Great Exhibition of 1851 was not the beginning of spectacle as a means of offering an entertaining distraction. Non-theater–based forms of spectacle had been around for a very long time. Indeed, the utilization of spectacle within the exhibitionary complex, if we call it that (Bennett 1995), predates the event by many decades (Quigley 1948; Altick 1978; Ozouf 1987; Castle 1995) and was to undergo further development thereafter (Luckhurst 1951; Richards 1991; Asendorf 1993; Friedberg 1993; Schwartz 1999). The year 1851 marks not an origin or a foundational beginning but a key start nonetheless, a coming together or, more precisely, what Foucault has called a *surface of emergence,* of the main elements that were to subsequently organize the modern practices of mass consumption by consuming subjects.[22] This utilization of spectacle involved organizing a way of seeing things, displaying interest (curiosity), valuing material culture, a zeal for classification, a concern with signs of progress and making the artifacts of industrialization recognizable in a particular way—as a panoramic totality into which one was immersed as imagining subjects able to read one's surrounding. One took possession of this space while at the same time being possessed by it. Other sites such as department stores, parlors, and museums that I will go on to consider later in this book are also spaces that are key to the surface of emergence of aspects of the consuming subject. What we see here at the outset is a start that informed those later spaces and which contained some element of each of them.

The Crystal Palace was a hybrid social space composed of elements from the theater, fair, winter garden, greenhouse, warehouse, museum, gallery, fantasy palace, bazaar, stocktaking, and catalogue. And spectators went to see a multi-perspectival spectacle of free trade, empire, national improvement, and international comparison. The exhibition was not driven principally by the desire to sell commodities but it had the effect of selling the idea of the commodity, not simply as a thing that could be consumed but as a way of seeing and as an expression of subjectivity. It did this through ordering curiosity about the values of classes of improved things into a new commodified totality (on museums and ordering regimes, see Hooper-Greenhill 1992). The concern with spectacle had to be worked out, its discourse established through a series of as yet incoherent material and visual discursive statements and techniques.

But the senses of both bewilderment and distracted interest, that of the browsing consumer (*flâneuse*), remained nonetheless, perhaps as a consequence of the de-territorialization of existing spectacular orders and their re-territorialization into something new and as yet unrecognizable.[23] In this book I want to accept that the resultant Victorian vision as Crary (1990), Richards (1991), and others have conceived it was indeed fetishistic but I also want to consider in a bit more critical detail what we generally understand that term to mean, not least because our understanding of (commodity) fetishism mostly relies on an earlier theorization of subject-object relations and an idealized contemplative and productive mode of reception it establishes that do not fit with this understanding of modern spectacle. In particular, like the nineteenth century that it describes, the preoccupation in theories of fetishism is with the relations of production rather than consumption (Baudrillard 1975) and those are then often transferred uncritically to the analysis of consumption practices and theories of the subject. The highly influential theory of spectacle on recent studies of consumption is particularly guilty in this respect (Debord 1977).

An important argument for our understanding of modern forms of spectacle must be that one cannot disentangle the subject from the scene, or to express it more clearly, the *surrounding* that it is constituted within. The constitution of the modern subject is expressed through an engagement with the material world that shapes that surrounding as a series of spaces of consumption. That, however, is something that has so far been missing in the analysis of commodity fetishism that begins with Marx (1939) and culminates in arguments that our whole society is nothing but a spectacle (Debord 1977) or a hyperreality (Baudrillard 1983). What we understand by fetishism has to address the subject-object relations that are highlighted by this process. It might be that spectacle becomes something that is lived through as a commodified totality rather than something that is seen from outside; in effect *it becomes panoramic* (on the history of the panorama as a form of visual entertainment, see Comment 1999), even panoptic (Foucault 1977). To acknowledge this is directly to challenge much of the Western Marxist understanding of commodity fetishism and spectacle that still dominates most recent post-Marxist understanding of consumer society. My intention theoretically in this book is to détourn that notion of fetishism rather than reject it outright.[24]

The Great Exhibition, in the way it was constituted as an immersing space of an improving industrial society, was like a giant panorama, and no one who visited it could see the edges or make sense of all the detail. They could only be overwhelmed by the detail that they were immersed within. In effect, we might say that the subject is constituted within spectacle, immersed in a world, extended into it (see Munro 1996), surrounded by objects, surrounded by the fetishes of that world, and that they engaged with them on such terms not only in that space but in all the spaces of consumer culture: notably shops, their homes, and in places of public display like museums in the making of their own subjectivity.

In many respects, therefore, a bewildered, distracted, and paradoxical confusion remains a central feature of the constitutive effects of modern forms of consumer spectacle. It thrives on the inability of viewers to recognize the boundaries of what is being represented to them and to see it in totality. One is immersed within the totality rather than seeing it as a whole. Rather than see the spectacle as a whole, one can only dwell within it and pay attention at a glance. Notwithstanding the valiant attempt of the organizers who brought together so many items, nor of the producers of the catalogue who tried to make everything knowable as part of a whole, the exhibition resisted being taken possession of as a whole by its viewers—jurors, lay public, Marx and Dickens alike, and yet it encouraged them to engage with it imaginatively as bewildered or distracted subjects nonetheless.

In effect, subjects within the consumer cultures of modern capitalism might be said to inhabit a peculiar world of paradox and bewilderment. They not only consume what they see but are also themselves made as consuming subjects in the process. The regime of curiosity that was generated out of this bewilderment that the panoramic spectacle immersed them within is one that is characterized by the effects of *taking possession*. While perhaps not directly conscious of this, Paxton's Crystal Palace does indeed express something of an awareness of what it meant *to take possession* (see also Nunokawa 1994). The building housed, without being a summary, its contents as a totality, as a panoramic spectacle. One could not see the objects within clearly from the outside (A. Miller 1995). They remained hidden, awaiting view inside. That is not to say that the Palace obscured the contents; rather, it invited one inside to come and immerse oneself within the panorama of a material culture of improvement, industrialism, capitalism, and empire. So too in a more uncertain manner did the exhibition itself: unwieldy in size; uncertain in its discourse of improvement; overly complex in its classificatory scheme both on the ground and in the catalogue, it invited spectators to take possession within the totality of the spectacle on offer through the imagination (on consumption as daydream, see Williams 1982; Campbell 1987) by immersing themselves in it, to take possession of its contents as a world into which one comes to know oneself in such an act.

To take possession of a panoramic spectacle within which one is constituted is also to take possession of oneself as a subject. We might say that this is a defining feature of a modern consumer society. The unfolding of consumer culture from this emergent form in 1851 was to take place over the next century and a half. The Great Exhibition as a panorama on improvement was one of the first statements of this idea. It was in the department stores, people's homes, and museums and galleries that different moments in the totality of that panorama of consumer culture were to be enacted and different fetishised acts of taking possession worked through and tacitly understood as a means of how to make oneself within a modern capitalist world. What becomes apparent in these spaces, and what I will seek to demonstrate in the following chapters, is that the central preoccupation of this taking possession (mediated as it is by spectacle/fetishism/phantasmagoria) and of a becoming-subject within capitalism, is a preoccupation with the act of transfiguring rather than producing value that cannot be simply reduced to the realms of either utility or exchange.

Chapter Two
Consumption and Spectacle

DÉTOURNEMENT

> [T]he reuse of prexisting artistic elements in a new ensemble.... The two fundamental laws of détournement are the loss of importance of each détourned autonomous element—which may go so far as to lose its original sense completely—and at the same time the organization of another meaningful ensemble that confers on each element its new scope and effect. (IS #3, Anonymous 1989, 55)

Modern capitalist life has, according to many commentators writing during the past couple of decades, become synonymous with consumption and a consumer culture. The interest and the supposed social relevance of the sites of consumption (like shopping malls) have waxed, as the sites of production (like factories) have waned (Shields 1989, 1992; Featherstone 1991; Lury 1996). And that world of consumption has increasingly been described by the concept of *spectacle*. Often beginning (after Walter Benjamin 1999a) with the early nineteenth-century arcades (see also Geist 1985), followed successively by the Great Exhibition in 1851, the Hausmannization of Paris in the 1860s (Clark 1984; Harvey 1985, 2003; Prendergast 1995), and the rise of the department store at the same time (Miller 1981), commodity culture has come to be seen as illustrative of the experience of modernity in general and to define the modern subject (Chaney 1983; Williams 1982; Frisby 1985; Bowlby 1985; Richards 1991; Friedberg 1993). The street life and culture of the metropolis, captured in the paintings of Manet and other Impressionists (Clark 1984; Crary 1999), the imprinting of newspaper text onto the city street (Fritzsche 1999), the poetry and flâneurie of Baudelaire, and the novels of Balzac, and later of Dreiser and Zola, have typically been taken as the key evidence for the shift in activity within consumer culture, from participation to spectating, brought about by capitalist-driven urban growth in the later years of the nineteenth century and its generation of a spectacle of the commodity.[1]

In such views, consumption has becomes indicative not just of modern urban culture but of the development of a new form of seeing and a new modern subjectivity as well (Crary 1990, 1999). Panofsky's recognition of the interpellating effects in the rationalization of sight created by the subject-object mirroring in the picture plane of linear perspective, discovered by artists in the fourteenth century (1991; see also Ivins 1953), has apparently been replaced today by the shop window (Friedberg 1993). And while it might have been the poets, novelists, and artists who were the first to recognize this in the nineteenth century, by the beginning of the twenty-first century we have all, it is argued, become modern consuming spectators mirrored as subjects in what we buy.

Later nineteenth-century consumer culture, that which arises out of the time and influence of the Great Exhibition of 1851 and the department stores of the 1860s, is often seen as the beginning for such spectacle-influenced ways of seeing and a relationship with the development of new and distinctly modern cultural forms—not least advertising (Leach 1993; Fritzsche 1999) and cinema (Friedberg 1993; Schwartz 1999; Butsch 2000), in which the undisciplined, mobile, and embodied crowd of earlier times (Altick 1978; Barrows 1981; Ozouf 1987) has become a distracted and static audience for the present. The idea that there is a relationship between new forms (and technologies) of visual representation and new ways of seeing is not a new argument (Ivins 1953; Benjamin 1973a; Malraux 1978; Lowe 1982; Gibson 1986; Crary 1990; Kellum 1996). It often assumes that new forms of disciplinary technique afford a visual environment in which we learn how to look at or to gaze upon an image effectively (as well as upon ourselves; see Foucault 1974, 1977). Likewise, the supposed shift from crowd to audience as a basis for experiencing a spectacle is premised on the idea, above all, of commodity culture's role in manipulating the subject. The key trope in much of this has become that of passivity. Beginning with the audience at the Great Exhibition, consumers as viewers are supposedly passive and distracted subjects susceptible to fetishistic forms of manipulation.

Within the idea of spectacle and of the gaze associated with it there has been something of a distinctive take on the question of mobility too. Key to this has been a displacement of the idea of mobility from the subject onto the object. If not moving images themselves as in film, then fractured, disorientating, and ever changing urban and consumption "screens" have become indicative of a mobile world of modernity that is available only to the gaze of a static modern subject (Kern 1983). This shift has seen an acknowledgment of the static, easily distracted subject with desires for the (mobile) image and its commodity forms.

In many respects, we can agree that modernity alters the character of experience fundamentally. We see with the advent of its de-traditionalizing forces that breakdown of experience as a totality (*Erfahrung*) grounded in the past of memory, custom, and epic narrative and the emergence in its place of a more fractured and fragmentary set of experiences of the now lived as a series of events whose character resists understanding and easy communication (*Erlebnis*; see Benjamin 1973c, 1999a; see also Simmel 1971a, b). With this shift in the character of experience such things as custom and tradition are overturned (Berman 1982; Lindroos 2001).

Koselleck (2004) sums this up in his analysis in the emergence of the narrative of historical time, as a major element in the making of the modern outlook. A premodern experience (*Erfahrung*) was characterized by the sense of a shared *topos* in which a community existed as a knowable whole for its members. Experiences in the present were felt to be the same as those in the past, changeless and reproducible in character and form. People dwelt in this shared *topos* in a time that was perceived to be continuous and natural and were able to experience the present as a present. There was no sense of emergence, trajectory, or novelty in such experience. There was no worldly outside (2004, 9ff; see also Anderson 1983); any sense of an end only came with death or God's intervention at the end of the world. With modernity comes the disruption of the social relations that underpin such a form of experience and its cultural expressions of *Gemeinschaft* and *Erfahrung* and with it the temporalization of history or the shift from natural to historical time as a response as people seek to reorientate themselves to radically changed circumstances. Such a discourse, Koselleck argues, "abbreviates the space of experience" (2004, 22) in a world now perceived to be ever accelerating and ungraspable as a knowable whole. The disorientating character of the advent of modernity described in such terms has been much explored by social scientists in recent years (for overviews, see Berman 1982; Clark 1984; Frisby 1985). With it comes an experience that is principally felt as lack, something captured in the powerful tropes of alienation, loss of community, inauthenticity, fragmentation, and so on that have developed largely through the idiom of Romanticism over the past two centuries. And it is consumption that is assumed to be central to this process of change in experience.

Where once the spectator experienced the world very much as a part of a carnivalized crowd with all its disruptive theatricality (Altick 1978; Bakhtin 1984; Sennett 1977; Agnew 1986), this has apparently now been disciplined into a static form of viewing spectatorship particularly as capitalism has ripened into a stage of (cinematic) lateness (Stallybrass and White 1986; Bennett 1995; Jameson 1991; Schwartz 1999). Indeed, this idea of the bombardment with fetishized images and scenes is later assumed to lead to a culture of the sign-image, of simulation and hyperreality as a totality (Baudrillard 1983, though see also Simmel's 1903 essay on the metropolis, 1971b). All the same, we need to question much that remains unacknowledged in these arguments with spectacle and with the changing character of capitalism. My intention here is to bring these issues about commodity culture together for further analysis. But my concern here is not so much with the issue of the gaze as such as it is with that of what we understand by the term spectacle and how it operates in the constitution of modern consuming subjects.

SPECTACLE AND THE ANALYSIS OF CONSUMPTION

Interestingly, the issue of spectacle only really begins to come to prominence in the analysis of capitalist society during the time of the consumer boom of the 1980s; a time, in particular, in which the former theoretical, as much as political, certainties of Marxism, and its productivist theory of fetishism, were beginning to melt into the postmodern air (or melt into the sign at least, see Baudrillard 1981; Zizek 1989; for an overview, see Pietz 1993). But if we look in more detail at some of the recent writing on this urban consumer culture (from the past twenty years) we begin to find at least a lasting influence from Marxism, albeit one derived from one of its more obscure theoretical backwaters. We see around this time not only the appearance of a word—*spectacle*—that had not been applied to consumption in this way before but also a name—Guy Debord—appearing in these analyses. The belated discovery of Guy Debord, a one-time leading member of the subsequently influential group of 1960s avant-garde radicals known as the Situationists, or *International Situationiste* (Gray 1974; Bonnett 1989; Bracken 1997; Jappe 1999), and of his 1967 book *Society of the Spectacle* in particular (1977; new translation in 1995) at some point during the 1980s, has shaped much of the discussion of consumer culture as spectacle thereafter and continues to do so today.

Perhaps the first to make this acknowledgment outside of France was T. J. Clark in his *The Painting of Modern Life* (1984). This influential book, by a one-time member of the Situationist group,[2] discusses the shaping of modern ways of seeing that are first articulated by the Impressionist's reception of the changing metropolitan character of Paris during the 1860s. In it, Clark acknowledges his broadly Marxist approach to reading bourgeois culture but rather than draw directly on Marx's analysis of alienation and commodity fetishism or on the well-known writings of Lukacs on reification (1971) or Marcuse on false needs (1968) that were all common currency at the time, he refers, instead, to a then little-known French avant-garde group of the 1950s and 60s—the Situationists, of whom Debord was a leading member and the leading theorist.[3]

Consumer culture and its urban expression is, for Clark (as it is for Debord), both an ideological construct and an expression of capitalist relations of power. Spectacle is about ways of being rather than just about ways of seeing. And that way of being is understood to be ideologically expressed through the development of what Debord called the *spectacle*. As Clark puts it:

> About the concepts of "spectacle" and the "spectacular society" it is not so easy to be cut and dried. They were developed first in the mid-1960s as part of the theoretical work of a group called the Situationist International, and they represent an effort to theorize the implications for capitalist society of the progressive shift within production towards the provision of consumer goods and services, and the accompanying "colonization of everyday life." The word "colonization"

> conjures up associations with the Marxist theory of imperialism, and is meant
> to. It points to a massive *internal* extension of the capitalist market—the inva-
> sion and restructuring of whole areas of free time, private life, leisure, and per-
> sonal expression which had been left, in the first push to constitute and urban
> proletariat, relatively uncontrolled. (1984, 9, emphasis in original)

He goes on:

> The concept of spectacle, in other words, was an attempt to revise the theory
> of capitalism from a largely Marxist point of view. The most celebrated of Situ-
> ationist metaphors—it comes from a book by Guy Debord—is meant more
> soberly than it may seem at first sight: "The Spectacle is capital accumulated
> until it becomes an image." (1984, 9)

Apart from another mention of the following page, Clark makes no further reference to Debord or his work in the rest of his analysis. It is clear, however, that this
argument is central to his reading of Impressionism, particularly the paintings of
Manet, and its relationship to the development of the "Haussmannized" capitalist
city. According to Clark, the Impressionists' vision expressed a new (alienated and
commodified) way of seeing the changing urban world. What they witnessed and
tried to capture in their art was nothing less than a profound change in the *relations of production* within a capitalist society made visible in the material changes to
the urban form of the city (1984, 10). Those relations of production were manifest,
in particular, in the processes of Haussmannization begun in the 1860s (see also
Harvey 1985) and they transformed not only the urban fabric of Paris (through
its boulevards, world fairs, and department stores) but also the experiences of its
inhabitants and the class dynamics of the city through which those experiences were
lived. Spectacle, in this analysis, is not about seeing per se but the way in which seeing is shaped by the capitalist relations of production. In the opening thesis of his
Society of the Spectacle, itself a détournement of the opening lines of Marx's *Capital,*
Debord says:

> In societies where modern conditions of production prevail, all of life presents
> itself as an immense accumulation of spectacles. Everything that was directly
> lived has moved away into a representation. (1977, thesis #1)

In modern capitalist society, a society seen to be defined more by consumption than
by production, the separation between a lived reality and its representation becomes
total. As Debord himself acknowledged, we are returned back to Feuerbach's concern with appearance and illusion.

> But certainly for the present age, which prefers the sign to the thing signified,
> the copy to the original, fancy to reality, the appearance to the essence…illusion

only is sacred, truth profane. Nay sacredness is held to be enhanced in proportion as truth decreases and illusion increases, so that the highest degree of illusion comes to be the highest degree of sacredness.[4]

Debord gets a further name-check in 1985 with the publications of Rachel Bowlby's equally influential work on gender and consumption, *Just Looking.* In this work on the Parisian consumer culture of the latter half of the nineteenth century, seen through a reading not of Impressionist painting this time but the novels of Drieser, Gissing, and Zola as well as some of the catalogues and advertisements from the time, Bowlby also makes reference to Debord's work as an influence on her own. On the first page of the book she acknowledges Debord's influential conceptualization of spectacle (although Freud is actually more central to her main concern: an analysis of the constitution of femininity within this consumer culture). Referring to the experience of consumer activity in the 1850s and of the world fairs in particular, in a somewhat looser reading of the concept of spectacle than Clark's, she says:

> No longer do goods come to the buyers, as they had done with itinerant hawkers, country markets or small local stores. Instead, it is the buyers who have taken themselves to the products: and not, in this case, to buy, but merely to "see" the things. In the late 1960s, Guy Debord wrote forcefully of the "spectacle de la merchandise" crystallizing the way that modern consumption is a matter not of basic items bought for definite needs, but of visual fascination and remarkable sights of things not found at home. People go out of their way to look at displays of the marvels of modern industrial production: there is nothing obviously functional in a tourist trip. And these exotic, non-essential goods are there to be seen by "tout le monde": no longer are luxuries a prerogative of the aristocracy. (1985, 1)

Strictly speaking, a Marxist account of spectacle would take issue with Bowlby's somewhat unclear use of the term as it is expressed here. Rather than see spectacle as the creation of a new emphasis on viewing an increasingly democratized class of once luxury commodities, it would emphasize instead the centrality of spectacle as a source of *mediation*—in the way in which spectacle, the social relations within capitalism, become mediated by images. For Bowlby, luxury becomes an alluring and glamorous unreality found in the department stores of the time; an environment in which women, in particular, are encouraged to develop their consumer subjectivity (see also Williams 1982; Wilson 1991; Nava 1997). Debord was never an orthodox Marxist, but all the same, the totalizing character of his use of the word *spectacle* was never intended to refer solely to the experience of luxury consumption and its fantasy-inducing world for the feminine consumer. He had in mind an understanding of spectacle framed by the Hegelian notion of totality and, in particular, Lukacs's incorporation of it into the Western Marxist canon (on the theme of totality, see Jay 1978) and he wanted to use it generally to address issues of power and alienation in postwar capitalist (and indeed socialist) society through the use of this term (Debord 1977, 1990).

During the 1980s and early 1990s the turn to the study of consumption and urban culture in texts like these, Debord's work, then, is treated as something of an insider secret, known outside France by only a few one-time radical students and arty academics for whom the "events" of Mai '68 and their aftermath in politics and art often figure prominently as a source of influence for their post-Marxism. He tends to crop up in the early pages of these texts as providing a suggestive term—rather than as a theorist whose approach is worthy of detailed analysis (see also Crary 1984, 1990; Richards 1991; Friedberg 1993). The Situationists' extensive analysis of a mature capitalist society—for all its problems that I will discuss below—and the need to focus on the sites of everyday life (including consumer sites) as the source of revolutionary impetus are largely ignored in this work (Gray 1974; Knabb 1989). As a consequence, the full significance of what Debord, right or wrong, was trying to say about spectacle often gets lost in the rather cursory treatments of his work in these influential accounts of consumer culture.

Certainly by the mid-1990s, though, Debord was becoming less of a shadowy radical outside of the academy and more someone who began to be recognized (recuperated?) within academic debates (Plant 1992); something, no doubt, aided by his suicide in 1994. Much to the chagrin of the remnants of a radical art/politics tradition who seem to want to keep Debord as their property (for instance, Bracken 1997), his analysis has been brought out into the open and has come to be seen instead to prefigure (wrongly, some would suggest; see Crary 1984, 1999) that of Baudrillard, de Certeau, and other postmodernists writing on consumer culture and the role of the image within it (Plant 1992); someone who also, alongside his one-time friend Henri Lefebvre, developed a critical understanding of the importance of analyzing everyday life within capitalism (Lefebvre 1971; see also Shields 1999) as well as a prominent figure in one of the more influential underground avant-garde cultures of the late twentieth century (Marcus 1989).[5] There has been a special issue of the journal *October* (1997) dedicated to the recent reception of Debord's work and several recent biographies. And most recent works on urban consumer culture and its development in the nineteenth century, as well as on audiences in general, have been a little more detailed in their use of Debord's concept than these early contributors (for instance, Sadler 1999; Coverley 2006). All the same, his analysis of spectacle, much like the theories of commodity fetishism and reification on which it draws, are often taken as given in the understanding of consumer culture that makes use of this term—assumed as an established theoretical truth rather than an argument, a particular take on the theory of commodity fetishism, that might be subject to scrutiny. As a consequence, Debord has become something of a protean figure, used to fit whatever form of analysis of spectacle people want to make.

Thomas Richards, for example, has sought to use Debord's analysis to understand the beginnings of commodity culture in Britain after the Great Exhibition of 1851 (1991). In this otherwise important work, Richards sees Debord providing a semiological understanding of the commodity somewhat akin to Barthes's more diffuse analysis of cultural myths (1983). Here, Debord is seen as analyzing capitalist society through its representations. Representation, constituted in a spectacular manner, Richards argues, has come to mediate all social relations and to extend the fetishistic character of the commodity into all areas of life through the pervasiveness of the image. While this latter point may well represent something of Debord's position, there is little in Debord's text to support Richards's claim that he was engaged in any overt semiological analysis of commodity culture pace Barthes (for a similar point, see Crary 1984, 1997), although this was indeed something Baudrillard was to carry out in his Debord-influenced first book *Les Systeme D'Objects* in 1968 (Baudrillard 1996). A committed humanist, Debord loathed any form of structuralist or semiological analysis—seeing it as something like the official ideology of a society of the spectacle (see 1977, 196). While he does state that "every individual commodity is justified in the name of the grandeur of the production of the totality of objects of which the spectacle is an apologetic catalogue" (# 65), he does not subject any individual commodity, or image of commodity relations, nor their totality, to semiological analysis in the manner in which Richards suggests. The only place where Debord might be said to engage in anything approaching semiological analysis (and then it is never imagined as part of a structuralist or post-structuralist project) is through his use of the technique of détournement, most notably in the numerous films that he made (Levin 1989).[6] The second point that Richards makes, however, is indeed correct. For Debord, capitalism has become a society dominated by the power of representation. His theory, however, is a theory of ideological mediation and of the manifestation of alienation within the representational order of capitalism rather than just in the conditions of production, and it is in no way a study of capitalism as a system of visual signs. Richards himself goes on to develop an interesting analysis of the semiotics of spectacle (1991, 58) but we should be wary of attributing such a move to Debord.

The second important factor in Richards's analysis is his point that seeing the commodity through the semiotics of spectacle is something that develops over a period of time and is something that had to be learned by consumers. Spectacle, then, has a history. It is shaped within certain phases of capitalism; for Debord it is the product of a capitalist society in which abundance rather than scarcity has become a problem. But spectacle is also a figure of stasis and the illusion of change (Debord 1977, 71)—a kind of eternal recurrence already analyzed by Benjamin's account of fetishism and the commodity (1999a; see also Wolin 1982; Buck-Morss 1989).[7] What neither Debord nor Richard acknowledge, however, is the history and the role of spectacle within popular culture before they become somehow magically commodified some time after 1851 (see, for instance, Altick 1978). Indeed, Debord stands in a long tradition in France, and not an especially Marxist one, that critiques not only consumption as an activity but also theatricality and the uses of spectacle as a source of power. It is a tradition that takes in Rousseau, Quatremère de Quincy, and numerous late-nineteenth-century sociological critics of consumer culture (including Durkheim) who tend to see these factors as variously leading to an erosion of more authentic forms of art or forms of social solidarity (Williams 1982; Maleuvre 1999).

One further influential recent text on nineteenth-century society, spectacle, and urban culture is Jonathan Crary's *Suspensions of Perception* (1999). This too makes passing use of Debord (see also Crary 1984, 1990, 1997). In an innovative genealogy of visual attention and its relation to subject formation, analyzed by reading nineteenth-century arguments on attention in academic psychology alongside developments visible in the art of Manet, Seurat, and Cezanne, Crary suggests that central to Debord's analysis of spectacle (alongside Foucault on surveillance) is not so much a concern with the allure of images or signs (pace Bowlby and Richards) but its role in constituting a society based on a principle of separation.

> Debord's work is often associated with the more facile meanings of the book's title, disregarding an essential characterization of the society of the spectacle: rather than emphasizing the effects of mass media and visual imagery, Debord insists that spectacle is…the development of a technology of separation. It is the inevitable consequence of capitalism's "restructuring of society without community."…. Spectacle is not primarily concerned with a *looking at* images but rather with the construction of conditions that individuate, immobilize and separate subjects, even within a world in which mobility and circulation are ubiquitous. In this way attention becomes key to the operation of non-coercive forms of power…. Spectacle is not an optics of power but an architecture. (1999, 73–75, emphasis in original)

Crary's own analysis seeks, then, to offer a genealogy of attention and distraction and its relationship with subject formation under such conditions of societal separation and erosion of community. He is certainly right to emphasize this aspect of Debord's work because it is certainly missing from most of the other accounts mentioned so far. Whether Debord's analysis can be fitted, however, into Crary's more broadly Foucauldian analysis of power remains rather debatable. His promise of a synthesis, while suggestive, remains undeveloped (just as it had been in his earlier work, 1990) in an otherwise important work on visual culture and the apparent immobilization of the subject in the late nineteenth century. Certainly Debord and Foucault were both concerned with the techniques of separation within modern society, but philosophically their projects have little else in common.

In all of these highly influential texts that have shaped our current understanding of the development of the consumer culture of modern society, a number of things stand out: (i) society (after Debord) is seen as one dominated by spectacle as a form of mediation, (ii) Debord is mentioned but there is little systematic analysis of his arguments, (iii) Debord is taken to be right (at least superficially) and the idea of a society of the spectacle has become commonplace in understanding consumer society. In this chapter, I want to acknowledge but also problematize the concept of spectacle, I want to provide something that is more than a cursory reference to Debord's work, and I want to argue that his theory is open to all sorts of questions that do not allow it to be treated like some kind of established fact. Seminal though his work might be in understanding consumer culture, Debord's theory was the product of a particular time and place and a particular set of issues, and these have not all traveled as well as the concept of spectacle itself. It is ripe, if not for critique in the ideology-critique sense, then certainly for détourning in the manner that Debord himself would understand.

THE SOCIETY OF THE SPECTACLE

Debord does not develop a critique of capitalism through the normal Marxist conventions of critique; rather, he starts from the artistic practice of détournement in his work. Détournement (a detour) was originally an artistic practice probably begun by Marcel Duchamp when he painted a moustache on a copy of Leonardo's *Mona Lisa* and called it L.H.O.O.Q (when the letters are spoken in French they sound like the sentence, in French, "she has a hot ass") and exhibited it as his own work. Others might, with some justification, suggest that as a practice it really begins with the writings of Lautremont in the 1870s. Nonetheless Dadaist in its inspiration, such a technique of détournement challenges the idea of artistic originality, aura, and singularity in art. It came to be seen as a key practice within the post-Second World War artistic avant-garde "fallout" with/from Surrealism, and with the group of artists know as CoBrA in particular, and especially with the paintings of the Danish artist Asger Jorn.

Jorn, a good friend of Debord, was particularly fond of buying cheap, aesthetically worthless paintings by unknown artists from flea markets and then partially over-painting them with his own abstract and childlike images, then signing them (often next to the original signature) and selling them as original works—creating a deliberate tension between the pictorial kitsch of the original and avant-garde abstraction of his own over-painting in the process (Atkins 1978; Wolin 1989a). But détournement can be practiced with text just as well as with painted images. Debord's *Society of the Spectacle* (La Societe du Spectacle) (1977 [1967]) is itself, substantially, a détournement of other works in the critical theoretical tradition: Hegel's *Phenomenology of Spirit*, Feuerbach's *Essence of Christianity*, Marx's *Capital, Volume 1*, and Lukacs's *History and Class Consciousness*, as well as other sources, notably from French literature, are the key materials (Jappe 1999, 60). Sometimes the similarities are deliberately and provocatively overwritten directly from these other texts and then subtly changed so that the apparent plagiarism can be seen. Most famously, the opening thesis:

> In societies where modern conditions of production prevail, all of life presents itself as an immense accumulation of spectacles. (Debord 1977, 1)

As in:

> The wealth of those societies in which the capitalist mode of production prevails, presents itself as "an immense accumulation of commodities." (Marx 1938, 1)

Not only is Debord making direct reference to the opening lines of *Capital*, he is also deliberately copying a sentence where Marx had himself engaged in an act of self-plagiarism (using words from his own earlier *Critique of Political Economy*). Debord was not writing an academic text with all the niceties of acknowledgment and referencing associated with that but a revolutionary manifesto in the avant-garde tradition. Part parody but deadly serious, didactic, self-regarding in its importance (André Breton is clearly his role model), Debord was engaged in an analysis of what he saw as a new moment in the development of capitalism and he drew on all his knowledge of the post-Hegelian tradition of critical analysis to shape the style and presentation of his theory of it: this is not presented as argument, rather, as logical fact beyond contradiction. Pure in form, revolutionary in intention, no deviation could be allowed; any attempt at interpretation or to make use of the argument for anything other than revolutionary means was to be seen as an example of the recuperating capacity of the spectacle itself trying to nullify any critique (Debord 1990, 1991; Debord and Sanguinetti 1990).

Debord as "leader" of the Situationists modeled himself on those from a revolutionary tradition from whom he drew some inspiration: Breton within the Surrealists and Marx during the years of the First International (around the time of the 1872 Hague conference when he managed to outmaneuver most of his enemies, notably the anarchists grouped around Bakunin). The history of all three groupings is not just one of radical activity but of splits, expulsions, intrigues, public denunciations of deviant members (and poor translators), and attempts by a leading figure to impose the purity of his vision upon "his" movement (Home 1988; Plant 1992). In a word, Debord wanted a total critique of what he saw as a totalizing society that aimed at the complete colonization of all areas of autonomous human life by the commodity form and he wasn't prepared to allow anyone to introduce any deviation from that (Debord and Sanguinetti 1990). It is in such a context that his arguments need to be understood. The theme of totality is key.

While it is, without doubt, the first 72 theses of Debord's book that are central to his analysis of capitalism as a society of spectacle (out of a total of 221 theses) and also to his subsequent influence on those writing about consumer culture, the key to understanding the whole argument is, I would argue, thesis 121, found, in my view, in what reads today as the least interesting chapter entitled "The Proletariat as Subject and as Representation." In this section, Debord provides a history of the revolutionary movement opposing capitalist society since the nineteenth century. He celebrates its high points, denounces the failings and compromises, rails against the scientism of contemporary Marxism (theory not derived directly from struggle), discusses the appeal but also the weaknesses of anarchism, outlines moments in the betrayal of the revolutionary working class by party functionaries, and ends up defending, like the young Lukacs (and also the postwar libertarian socialist group Socialisme ou Barbarie, with whom he had some association)[8] a libertarian-communist position (something Leninists would once have called "left-wing communism") based, in principle, in the idea that revolutionary organization is born in the spontaneous necessities of class struggle (situations/the event) rather than in either scientific theory or the party. Somewhat ironically, this celebration of the contingencies of spontaneous struggle and the forms it generates (Debord's "Marxism" is closest to the "anti-statist" Marx found in *The Civil War in France*) requires, for Debord, an incontestable theoretical analysis of the conditions it is challenging. That challenge is not just of capitalism per se but of capitalism's attempt to totally colonize all areas of social life. Not content with transforming the forces of production, capitalism (seen by Debord as an autonomous and functionalist system) seeks to intervene in transforming the relations of production too—particularly in the arena of consumption. Its success in doing this would undermine, according to Marxist understandings of social change and conflict, any possibility for new contradictions emerging between the forces and relations of production. Capitalism would become total, determining all areas of social life. The only response, for Debord, can be total and uncompromising critique of the most fundamental mechanism through which capitalism seeks to exercise this form of domination: the spectacle. This, then, is his key thesis:

> The revolutionary organization can be nothing less than a unitary critique of society, namely a critique which does not compromise with any form of separate power anywhere in the world, and a critique proclaimed globally against all the aspects of alienated social life. In the struggle between the revolutionary organization and class society, the weapons are nothing other than the essence of the combatants themselves: the revolutionary organization cannot reproduce within itself the dominant society's conditions of separation and hierarchy. It must struggle constantly against its deformation in the ruling spectacle. The only limit to participation in the total democracy of the revolutionary organization is the recognition and self-appropriation of the coherence of its critique by all its members, a coherence which must be proved in the critical theory as such and in the relations between theory and practice. (1977, 121)

This is not the Debord that usually gets quoted in academic writing on the salience of his work for understanding consumer society (such as those works discussed above). Spectacle is constituted here as a unitary and totalizing concept because only such a concept, for Debord, could ever be an effective weapon against a unifying and totalizing society that capitalism seeks to become. Debord's understanding of spectacle is not, then, derived from empirical observation of contemporary consumption practices, branding or advertising techniques, nor from semiological analysis of its images, but from the necessities of class struggle in a world where all previous areas of autonomous social life where struggle might possibly emerge are seen to be in the process of being colonized by capitalism.

Debord diagnoses the key failings of revolutionary organization and activity up to now as not having generated a sufficiently unitary and totalizing critique of capitalism that matches its totalization within social life. He seeks to redress that himself. In other words, Debord develops the concept of spectacle as a means of imposing an understanding on the totalizing effects of capitalism in order that those who then seek to change things will know what it is they have to attack as a totality. As the Situationists themselves (and there were never more than about twelve of them at any one time in the history of their organization) are seen by Debord as the only uncorrupted embodiment of revolutionary struggle, this statement is seen not as an abstraction derived from the scientism of a theory removed from struggle but rather the product of revolutionary praxis itself: the praxis of their group—apparently. The functionalism and reductionism behind such a move are clearly evident and should be recognized as such at the outset of any analysis of Debord's theoretical approach. Debord's argument about the nature of spectacle should be assessed in light of this starting point.

Beginning with the argument that alienation in modern capitalist society (since the 1920s)[9] has become total in an all-pervasive regime of representation, he goes on to suggest that this regime of representation has developed a degree of autonomy in the form of spectacle. Spectacle does not consist in the distorting of vision itself but in an alienated way of seeing in which seeing and doing have become separate activities. This separation produces, for Debord, distracted passivity and acceptance of the spectacle as an expression of the relations of power within a capitalist society. The dynamics of capitalist production, alienating in their effects, shift from (i) an alienation of being to having in early capitalism to (ii) an alienation of having to appearing in the late twentieth century (1977, #17). In this respect, mediated rather than lived experience can be said to be all encompassing. The totality of mediated experience, spectacle, becomes the negation of human activity (#27), the isolation of the individual from communal life except through mediated communal life, and the source of looking in a culture of consumption. He uses the term contemplation to describe the only possible activity for the spectator in Debord's view (#30). However, this is not critical, disinterested contemplation in the Kantian sense but a distracted form of looking that is susceptible to manipulation.

Despite his claim that spectacle is not about the image per se but about mediated relations of power, Debord repeats his central claim, over and over again, that in modern capitalism the lived has been replaced by the seen. Above all, this is taken as a historical development within the process of commodity fetishism. For Debord, commodity fetishism has a history tied to the changing forces and relations of production. Commodity fetishism, as described by Marx, is no longer effective in its classical formulation in describing the conditions that exist in a society of consumer abundance, where, in order for the circuit of capital to be maintained, workers have to more and more become consumers and not just producers. For Debord, spectacle is not just another word for fetishism but a historical manifestation of a form of commodity fetishism in a society where the relations of capitalist production have extended to the arena of consumption as well. This is a society conceived in the nineteenth century but only brought to fruition in the economic boom of the 1920s, brought to a temporary halt between 1929 and 1945, and which reemerges in the 1950s and quite late and rapidly in France at that (see Jappe 1999). In other words, for Debord, Marx describes the process of fetishism in the era of the early factory system where consumption is relatively primitive, Lukacs's in the era of Fordism in which mass consumption is only just beginning to be possible, and Debord in a society where mass consumption has become paramount to the survival of capitalism itself.

In developing this position he draws extensively on Henri Lefebvre's work on everyday life (Debord, though never himself a university student, audited Lefebvre's classes in the late 1950s; see Jappe 1999; Ross and Lefebvre 1997). In particular, he draws on and develops Lefebvre's postwar analysis of the importance of consumption and everyday life rather than the factory as a site for the future development and reproduction of capitalism (1971). In this argument, capitalism produces an abundance of commodities that will remain unsold if people cannot be persuaded to buy them. It seeks therefore to colonize more and more areas of social life (everyday life), which, during Marx's lifetime, (except for the poorest in society) still remained somewhat outside of the effects of capital (hence all the need for disciplining an uncommodified popular culture in the nineteenth century; see Thompson 1968; Burke 1978; Yeo and Yeo 1981; Stallybrass and White 1986; Bennett 1995). In other words, the spectacle is a leading part of the transformation of the relations of production in a mature capitalist economy. For Debord, the fetishism of the commodity becomes total under such conditions.

For Debord (following Lefebvre and possibly also Adorno) this is a world that is alienating not just in the sense of transforming being (sensuous human activity) into having but, as we have seen, into appearance. Just as for Marx the site of the most profound alienation—the factory—was also the most likely site for resistance, so, for Debord, it is the sites of consumption that become not only ones of alienation and spectacle but also, potentially, of resistance and ultimately the overthrow of capitalism too. The fact that this might have happened in France in May 1968 was seen as a vindication of his theory by Debord and did something to elevate its status thereafter.

In retrospect we can say that the influence of the Situationists on those events was certainly real but minor: their early writings had influenced a student strike in Strasbourg in 1966 and they were invited by the students, at the university's unwitting expense, to produce a pamphlet (supposedly written by the protesting students) critiquing capitalist society—*On the Poverty of Student Life*—during those events. This created something of a scandal at the time and was to lead to Situationist ideas developing some notoriety and to have some influence on a group of radical students at Paris-Vincennes who began their own protests along similar lines against the University in March 1968. This, after arrests and threatened expulsion of the students (apparently a false rumor that Lefebvre claims that he started to whip things up a bit; see Ross and Lefebvre 1997), was to lead to the student riots in Paris and a general strike in support of them during May of that year (Gombin 1978). Their journal, *International Situationiste* (of which twelve volumes were produced between 1958 and 1970), particularly its extensive use of détourned images and cartoons, was also to influence the style of many of the posters and graffiti that appeared on the walls of Paris during those events. And while Debord and other members of the Situationists participated in the various actions and committee discussions surrounding the protests, their influence during the events did not extend much beyond that (Vienet 1992). Their subsequent notoriety does though. They have become almost synonymous with Mai '68 and it is largely because of that that anyone has ever heard of Debord.

Central to Debord's critique of the spectacle is the theme of banalization (1977, #59). In ways that echo Adorno and Horkheimer's earlier critique of the culture industry (1979)—a term that in many ways prefigures that of spectacle—Debord analyzes spectacle in terms of (i) its debasement of culture, (ii) the rise of celebrity, (iii) as a condition of a bureaucratic society, (iv) the creation of false and manipulated conflicts, (v) of continuous change within the same commodity form, and (vi) in the denial of individual autonomy. But whereas the pessimistic Adorno sought refuge in the negative moment of autonomous art—the last area of non-commodified social relations, Debord, at least in 1967 (though not in the 1988 sequel; see Debord 1990), had already rejected art as part of the spectacle and believed that resistance was still possible within the daily life of a consumer society. The key question for him was how to release it: "How to turn consumer passivity into revolutionary activity?"

These arguments are established in the first seventy-two theses of the book. These central claims are then repeated in the rest of the book in relation to a number of further issues. After the chapter (4) on the history of revolutionary struggle where the theme of totality and praxis are introduced and a libertarian or council communist position is outlined, Debord goes on to discuss the impact of the spectacle on our understanding of time and space, on avant-garde art, and on forms of revolutionary struggle. Following Lukacs, Debord sees a major consequence of the spectacle as the spatialization of time. The relationship between spectacle and stasis is again apparent. He provides us with a Hegelian and Marxist (and indeed rather Eurocentric/French) view of history and discusses the relationship between modes of production and the prevailing forms of social time. This analysis is all rather conventional (i.e., acknowledging the link between Feudalism and the conception of cyclical time) until we get to his remarks on what, in effect, amounts to a condition of globalization (though Debord doesn't actually use that term). Time in a global economy becomes universal and this is seen as a necessary condition of spectacle.

> With the development of capitalism, irreversible time is unified on a world scale. Universal history becomes a reality because the entire world is gathered under the development of this time. But this history, which is everywhere simultaneously the same, is still only the refusal within history of history itself. What appears the world over as the same day is the time of economic production cut into equal abstract fragments. Unified irreversible time is the time of the world market, and, as a corollary, of the world spectacle. (1977, #145)

The condition of globalization is the condition of spectacle not simply because of the penetration of capitalism into all markets in the world but also because of its imposition of a singular irreversible sense of time upon the world. Debord goes on to analyze what he calls spectacular time in terms of false consciousness (i.e., the pseudo-cyclical time of the working day and of the life of a commodity) and in terms of its spatialization. For Debord, lived time is historical, whereas spectacular time is spatial. The spatialization of time is constituted through forms of social stasis and separation.

Perhaps the most interesting part of *The Society of the Spectacle*, indeed of the whole Situationist project, is what it has to say about social space. At a time when Lefebvre was only just beginning to formulate his own ideas on the city and on social space, *La Production de L'Espace* was not published until 1974 (1991 in English) and almost twenty years before the advent of Marxist geography in the 1970s, Debord already had a coherent understanding of the social space of a late capitalist society from around 1953 when he (and about three others) were members of the group the Lettrist International that was a forerunner to the Situationists (Bonnett 1989; Sadler 1999). In fact, the idea of the spectacle is a theory that is much more concerned with the effects of capitalism on social space than it is on its use of images to manipulate consumers. The chapter in *Society of the Spectacle* on space (7) is a summary of about fifteen years of writing on social space that begins with the post-Surrealist text "Formulary For a New Urbanism" by Debord's friend Ivan Chtcheglov in 1953 (1989) through numerous articles and détourned artworks (by

Debord and Jorn) on urban planning, zoning, traffic, the loss of historical space, and the 1965 Watts riots.

Debord's analysis of social space highlights a number of themes: the unification of space as capitalist space through spectacle (1989a); the rise of zoning and planning (1989c); the banality of contemporary urban life; urbanism as the ideology of capitalism; a critique of the functionalism of modernist architecture; the attempt to separate the city from the flow of history; the disappearance of the town/country distinction; and above all of urban life as premised on conditions of individual separation and stasis. There is as much of a subtle blend of ideas from Surrealism, the Chicago School, and Lewis Mumford in this analysis as there is the influence of Marx, and it is perhaps this hybridism that makes this area of Situationist writing most worthy of attention today (Sadler 1999).[10] Beyond the chapter on space within *The Society of the Spectacle*, the relationship between social space and spectacle is clearly apparent in Situationist critiques of capitalist society as well as in their preferred forms of resistance to it. While they (and Debord in particular) were at pains to point out repeatedly that spectacle had invaded all areas of society, their analysis of spectacle mainly focuses on three arenas: the city, cinema, and, more abstractly, on everyday life. It is in these areas of analysis that their critique of separation, the spectacular constitution of space and sense of opposition between revolutionary mobility and consumer passivity, are most clearly articulated.

For the Situationists, the Baudelairean tradition of flâneurie becomes the dérive (drifting). Often in groups, they would set off into unfamiliar areas of Paris hoping to be inspired by the atmosphere and the vitality that this might convey. They hoped it would reveal an older Paris, an uncommodified city with traces of authentic life that could be set against the newly zoned and planned urban forms of consumer capitalism and thereby act in the manner of a détournement of its spectacular appropriation of social space. They sought to turn the practice of dérive into a new form of urban imaginary: psychogeographie. Through the use of dérive, détourned maps, articles critiquing the new vision of 1950s urbanism, and later on through films, they sought to capture an experiential, lived, and mobile city that could be used against the visions of the planners, capitalists, and bureaucrats.

> Psychogeographical research, "the study of the exact laws and specific effects of the action of the geographical environment, consciously organized or not, on the emotions and behaviour of individuals." (Debord 1989, 23)

Through the dérive, one could allow the city to become a force of seduction and promise that, once practiced, would allow the stroller to construct a psychogeographical understanding of the city that could be used to then see through the ideology and false consciousness of urbanism. The practice of the dérive, the psychogeographical imaginary, persuaded Debord and the other Situationists of the need for a total critique of the modern capitalist city, and that critique was to go under the name of unitary urbanism, which was imagined as a form of adventure (Sadler 1999; Coverley, 2006). In a paper written by Kotanyi and Vaniegem, the Situationsts set out their theory of unitary urbanism along lines already developed in writing about the dérive and psychogeographie (1989, 65–67). Many of the themes that Debord was later to develop around the spectacle are presented there too: urbanism as an ideology rather than a practice, the capitalist domestication of space through planning and false participation, traffic as an expression of individual isolation, cities as an expression of reification. They go on to highlight the forms of praxis that will challenge all of this: dérive, détournement, and the construction of situations (see below). Through a critique of the city, they believed that a critique of capitalism could be developed just as earlier Marxists had tried to critique the conditions of the factory for similar ends.

> The situationist destruction of present conditioning is already at the same time the construction of situations. It is the liberation of the inexhaustible energies trapped in the petrified daily life. With the advent of unitary urbanism, present city planning (that geology of lies) will be replaced by a technique for defending permanently threatened conditions of freedom, and individuals—who do not yet exist as such—will begin freely constructing their own history. (Debord 1989d, 67)

The early practices of the dérive through Paris and other cities were latter dropped and came to be seen as of little use beyond that of experiment. They were to be replaced with a more general argument about the idea of intervention in the wider arena of everyday life as it had been analyzed by Lefebvre (1971).

Lefebvre's analysis of everyday life, begun in the 1940s, was to have a lasting impact upon French sociology (see, for instance, de Certeau 1984) and was to shape the critique of consumer capitalism put forward by Debord and the other Situationists as well. In part, the analysis can be seen as an ongoing concern among Marxists with the crisis of revolutionary consciousness that began to be acknowledged in the early years of the twentieth century. If ideology and the false consciousness that it afforded stopped workers recognizing their real interests, the question became not only how to overcome this but also to try and recognize all the areas in which the capitalist relations of production were being supported ideologically. Lefebvre was one of the first Marxists to throw off the productivist bias that had come to define Marxism since Marx's own day.

Another influence in shaping views about contemporary capitalist society was the group of libertarian socialists known as Socialism ou Barbarie who also developed an understanding of contemporary capitalism around this time that diverged from the then orthodox, productivist French Communist Party model. This small group, whose members at one time included Cornelius Castoriadis, Claude Lefort, and Jean-Francois Lyotard, was to also influence Debord's arguments about everyday life, especially its bureaucratic characteristics (Gombin 1978). If Lefebvre's major concern was the increasing significance of consumption in shaping everyday life and the kind of banality in culture that it promotes (1971; see Shields 1999), Socialism ou Barbarie set out to analyze the changing character of work, recognizing the need to move away from a simple capitalist/worker dichotomy in order to take account of the new managerialism, as well as the technocratic and bureaucratic nature of postwar Fordist industry and rise of the service economy. They rejected a simplistic proletarianization thesis in favor of an argument that recognized that power was not just concentrated in the hands of the owners of capital but also in the hands of a new managerial class: not owners but "order givers." The workers, in contrast, were not simply defined as those who had to sell their labor power (this applied to many managers too) but those who had to take orders rather than give them in their place of work. Debord recognized early on the shifting character of postwar capitalist society and was to incorporate ideas from both Lefebvre and Socialism ou Barbarie into his own work. People were becoming more prosperous and secure yet their lives were becoming increasingly bureaucratic, isolated, and banal at the same time, he believed. Any form of revolutionary change could only emerge out of those conditions of prosperity rather than out of the immiseration of the working class.

While his earliest writings show him mainly concerned with distancing himself from a radical avant-garde artistic tradition, the one element he was to retain from that was the idea of shock and intervention as a means of challenging the established norms of bourgeois society. He tried to adapt that to fit with his analysis of the spectacle as pervasive within all areas of social life. This Dadaist theme, coupled with a political and social analysis of consumption and bureaucratic capitalism, was to shape his approach to the question of everyday life and to the type of resistance it might encourage. The idea of *the situation,* or event, is what he came up with as an answer:

> Our specific concern is the use of certain means of action and the discovery of new ones, means more easily recognisable in the domain of culture and mores, but applied in the perspective of an interaction of all revolutionary changes. (Debord 1989b, 17)

While not a definition of a situation, this quote shows something of the artistic milieu that Debord was writing from and his attempt to apply some of its theater of action to broader social issues. In this piece, he goes on to critically discuss the limitations of Dada and Surrealism (the two traditions in modernist art from which the Situationists, despite their hostility to them, do draw on for their not inconsiderable influence). He then goes on to critically discuss the postwar milieu with which he was loosely associated, CoBrA and the Lettrists (Home 1988; Plant 1992; Jappe

1999), before going on to define a "situation" and convey its significance within a Situationist political project.

> Our central idea is that of the construction of situations, that is to say, the concrete construction of momentary ambience of life and their transformation into a superior passional quality. We must develop a methodical intervention based on the complex factors of two components in perpetual interaction: the material environment of life and the comportments which it gives rise to and which radically transform it. (Debord 1989b, 22)

Exactly what momentary ambiences are and the nature of their passional quality is not specified. What is hinted at (more so given the Dadaist legacy) is a theatricality of action and intervention that disrupts the stasis of routine by aiming to produce a shock of recognition into the false reality that is being challenged. At this time of writing (1957) the dérive and its psychogeography are seen as the main forms of situations that might be engaged in. In his later writing, Debord was to see these examples of situations as rather innocent, still overly influenced by an avant-garde playfulness and not an expression of political maturity. But his discussion of the need to construct Soviets (workers councils) as a means of furthering the revolutionary struggle that is at the center of *The Society of the Spectacle*, his ideas of how they come into being (through situations), and on the idea of praxis as autonomous from any body of doctrine, class of intellectuals, or party machine, retains more than a trace of this spontaneisist position.

A summary of Debord's analysis, then, might go something like this: *Everyday life, a false and passive reality, and the increasingly bureaucratic character of work, despite the prosperity it brings for individuals, reinforce and reproduce alienating capitalist relations of production that generate an ideology of a good society. In late capitalism, that ideology as a form of fetishistic mediation has developed both as a functional totality and as autonomous from the control of any one class and has become an independently acting spectacle. Only the construction of situations can challenge the spectacle. In the first instance this will probably only be carried out by a small revolutionary elite but rather than try and organize the masses as Communist parties tried in the past, they will seek to inspire and educate them instead until people begin to construct their own situations, organize themselves spontaneously and then develop a revolutionary consciousness out of their organization.* For Debord, Mai '68 was a vindication of this theory, at least for a while, until a level of pessimism about the total integration of spectacle into all areas of life began to color his analysis toward the end of his life (1990).

The legacy of this position outlived 1968 and Debord himself. The growth of all manner of new social movements across the Western world since 1968, and the emphasis they often place on the spontaneous politics of direct action as a means of bringing about change, often through highly theatrical forms of protest and media campaigning, is in many respects Situationist. Certainly in some cases the influence is a direct one (Klein 2001). Contemporary anticapitalist protest and culture jamming come straight out of the Situationist project and its ideas about, and uses of, spontaneous direct action and owe much more to Debord than they do to Ghandi, the other great advocate of direct action as a form of protest to bring about change.

SITUATIONS, MOVEMENT, SPECTACLE

The Situationist project is, above all, a kinesthetic project—that is both its imaginative strength and its major limitation. It celebrates the values of community, movement, and action against isolation, passivity, and spectatorship but it cannot imagine those attributes outside of its own narrowly defined view of what constitutes activity. Indeed, I would contend that it is the theory of spectacle's own fetishism of action as well as its totalizing of the idea of passivity that constructs the consuming or viewing subject as passive rather than what consumers do themselves.

To begin, Debord has no real theory of desire. While his fellow Situationist Raoul Vaniegem devoted considerable attention to matters of pleasure, libidinal desire, and freedom and tried to make them central to the Situationist project (1983, 1990), desire in Situationist ideas is found only in action as struggle. This is a Surrealist move but whereas for them the mobile subject encountering an unfamiliar world would find his or her unconscious desires stimulated and released in a burst of surreal imagination, for the Situationists, this activity is supposed to lead instead to consciousness and recognition of real interests. In the theory of spectacle, the fetishistic spell that the commodity casts is not one of fulfilling some unconscious sense of lack as in the Freudian and Lacanian traditions, but of making people passive, isolated, and immobile and of the commodity then becoming their way of connecting with a sense of community, action, and self. Debord's approach, with the centrality it gives to ideas about the dérive, psychogeographie, and the creation of situations, derives from Lukacs's abstract theory of consciousness in *History and Class Consciousness* (1971) rather than from any recognition of embodied desire or practice. For Debord, the body and its sensuous pleasures will only be fulfilling, rather than a source of false consciousness within a society of the spectacle, after they have been reconciled with a conscious recognition of real interests—i.e., in struggle and in the overthrow of capitalism. On the theme of desire he offers something akin to a synthesis of Dada and Lukacs. The Situationists, and Debord in particular, are pretty much summed up by that combination of ideas.

While in many respects Debord places himself at the center of the Western Marxist tradition and its concern with the crisis of consciousness, his refusal of an analysis of desire makes him quite different from the likes of Adorno, Benjamin, Marcuse, Fromm, or others for whom psychoanalytic approaches to desire are what is missing in Marx (Ollman 1979). Apart from a few passing references to the work of Joseph Gabel's book *False Consciousness* (1975; see Debord 1977, #219) a work on the Marxist concept of false consciousness understood through an analysis of schizophrenia, there is little to suggest that the psychoanalytic tradition had any influence on Debord whatsoever. This is not necessarily a problem in itself. What is more problematic is the cast that it gives to the idea of fetishism and to how its spell is supposed to be broken. The key question for Debord is the nature of mediation.

Dada was about shock and intervention. It wanted to destabilize bourgeois taste and ideas about art through the use of nonconventional techniques and media. Although restricted to the arena of art works, it achieved some success, for a period, in unsettling a sense of convention in art as well as in providing a few lasting artistic techniques such as the ready-made and collage (Motherwell 1989). Debord spent much of his time distancing himself from the artistic legacy of Dada, and though some of the détourned artworks he did with Jorn in the 1950s make use of collage (Sadler 1999), he later repudiated them and spent much of his subsequent time within the Situationist group organizing the expulsion of any members who sought to express their activities through art (Home 1988). What he retained from the Dada movement was the idea of détournement—itself the principle behind creating situations—as the basis for critique and change.

The practice of détournement hopes to bring forth a shock of recognition in the unreality of what is taken as real in any cultural context, whether that be in the world of established artistic conventions or consumer society. Conventional and everyday media—newspapers, advertisements, billboards, and film or video—could make use of this technique. But to encounter, over and over, images that have been subjected to such treatment does not bring forth a recognition of the false reality, the fetishism expressed in those images, rather, it becomes something of a banal joke after a very short time.

Despite the sophistication of Debord's analysis of the spectacle, his analysis of the consumer as subject is mechanistic and crude; an example of the worst form of mass cultural analysis that treats distracted audiences as cultural dopes. Individuals are nothing more than isolated members of an audience; that is the sum total of their subjective experience in Debord's analysis. In effect, they exist outside of their own experiences and are nothing but a functional product of a functionalist spectacle—it is seen to take possession of them rather than to constitute them as subjects through the activity of taking possession. They cannot encounter the world other than as isolated and static members of an audience unless they engage in the practices of détournement as revolutionary activity themselves. Only though that practice do they become active and mobile and begin to develop their desires and start to demand more from society than its spectacular forms of consumption and entertainment offer.

In the Situationists' world in which all social relations are believed to be mediated by fetishized images, it is the image that has to be challenged, particularly where those images constitute a totality, a spectacle. The practice of détournement, the diversion of the image, seeks to challenge spectacle through the construction of a rupturing event. This does not necessarily just mean the détournement of particular images, advertisements say, although that was a part of Situationist practice, but of détourning the idea of mediation itself. To constitute mediation as a cinematic spectacle and to attribute to that spectacle a fetish character that is total and to then construct a total critique of that form of mediation as a means for engaging in both theory and practice is to be captured by the spectacle one is constructing.

Situationist politics is a fetishistic politics that cannot escape from the logic of its own critique—it can only know the world through spectacle and cannot imagine any other ways in which it capitalism might be lived. Ordinary lived reality, beyond politics, may indeed exhibit signs of treating the mediating images of social relations for the thing themselves but never so totally as the Situationists do. We need to explore further the bewildering and distracted nature of spectating that consumer culture generates if we are to avoid this trap.

Debord was not only trapped in the Dadaist fascination with challenging the media of images but also in Lukacs's transformation of alienation—a specifically defined area of life associated with production in Marx, but equivalent to all forms of social objectification in Lukacs. In interpreting Marx through Hegel (at a time when the 1844 manuscripts had yet to be rediscovered), Lukacs, like his one-time mentor Simmel, assumes any form of objectification of subjective expression as alienation and not just that defined by production within capitalism. This is because that rationalization process within Western society, for Lukacs, has generalized the conditions of the mechanized factory to all areas of social life and thought.

> This fragmentation of the object of production necessarily entails the fragmentation of its subject. In consequence of the rationalisation of the work-process the human qualities and idiosyncrasies of the worker appear increasingly as mere sources of error when contrasted with these abstract special laws functioning according to rational predictions. Neither objectively nor in his relation to his work does man appear as the authentic master of the process; on the contrary, he is a mechanical part incorporated into a mechanical system. (1971, 89)[11]

Debord simply takes that formulation out of the arena of production and applies it more generally and more totally to consumption and everyday life, which are seen to be more significant in the capitalism of postwar Western societies. Likewise, Lukacs also locates desire in action, seeing the bourgeois life-world as a contemplative one and imagining that the proletarian life-world will become more active because of its location within capitalist social relations. Only active struggle by the proletariat will change things; above all, Lukacs believed in reconciling subjective and objective life. Lukacs was later to go on to criticize himself on this position (1971), but Debord remained faithful to the position set out in *Society of the Spectacle* for the rest of his life, indeed arguing that its totalizing tendencies were becoming even more total as time went on (1990).

If Debord doesn't have a theory of desire, he doesn't have much of an understanding of the lived reality of subjects either. His consumer subjects are little more than theoretical abstractions. This was a point made by Christopher Gray, himself a one-time member of the Situationists, in his own introduction and commentary in an early set of translations of their writings.

> What was basically wrong with the S.I. was that it focused exclusively on an intellectual critique of society. There was no concern whatsoever with either the emotions or the body. The S.I. thought that you just had to show how the nightmare worked and everyone would wake up. Their quest was for the perfect formula, the magic charm that would disperse the evil spell.... In the last analysis they made the same mistake as all left wing intellectuals, they thought that everyone else was plain thick. (1974, 166–67)

More recently Debray has offered a similar critique.

> With the advent of participatory or interactive communication in groups or en masse—as in rock concerts, sporting events and popular attractions like Disneyland...—the theatrical setting, and arrangements, namely face-to-face relations of scene and public, screen and watchers, are abolished.... The society of the spectacle, which reached its apogee in the century of Louis XIV, has not withstood the harsh attacks, sharper and sharper, of the photographic onslaught. We live out its death agony and undergo its effects on a daily basis. The problem today is not the distance brought about by spectacle but the engulfing, fleshy communions of non-spectacle, by this I mean live broadcasts, the new "immediacy" and "performance art." The transition from film to television, from device to projection...to one of broadcasting into the home, from work characterised by deferment to the visual documentation of life in real time, marks precisely the moment when the image ceases to be a spectacle and becomes a vital milieu, removing the founding difference between the seen and the lived. (1995, 138–40)

While the theory of spectacle, like all theories of false consciousness, is not about faulty cognition but about the masking of social reality by false appearances and how that comes to take on the character of the true social reality, the mechanistic and disembodied understanding of subjectivity ultimately fails to find a way out of the crisis of consciousness it seeks to challenge. Or, to put it in the form of a détournement...

The chief defect of recent materialism (that of Debord included) is that the thing, reality, sensuousness, is conceived only in the form of the objectivity of spectacle or of passive contemplation, but not as sensuous human activity, practice, not subjectively. Hence, in contradistinction to materialism, the active side was developed abstractly by Marxist-idealism—which, of course, does not know real, sensuous activity as such. Debord wants sensuous situations, really distinct from watched spectacles, but he does not conceive vision itself as situated sensuous activity. Hence in Society of the Spectacle *he regards the theoretical attitude as the only genuine human attitude, while non-theoretical practice is conceived and fixed separately in its dirty-massified manifestation. Hence he does not truly grasp the revolutionary significance of "embodied," of "everyday," activity.*

We need to explore in more detail the relationship among fetishism, mediation, subjectivity, and experience rather than accept the arguments Debord offers us and his formula that consumer society is a society of the spectacle. I turn to Marx and then to Benjamin in the next two chapters in order to do this. My aim is not to reject the idea of fetishism out of hand but to seek to use it in a less totalizing manner than Debord and others do when describing consumer society, and to relate it more closely to the idea of the active subject within consumer culture.

Chapter Three

Phantasmagoria and the Fetish

CONSUMPTION AND FETISHISM

If we are to better understand the character of the consumer culture that emerged in the latter half of the nineteenth century after the Great Exhibition, the mass consumer culture of industrial capitalism that continues to define our world, then we need to move away from totalizing theories of spectacle. The Great Exhibition showed how a social space defined by spectacle came to prominence in a particular form during the nineteenth century, one that was premised on ideas of panorama and totality and which involved novel understandings of subjectivity and objectivity. What a commodity is (see Marx 1938), its changing position within regimes of value (Appadurai 1986) and cultural codes (McCracken 1988), and its cultural biography, a consequence of its changing value position in time and space (see Douglas and Isherwood 1986; Thompson 1979; Kopytoff 1986), are all of significance to our understanding of the rather fluid and complex production of consumer spaces in which spectacle is constituted. In the previous chapter I challenged ideas that sought to use the term spectacle as a synonym for a totalizing theory of commodity fetishism. My main criticism, focused on the work of Debord (1977), was that the totalizing theory that has developed around this term and been applied to consumer culture treats consumers not merely as isolated subjects but as cultural dopes who engage in consumption in a passive, distracted, and thereby seemingly asocial manner.

But before moving on from this position to look at the spatialized character of consumption, I want to go back to where this theory of spectacle originated, as I believe that while some of the problems can be put down to Debord's theoretical style and his political machinations, others are to be found in the theoretical sources from which his ideas about subjectivity are first expressed. In particular, that means we need to consider the whole issue of fetishism on which the idea of a society of the spectacle is premised. In this chapter, therefore, I want to discuss what that well- used term means in the context of consumption. To do this principally requires that we engage critically with the use of the term fetish in relation to the commodity in the work of Marx (1938).

While the association of the term fetish with that of the commodity is an established one that begins with Marx, understanding of the term fetish, however, predates the publication of *Das Kapital* in 1867. What the term means, both before and after Marx, remains complex and contested, requiring some unraveling here. Discourses surrounding the pidgin term *fetisso* go back to the sixteenth century, and for at least the past 250 years the idea of the fetish has had an important place in a number of different and well-known fields, notably anthropological studies of religion and psychoanalysis as well as in Marxist political economy (for an overview, see Cohen 1978; Ellen 1988; Pietz 1993). It has also, more recently, figured significantly in discussions of modernist art, female sexuality and sexual politics, and in film studies too (see, for instance, Apter 1991; Apter and Pietz 1993; Mulvey 1996). Clearly some of these debates are beyond the scope of this book and while differing in their interpretation of the term fetish, what we can say is that what all these approaches have in common, at least in the original conceptualization of fetishism, is a concern with how an object comes to be seen as an active force that has some power-effect on subjects (Pietz 1985, 7). In each case, we might add, relationships with the fetish are understood through a form of knowledge premised on the idea of *fascination* or *curiosity* (Bann 1995; Mulvey 1996). In a sense, a fetish is an object with mystery and allure, something that is not what it purports to be, an object that conceals and at the same time reveals a displaced absent/present active material force that is able to somehow constitute a viewing subject through its attributed agency, variously as fetish worshipper, sexual fetishist, or producer/consumer. What has often followed from these varied analyses is the *Othering* of these forms of subjectivity that are associated most closely with fetishism. While there have recently been attempts, notably by feminists, to revalorie sexual fetishism as a counter-hegemonic source of empowered identity for women (Apter 1991; Mulvey 1996) and not simply treat it negatively as a male perversion, the same cannot really be said yet for the consumer and his or her susceptibility to commodity fetishism.

In Western societies the fetish is not typically seen as an agent within the process of rational subject formation but rather as a form of distorted understanding associated with some kind of errant subjectivity conceived as primitive, individualist, or perverted. To suggest that the fetish, in the context of consumption, might be connected up to other ways of knowing the subject is to challenge the way in which the fetish is understood, and that means we must look at those who have most clearly developed a systematic critique of fetishism through their understanding of capitalism as a *mode of production*. Typically, then, the conventional approach to fetishism, established since the Enlightenment, has involved the act of witnessing what others do with objects and then making a critical judgment about their flawed attributions of agency, particularly those concerning a person's apparent attribution of agency and causal powers to things themselves.

This critical approach has been established in Western thought across many centuries, initially in the sixteenth century, and has developed since then to the point where fetishistic knowledge is now assumed almost unquestioningly to be the antithesis of all enlightened forms of rational understanding. While more sophisticated understandings of fetishism, such as Marx's, have gone on to suggest that it is the visualized reality that is distorted by fetishism and not the cognitive abilities of subjects constituted within that false reality, the model, based on the idea of an error of causal explanation, has remained intact nonetheless even in this work.

In this chapter, following William Pietz, I explore something of the genealogy of the discourse of the fetish and look in detail at Marx's understanding of commodity fetishism in relation to it. I highlight, in particular, the significance he gives to the early nineteenth-century version of the magic lantern show, the phantasmagoria, as the trope for understanding the regime of curiosity of the fetish. This is significant not only because of what it tells us about Marx's understanding of fetishism but also because it is within this spatial framing that the modern concept of spectacle has its beginnings. I argue that this is premised on a particular understanding of subjectivity that draws on the earlier reception of fetishism during the Enlightenment and before and that it fails to take into account the changing constitution of the subject that emerges during the nineteenth century. This is somewhat surprising as much of Marx's own work can be seen as one of the preeminent examples that emerged from this particular humanist and Romantic discursive moment (Gouldner 1973) that challenged directly the de-corporealized rationalism of the Enlightenment and earlier baroque scientific thinking on which the theory of fetishism had previously been premised (Howes 2003). While Marx makes much of the creative powers of the subject as producer within a material environment, and makes a clear distinction between alienation and objectification in his analysis, through this trope of the phantasmagoria he simplifies the power effects of objects as fetishes upon alienated subjects. The reason he does this is because of his emphasis on the importance of production (an alienated source of creative subject powers) and exchange value over symbolic exchange, consumption, and use value (the realm of the object) in his analysis of capitalism (Baudrillard 1975; Howes 2003). Through this analysis he creates what might be called a *production view of the subject*. I want to challenge this view and develop an alternative in subsequent chapters of the book—*a consumption view of the subject* (see also Munro 1996).

THE COMPLEX SPACE OF THE FETISH

The term fetish emerged from an "unstable space" or paradoxical space of betweenness rather than from any singular definite location (Spyer 1998). It derived, in particular, from the encounter of two peoples through a shared interest in the value of material culture in an uncertain "intercultural" space: initially the space of commerce between Portuguese explorers of the sixteenth century and the African peoples they began to trade with on the Mina coast of West Africa as they navigated their way south (Pietz 1985, 6). These traders observed that the people of that area seemingly worshipping objects that they assumed to have god-like powers. These objects, which, in fact, had many different forms of significance within that culture, were often enrolled within the trading process itself between these two peoples. In order to trade with the Africans, the Portuguese traders had to form a contractual arrangement that, in order to be deemed trustworthy for the Africans, required of them that they swear an oath on the fetish object (Pietz 1985, 1987). The pidgin term given to these artifacts in this intercultural space was *fetisso*. This term derived from the Portuguese word *feitiço* that referred to magical practices. This word, in its turn, derived from the Latin *facticius*, meaning "something manufactured" (Pietz 1985, 5).

From that initial set of uncertain encounters and the establishment of trading relationships, Pietz suggests that we can see the development of a series of phases through which the fetish comes to be understood within Western society (1985, 5). In the first phase (sixteenth and seventeenth centuries), one of encounter and exchange in this uncertain intercultural space, the Portuguese found that the Africans appeared to worship objects of cultural value. Some objects appeared to have religious value, others acted more like talismans, some were of erotic or aesthetic value, others were used for oath-swearing such as in contract-making activity, and some had economic value and were traded (notably gold objects) (Pietz 1988, 109). This hybrid mix of objects and values was seen as a puzzle to the Portuguese who noted that any artifact appeared to be able to assume the status of a fetisso for the Africans and they seemed to be able to transfigure its value at will through their relationship with it. The arbitrariness was a puzzle to them. Clearly objects of value, there appeared to the Portuguese to be no visible significance as to how that value was derived. It would seem that for the Africans it was the object as signifier that was important, whereas for the Portuguese, it was what it signified that mattered most. For one, the figural qualities of value mattered and allowed for its fluid movement within different spaces of cultural exchange, for the other—the Portuguese, the object as an enunciation of a discourse of exchange value was what mattered most; gold, above all, being the emblem of such a discourse.

Such puzzlement at the paradoxical status of the fetisso continued among the northern European Protestant traders who began to displace the Portuguese and to trade in the area from the seventeenth century onward. More schooled in the Protestant critique of idolatry than their Catholic Portuguese predecessors, they tried at first to see these objects as akin to the idols that they hated in Catholicism. However, the seemingly arbitrary signification for the Africans remained problematic to the

Protestant mindset and did not allow for this position to be held unquestioningly as a basis for critique. Unable to adequately situate these objects within a critical Christian discourse of idolatry, therefore, the initial confusion began to give way to a more sustained critical tone as the Europeans, unable to derive any sense of value from their own logic of understanding of the significance of idols, began to assume that the fault must instead be with the reasoning capacity of the Africans themselves. As a consequence, they came to be seen as irrational, arbitrary, and foolish in their unsystematic attribution of power and significance to things (Pietz 1987); or, in a word, as primitive. This phase of encounter ends with early eighteenth-century texts such as Bosman's 1703 *A New and Accurate Description of the Coast of Guinea* (1967), in which we find expressed a critique of African religious beliefs as irrational and founded on superstition and interest (see Pietz 1988).

Thereafter, a second phase emerges in the discourse of the fetish in which Africans come to be Othered through an increasingly racist depiction of their figural forms of understanding and religious beliefs as primitive and illogical. De Brosses's landmark text of 1760, *Du Cult des Dieux Fétiches,* firmly establishes this view of primitive religion centered on the fetish within an Enlightenment consideration of rationality and societal development. He offers the first systematic attempt to try to understand fetishism as a particular religious belief system and seeks to locate it within a general theory of religious development. For Enlightenment thinkers like de Brosses, African fetish worship appears to demonstrate an error in understanding the principles of causality, whereby objects themselves are assumed to have magical powers (Pietz 1988, 116). In line with the normal/pathological model of establishing categories of identity that Foucault has described in the modern European context around the categories of sanity, illness, criminality, and sexuality (1974), the fetish-worshipping African comes to be seen as the unenlightened antithesis of the enlightened European subject; in fact, perhaps *the* preeminent Other in the establishment of the modern discourse of reason, at least as prominent as the mad or the Oriental (Said 1979). If the Oriental was the exotic spatial Other to Western eyes, then the African became the primitive or temporal Other. Orientalism and African fetishism each has its own imaginary geography: east (exotic) and south (backward). We should locate both terms within the same discursive formation of the rational Western subject. The term fetishism has subsequently been understood as a source of causal error associated with a simplistic attribution of agency to things, in particular giving things magical powers or special qualities that they do not possess in themselves. Subsequent Western scientific understandings of fetishism have their beginnings, therefore, in this racist discourse of the "primitive" Other.

A third phase in the use of the term fetishism, according to Pietz, occurs during the nineteenth century when this earlier Enlightenment concern with primitive religion developed within different emerging social sciences, most notably in anthropology, psychology, and, of course, in Marxist political economy. In anthropology,

August Comte took up De Brosses's developmental view of religion and worked it into his positivist study of society as something thought to be in a process of passing through different and advancing stages of development (fetishism/polytheism/monotheism; Ellen 1988, 214). Subsequent evolutionary theorists such as Spencer and Lubbock similarly adopted this view of primitive belief systems and applied it to understanding the trajectory of societies.

Such a view did not hold for long without challenge, however, as anthropology refined its conceptual understanding through ethnographic research. Distinctions began to be made over the practices involved in fetishism within different cultures, and over whether it was the object itself that was attributed special powers (fetishism) or a spirit working through it (animism). Subsequent anthropological work rejected this earlier evolutionary approach to cultural matters and more generally to the usefulness of the idea of fetishism itself. Durkheim, for instance, in his groundbreaking study of elementary religious forms, relegates fetishism to only half a page of dismissive discussion (1971, 175). Nonetheless, there remains ongoing debate in anthropology around this term (Ellen 1988), sometimes combining it with Marxist usage (see, for example, Taussig 1980, 1992).

In psychology, the term fetishism was adapted from readings of both Enlightenment theory and early ethnology and applied to understanding deviant and "primitive" or regressive forms of sexual rather than religious behavior. The notion of a sexual fetish, understood as a figure of perversion, applies where an object, or a part of the body, becomes the subject of erotic attachment. This argument was first developed by Richard von Krafft-Ebing in his 1886 study *Psychopathia Sexualis* (1965). It was Freud, however, who most famously went on to analyze fetishism and to develop the psychoanalytic conceptual understanding of it that is the basis of what we have today. In two works, *Three Essays on the History of Sexuality* (1905) and *Fetishism* (1927) (see Freud 1977a, 1977b), he argued that fetishism be seen as the result of an Oedipal crisis in which the male child's fear of castration, which arises from first seeing the female genitals as an infant, is unresolved and remains present in the adult. For the fetishist, the fetish stands in for the missing penis of the mother, the absence of which the fetishist seeks to disavow by substituting its lack with an object, body part, or item of clothing that takes its place. As with early ethnographic research, fetishism is understood in this context as a primitive form of sexual development; as a perversion or an aberrant condition that has not achieved a fully developed (adult) state.[1]

Finally for Pietz, the fourth stage in the discourse surrounding fetishism is the one we have today where there have been attempts at theoretical unity, bringing together these different nineteenth-century approaches (see, for example, Baudrillard 1981; Zizek 1989). While there are important insights to be drawn from both of these anthropological and psychoanalytic perspectives, it is Marx's discussion of fetishism in the first chapter of *Capital*, part of Pietz's third phase, that has come to dominate understanding of fetishism in the economic context. In that we find an articulation of nineteenth-century anthropological ideas about religion with those of political economy, around a theory of value, and I want to concentrate on that here.

MARX AND COMMODITY FETISHISM

Marx's famous discussion of commodity fetishism in Chapter 1 of *Capital* is also based on this earlier Enlightenment and anthropological perspective on the fetish. According to Pietz, Marx studied work on religion, including De Brosses in 1841, and first used the term in a derogatory way when referring to the illusory ideas of some of his Hegelian opponents (1993, 134). Later on, the theory of commodity fetishism developed beyond a term of abuse but it remained, above all, a theory of visual illusion associated with the "fantastic" and "monstrous" spectacle of the alienated object-world of the commodity that capitalism conjures up (see also Keenan 1993; Derrida 1994). Marx drew on the earlier denigration of fetishism within scientific studies of religion and used a popular mechanical visualizing apparatus for creating spectral illusions as the metaphor through which he developed a critique of the illusory concealment of the creation of value in capitalist societies. The effects of this have not been inconsequential. This emphasis on illusion as the basis of capitalist reality becomes an ever more explicit theme in later writings in the Marxist and post-Marxist tradition, notably in the work of Debord (1977) and Baudrillard (1981) but is already apparent in Marx and successive Marxist commentators who place commodity fetishism at the center of their critical analysis, notably Lukacs (1971), Adorno (1981), and Benjamin (1999a, 1999b, 1999c). It is a theory of fetishism that positions subjects and objects (commodities) in a particular way, reading the commodity and commodified culture as an illusory representation of the world of production; something that seemingly involves consumers in the worship of the misleading figural or signifying qualities of material culture.

Marx himself, however, did not extend his analysis of commodity fetishism to the whole of consumer society. Rather, he limited his analysis to the realm of capitalist production and the status of exchange value within it. Nonetheless, Marx's famous analysis of commodity fetishism has the central trope of visual obscuring or concealing within an apparently simple and recognizable image. However, this is not to suggest that his theory of fetishism presumes that the fault is in the consciousness or cognitive abilities of subjects within capitalism. Rather, the illusion arises because in capitalist societies people do see a true picture—but a true picture of a false reality.

For Marx, fetishism occurs where the value of a commodity, the product of real social relations that are the outcome of sensuous human activity (subjectivity is conceived here in terms of production as Homo Faber), comes to appear as a thing independent of the labor that produced it. Exchange value appears to derive from the thing itself rather than from the social relations of production in which it is produced. For Marx, in a capitalist society, the real social relations that operate between people are replaced by imaginary ones that appear to occur between things. Within capitalism, the relations of production through which use values are turned into exchange values by human labor come to be objectified in the commodity, and the involvement of labor in the creation of value is thereby obscured— as the abstraction of labor power. Fetishism, for Marx, has to do with the relationship between people and things through which this obscuring relationship or substitution occurs.

For Marx, human beings, workers, produce value through their labor power, but in a capitalist society this goes unrecognized. Whereas in other modes of production such as feudalism, the production process makes the social relations on which that society is based visible to all, in capitalism, Marx believes, those social relations are concealed. Because the value of a commodity that is bought and sold in the market appears to be established there, the role of production and of the workers' labor as the real source of exchange value comes to be hidden. As a consequence, social relations in a capitalist society appear to emerge within the processes of exchange rather than production. It appears as if the value of a commodity derives from the commodity itself rather than from the work that went into producing it.

Yet, for Marx, it is workers who produce value through their socially necessary labor. In fact, under capitalism they produce more value than the costs involved in maintaining their ability to continue working. However, because this labor power is itself sold to the capitalist as a commodity in return for a wage, it is the capitalist who gains the surplus value that is produced and not the worker. The capitalists are able to sell the commodity for more than its costs, including the cost of labor. Because value appears to derive from the commodity, this comes to be seen as natural and right. It is, then, this quality of commodities that Marx associates with the idea of the fetish. Here is the famous passage in full from *Capital* where he develops the term:

> A commodity is therefore a mysterious thing, simply because in it the social character of men's labour appears to them as an objective character stamped upon the product of that labour; because the relation of the producers to the sum total of their own labour is presented to them as a social relation existing not between themselves, but between the products of their labour. This is the reason why the products of labour become commodities, social things whose qualities are at the same time perceptible and imperceptible by the senses. In the same way the light from an object is perceived by us not as the subjective excitation of our optic nerve, but as the objective form of something outside the eye itself. But in the act of seeing, there is at all events, an actual passage of light from one thing to another, from the external object to the eye. But it is different with commodities. There, the existence of the things qua commodities, and the value relation between the products of labour which stamps them

as commodities, have absolutely no connection with their physical properties and with the material relations arising therefrom. There it is a definite social relation between men that assumes, in their eyes, the fantastic form of a relation between things. In order, therefore, to find an analogy, we must have recourse to the mist-enveloped regions of the religious world. In that world the productions of the human brain appear as independent beings endowed with life, and entering into relation both with one another and the human race. So it is in the world of commodities with the products of men's hands. This I call the Fetishism which attaches itself to the products of labour, so soon as they are produced as commodities, and which is therefore inseparable from the production of commodities. (1938, 42–43)

Marx suggests we need to turn to religion as an analogy to understand the mystical power of the commodity fetish. We need to turn, in effect, to the established Enlightenment approach to anthropological investigation of fetishism as a false and primitive form of understanding as set down by Bosman, De Brosses, and others.

Marx had, in his early writing, already made reference to the concept of fetishism. It first appears in a critique he makes of an article on religion that had appeared in the *Kölnische Zeitung* in 1842. His understanding of fetishism there has a strong Enlightenment influence in its treatment of religion.

Fetishism is so far from raising men above his sensuous desires that, on the contrary, it is "the religion of sensuous desire." Fantasy arising from desire deceives the fetish-worshipper into believing that an "inanimate-object" will give up its natural character in order to comply with his desires. Hence the crude desire of the fetish-worshipper smashes the fetish when it ceases to be its most obedient servant. (1975a, 189)

Fetishism is seen here is a product of sensuous desire (figural knowledge) rather than rational thought and as a consequence is associated with the idea of illusion or fantasy. Similarly, in his discussions of private property in his 1844 *Economic and Philosophical Manuscripts*, he refers to the detractors of eighteenth-century Enlightenment political economy as primitive fetish-worshippers.

The subjective essence of private property, private property as activity for itself, as subject, as person, is labour. It therefore goes without saying that only that political economy which recognized labour as its principle (Adam Smith) and which therefore no longer regarded private property as nothing more than a condition external to man, can be regarded as both a product of the real energy and movement of private property (it is the independent movement of private property become conscious for itself, it is modern industry as self), a product of modern industry, and a factor which has accelerated and glorified the energy and development of this industry and transformed it into a power belonging to consciousness. Therefore the supporters of the monetary and mercantile system, who look upon private property as a purely objective being for man, appear as fetish-worshippers, as Catholics, to this enlightened political economy, which has revealed—within the system of private property—the subjective essence of wealth. (1975b, 341–42)

For Marx, fetishism is a trope for the illusory belief that does not recognize the subject as the producer of value (or private property) in the object. This is a theme that is constant throughout his work. The metaphors the Marx uses when discussing fetishism are visual ones: delusion, illusion, and Catholic idolatry. Something is getting in the way of the rational eye/knowledge that is stopping us from seeing the true subjective process of value production. The attribution of the value-producing agency to objects is getting in the way. In *Capital* he goes on to suggest that it is the *thing as image* that is concealing the truth like some opaque screen.

> The mode of production in which the product takes the form of a commodity, or is produced directly for exchange, is the most general and the most embryonic form of bourgeois production. It therefore makes its appearance at an early date in history, though not in the same predominating and characteristic manner as now-a-days. Hence its Fetish character is comparatively easy to be *seen through*. But when we come to more concrete forms, even this appearance of simplicity vanishes. Whence arose the illusions of the monetary system?.... And modern economy, which looks down with such disdain on the monetary system does not its superstition come out as clear as noon day, whenever treated as capital? (1938, 54, emphasis added)

If we look closely at the first quote above from *Capital* and include alongside it the original German, we see precisely how Marx imagined the fetish to work. The social relations that are constituted through commodity production are understood as a form of illusory and ghostly visual entertainment that became popular at the end of the eighteenth century.

> There is a definite social relation between men, that assumes, in their eyes, the [phantasmagoric] fantastic form of a relation between things. (1938, 43)

> [Es ist nur das bestimmte gesellschaftliche Verhaeltnis der Menschen selbst, welches hier fuer sie die phantasmagorische Form eines Verhaeltnisses von Dingen annimmt.][2]

Die phantasmagorische Form. Moore and Aveling's 1887 English translation from the third German edition drops the precision of "phantasmagoric" for the vague yet more familiar English word "fantastic." Nonetheless it is there in the original, and phantasmagoria was a word used in English from the early nineteenth century. Marx was clearly aware of the phantasmagoria tradition that began in Paris in the late eighteenth century as an extension of the entertainment offered by magic lantern shows. He used the word a number of times throughout his work to refer to illusory spectacles.[3] If fact, he was very fond of using metaphors of optical tricks, ghostly apparitions, and mechanical visualizing apparatus when discussing matters of knowledge and ideology (see Derrida 1994). In *The German Ideology*, for instance, Marx and Engels make reference in a similar way to a visual apparatus as the metaphor for illusory ideological vision.

> Consciousness can never be anything else than conscious existence, and the existence of men is their actual life-process. If in all ideology men and their circumstances appear upside-down as in a *camera obscura*, this phenomenon arises just as much from their historical life-process as the inversion of objects on the retina does from their physical life-process. (1970, 47, emphasis in original)

The illusory world of the camera obscura and later the phantasmagoria that is an adaptation of this technical apparatus is how Marx explains the operation of both ideology and fetishism within capitalist society. Marx's use of phantasmagoria is not just a literary flourish but the governing trope in how he presents the "mystical" nature of commodity fetishism to us.[4] *It is his way of understanding the commodity's regime of curiosity,* a regime that he considers to be a false one. It is this issue that is, furthermore, developed significantly within the tradition of Western Marxism during the twentieth century, notably by members of the Frankfurt School who were concerned to understand not so much the processes of production within capitalism as its consumer culture (see Lukacs 1971; Adorno 1981; Benjamin 1999a, 1999b, 1999c). In using the metaphor Marx tries to demonstrate something of the bewildering capacity of the commodity and of the subject constituted in relation to it. We need to investigate this trope of the phantasmagoria further in order to see the form of visual understanding that Marx is placing at the center of his theory of commodity fetishism and the model of both subjectivity and objectivity that he is bringing into play around it.

PHANTASMAGORIC VISIONS

The original phantasmagoria was a form of popular spectacle that emphasized the principle of deception or concealment, in its mode of display, particularly through its association with the presentation of the figure of the ghost (on the history of the phantasmagoria, see Quigley 1948; Altick 1978; Barnouw 1981; Cohen 1989, 1995; Crary 1990; Castle 1995; Heard 1996; During 2002). The earliest phantasmagoria shows were shown in Europe, notably Paris, in the latter part of the eighteenth century. A combination of the earlier traditions of magic lantern show, Chinese shadow play, and magic displays, phantasmagoria involved the back projection of ghostly images onto a translucent screen (or, in some cases, smoke) hung in the middle of a darkened room around which an audience sat.

Francois Seraphin showed an entertainment that first used some of these elements to the court at Versailles in 1784. It was soon relocated to that center of popular entertainment, consumption, and political ferment—the Palais Royal—around the same year (see Quigley 1948, 76–77; on the Palais Royal, see Hetherington 1997).[5] The technique was taken up, popularized, and named as a *Phantasmagoria* by Paul Philidor, who held a show under that name in Berlin in 1789 (Heard 1996; During 2002, 102). However, the person who is more commonly given the credit for naming and inventing the phantasmagoria in 1798 was the Belgian entertainer Etienne-Gaspard Robertson, who apparently plagiarized the idea from Philidor (see Heard 1996) and whose shows caused a sensation in Paris in the aftermath of the Revolution (Quigley 1948, 77–78; Castle 1995, 144ff.; Cohen 1989; During 2002, 102ff.).

As much popular theatre as magic lantern show (assistants would sometimes move around the audience dressed as skeletons; Cohen 1989), Robertson's shows were dominated by the presentation of images of the recently dead figures from French history, such as Rousseau and Voltaire, and by leading figures from the Revolution, such as Marat. Their ghostly images were projected onto a screen in the middle of the room—as ghosts returning to haunt the spectators in the aftermath of the Terror.

The principle of concealment was established by hiding the projectors from view, something not done with earlier magic lantern shows. In effect, what was concealed was what *produced* the images. The images were intended to appear as if they just emerged and had a life of their own independent of any mechanical apparatus for projecting them as images. Typically, Robertson would ask a member of the audience whose ghost they wanted to see, he would throw an item (such as some leaves) on a fire to call them up, and then, as if by magic, the ghost would appear in all its spectral horror. In a room in which all the candles had been snuffed out, the audience was only able to see the ghostly appearances dance in the middle of the room. Not only could they not see the projector, they couldn't see the screen onto which they were projected either. The central concealment of production and the presentation of the images as independent entities make this at first glance a seemingly apposite metaphor for Marx. But what he doesn't really think about when using this term is how those shows might have been consumed.

Following the popularity of the phantasmagoria shows in Paris, they were soon to cross the channel to England. In 1801, Philidor resurfaced in London now operating under the name of Paul de Philipsthal (a one-time partner of Madame Tussaud, whose waxworks still exists today as a leading London tourist attraction; see Heard 1996; During 2002, 102) and introduced the phantasmagoria and exhibited it at the Lyceum in the Strand (Altick 1978, 217; Castle 1995, 150). Its popularity lead to many imitators in the early years of the nineteenth century, the first of whom was a clown called Mr. Bologna who performed at Covent Garden and set up his own phantasmagoria show called "Phantsacopia" following Philipsthal's success (Beresford Chancellor 1925, 119).

It was from these early London shows that the word first appeared in English in 1802 (*Oxford English Dictionary*). From there, it made its way into other languages, including German, in the early years of the nineteenth century. Indeed, one of the key sources for the popularity and spread of the word beyond the limited world of these magic shows and into a general discourse on societal illusions was Thomas Carlyle's *Sartor Resartus* (2000 [1833–34]), where he used the word to mean losing touch with reality in a more general sense (During 2002, 102), creating an illusory world more complex than allegory to unravel.

> We sit in a boundless Phantasmagoria and Dream-grotto; boundless, for the faintest star, the remotest century, lies not even nearer the verge thereof: sounds and many-coloured visions flit round our sense: but Him, the Unslumbering, whose work both Dream and Dreamer are, we see not; except in rare half-waking moments, suspect not. (Carlyle 2000, 43)

What the word's etymology might signify is of interest too, not least because of its aporial status. Three interpretations of the term have been offered (see Cohen 1989, 95).

- Most simply as "ghost-speak" or "speak to the ghosts"
- *Phantasma agoreuein*: to speak in public (from the agora—a place of public discourse that was also a market place) under the influence of allegory (Robertson's preferred definition)
- *Fantasme agourer*, which translates as "ghostly deceiver" or "deceiving ghost"

In effect, the slippage between each of these equally plausible definitions defines the phantasmagoria through paradox and opens up the idea of the speaking ghost/illusion/figure and the doubtful quality of what it might have to say, the space in which it says it, and the kind of language it offers. Concealment and uncertainty are central motifs. This was a space of intended bewilderment. The nature of the figure on display there is significant too. These were ghostly figures and not just any kind of image. The slippage in the word's etymology also suggests something else that is apposite to Marx's analysis: "phantasm agora" (Derrida 1994, 108). It is in the market place of illusion, image, and voice that the ghost appears as if to speak.

Marx is deeply suspicious of ghosts yet they continue to haunt his work (Derrida 1994). We might ask ourselves why. The ghost is the preeminent figure—a product of figural rather than rational discursive knowledge. Its ontological status is that of a source of figural revelation through which we encounter a concealed and possibly deceptive language outside of discourse (Derrida 1994; Gordon 1997). It is a figure that speaks through images and appearances, above all, and only reluctantly through words directly (think of the early sections of *Hamlet* and the difficulty that Marcellus, Horatio, and Hamlet have in getting the ghost of Hamlet's father to speak). It speaks in a manner in which images appear to speak within a dream: phantasme. This is suggestive of how commodities speak to consumers, as we will see in Benjamin's work (1999a) in the next chapter. But the question is how Marx treats these issues.

While perhaps initially shocked and amused by this apparition in their midst (spectral visions, ghost stories, and gothic novels were popular entertainment in England in the early years of the nineteenth century and were a central motif for the emerging Romantic imagination; see Castle 1995), we have to assume, given the skilled reception shown within a long history of theatrical entertainments and spectacles (see Altick 1978), that audiences were not so credulous that they couldn't see through these phantasms and recognize them for what they were—a source of entertainment that created a frisson of trepidation and excitement (see Agnew 1986). Certainly as a form of entertainment the phantasmagoria had long since become passé by 1867 when Marx published *Capital*, but its principle of presenting images of reality as if they were reality and concealing the true source of the production of those images was certainly a part of the nineteenth-century episteme and its concern with the optics of attention (Williams 1982; Crary 1990, 1999; Friedberg 1993) and with secular magical entertainment prior to the advent of the "magic" of cinema (During 2002). Understanding the attributed powers of the fetish through the trope of the phantasmagoria rests on an understanding of technique (object) and seeing (subject) and the character of the figure that mediates the two. We need to consider this issue further.

In an important recent work, Jonathan Crary has argued that an epistemic shift in the optics of attention, and of the form of subjectivity premised on it, occurred some time in the early 1820s (1990; see also 1999). Prior to that and throughout the course of the eighteenth century, the apparatus that was taken as the trope for understanding subject-object relations was that of the camera obscura. While the principles of producing an upside-down image on a wall of a room after light from outside has been projected through an aperture into that room might have been known for thousands of years and, indeed, was a noted phenomenon by many important philosophers and artists from Euclid onward, it was Leonardo da Vinci who was the first to make the important comparison between the technical principles of the camera obscura and the workings of the human eye (Lindberg 1976, 164ff.). After this, the camera obscura came to be seen as a metaphor for sight and for rational knowledge in the classical/Baroque age (Jay 1994). As a model it typified the regime of curiosity of the Classical age: viewing subjects looking onto a viewed object world that was separate and distinct.[6] That term continued as a metaphor for visual knowledge throughout the seventeenth and eighteenth centuries. It became the metaphor, moreover, not only for the principles of sight but also for the truth of vision (Crary 1990, 29) and a model for understanding the human subject as such. As Crary neatly puts it:

Beginning in the late 1500s the figure of the camera obscura begins to assume a pre-eminent importance in delimiting and defining the relations between observer and world. Within several decades the camera obscura is no longer one of many instruments of visual options but instead the compulsory site from which vision can be conceived or represented. Above all it indicates the appearance of a new model of subjectivity, the hegemony of a new subject-effect. First of all the camera obscura performs an operation of individuation; that is, it necessarily defines an observer as isolated, enclosed and autonomous within its dark confines. It impels a kind of askesis, or withdrawal from the world, in order to regulate and purify one's relation to the manifold contents of the now "exterior" world. (1990, 38–39)

Vision, Crary suggests, becomes de-corporealized as a consequence of this subject-object arrangement. In the camera obscura model of vision, a model contemporary with what Foucault has called the classical episteme, subjects are unable to locate themselves within the representation of the world. They no longer see themselves as within a world in which God looks over but are placed outside it in an abstract space looking onto that world themselves (Crary 1990, 41). In this "age of the world picture" (see Heidegger 1977c), the God-eye is displaced by the human eye in the privileged position of the viewing point; the human subject comes to be seen as independent of the natural object-world and sovereign as a consequence (Panofsky 1991; Alpers 1983; Rotman 1987; Foucault 1989; Jay 1994). This, Crary argues, becomes the model for understanding subjectivity that continues until the beginnings of the nineteenth century.

What happens in the late eighteenth/early nineteenth century, Crary contends following Foucault, is the emergence of a new modern episteme, one based, above all, on the reintroduction of the human body into the seeing process. No longer a mute part of the representation as it had been before the classical age, the corporeal desiring subject is now returned into the world as an active force able to affect change within it in a manner previously only attributed to God's intervention from outside. The subject becomes the main source of creative action in the world of things. As a consequence, the camera obscura model of the subject comes to be challenged fundamentally by this shifting subject-effect. Whatever else it might do, the camera obscura model does not allow the subject this creative potential. Indeed, by the time Marx and Engels were writing *The German Ideology* in 1846–47, the camera obscura, as we have seen, had come to be seen as the model of all things false, the antithesis of how it had been seen just a century earlier. It is now a metaphor for an inverted world where everything is erroneously turned on its head. It will no longer serve as an adequate metaphor for true understanding; rather, it becomes the metaphor for distortion, ideology, and later for fetishism.

The emergence of this new episteme is reflected in the beginnings of Romanticism. In that philosophical and literary movement this separate subjectivity begins to reflect not just on the world around it but on itself as well as a supposed unique source of agency (Gouldner 1973; Berman 1982). In effect, vision becomes subjectivized in this move (Crary 1990, 69). This shift reflects a move from a classical episteme, where the truth content that was apparent in the image of the world was accepted, to a modern one where, rather, it is the subjective interpretation of the world and subject that counts for everything (Foucault 1989). This shift is apparent also in the development of a post-Kantian hermeneutics in which that objective world is opened up not only to the possibility of interpretation but also to doubt (Gadamer 1975). Seeing is no longer automatically believing. In this process, vision is returned to the body, becomes a possible source of interpretive creativity, and can also be detached from the empirical world as a source of self-scrutiny and reflection. A product of self-reflection, then, it also results in a so-called crisis of representation in art that, according to Crary, is a consequence of this shift in subject-effect. The creation of an autonomous subjectivity (1990, 101) that is premised on this crisis is also the point, we might add, where a new regime of curiosity emerges and an earlier one is thrown into doubt. It is also the epistemic point at which post-Hegelian writers like Feuerbach and Marx emerge with very definite ideas about the relationship between the active, sensuous subject and the material world.

Of all the long list of mechanical devices used for creating images that begin with the camera obscura in the Renaissance and end, by way of the invention of photography, with the introduction of the cinematograph in 1896, it is the phantasmagoria that was in its heyday between 1795 to 1820, which synecdochically expresses the change and the uncertainty associated with this epistemological break and development of a new subject position (Castle 1995).[7] While its life as a specific form of a visual apparatus was short lived, it nonetheless was the start and main inspiration for a whole tradition in secular entertainment and magic shows in which the spectre figured as a key trope for illusion and wonder that lasted throughout the nineteenth century (During 2002). Through it a new regime of curiosity comes into being, a regime, moreover, that puts consumption rather than production center stage.

Synecdochically, the phantasmagoria presents a type of entertaining spectacle in between that of classical and modern forms of curiosity (Foucault 1989). It retains an interest with the things that fascinated the philosophers and artists of the classical (or Baroque) age: the anomalous, freakish, and the heteroclite—ghosts, in this case. But whereas before these were seen as objects within the world of things, increasingly they come to be seen part of the creative imagination and of the subjective interior instead. Deploying the magic lantern adaptation of the camera obscura (adding a lens to the aperture turns the image of the world the right way up), the phantasmagoria seeks not only to conceal its workings but to make this shift more credible and believable. The concealment is intended not so much to deceive a credulous audience of what produces images (as Marx assumes) but to act as a spur to their imaginations as they consume them. Whereas in the regime of curiosity that we might associate with the camera obscura it was the external world of things that had to be shown to be credible, in the phantasmagoria, it is the effects of the imagination that spring from an encounter with the world that are to be believed. *It is not that people needed to believe in what they saw as real or true but that they believed in the reality of the powers of their imaginations to construct an understanding of the world that mattered most.* The phantasmagoria seeks to confirm the powers of the subject, not the object, as a source of truth. This is not something that Marx allows for in his use of the term. But that is what subjects do, I contend, in the modern world of consumption (see also Campbell 1987; McCracken 1988). The phantasmagoria uses illusion not as a source of deception but rather as a spur to a self-conscious, active, and creative subjectivity, and it uses figural rather than discursive qualities to do this. It is an adapted camera obscura in principle but one where the camera obscura's principles of accurate depiction of reality are thrown into question at the same time. In this respect, the space of the phantasmagoria is a paradoxical one rather than an illusory one. It is a space in which truth and reality are thrown into doubt and require resolution through the actions of the subject interpellated as a consuming subject.

The technique of back projection that conceals the operation of the projector and the projection of ghosts—those most uncertain of figures—clearly expresses this interest in doubtful representation and encourages a focus on the imagination rather than on the object itself. The language of the *phantasma agoreuein/fantasme agourer* is that of ghosts speaking allegorically to us about our own imaginations. To deceive objectively is to convince subjectively—its uncertain space positions the viewing subject in a particular way: in a position of doubt but also in a position of critical self-reflection as an outcome of that doubt. In addition to the phantasmagoria there are other devices from this time that seek to achieve the same effect: both the panorama and the panopticon might be said to produce the same effects of self-reflection in the (bewildered) subject (Foucault 1977; Comment 1999). If the world is doubtful or uncertain, then that doubt needs to be removed, ordered, by the powers of imagination. The figure of the ghost is crucial in this.

As a figure of *unfinished disposal*, the ghost's power resides principally in its ability to haunt. To haunt is to remain or to return to where one does not belong—*unheimlich* (uncanny, but literally "unhomely") and revenant—it calls on people to reflect on their own debt to the life of the unsettled spirit and to their own conduct as possibly a cause of that lack of settlement (Derrida 1994). The ghost puts us in contact with another space, out of time, though the words it uses to do that do not come easily to it (Gordon 1997, 175). In effect, it puts us in touch with our own uneasy imagination. It is not just the specific question of the figure of the ghost that interests us here, however. It is more a question of the broader issue of the manner in which *the figural*—that which is seen as signifier but not represented, not a signified:

the apparition, image, trace, spectacle—speaks or *gives utterance*, through the object, to that which cannot be spoken clearly as discourse. Such an effect is suggested in the mediating powers of the commodity as fetish. It may be that the modern episteme not only brings with it a new subject-effect as Foucault has argued, but also a new object-effect too: a new object-effect that is expressed most clearly through the form of the commodity-fetish as a figure open to multiple interpretations through consuming practices.

At this point we can suggest that, above all, ghosts want to give us a message; their very being is determined by this overwhelming desire to communicate. They want to put us straight, make us remember what we have forgotten—the debt we owe them—so that they can then rest in peace (Derrida 1994). Yet the ghost's presentation of self usually has more to do with figural appearance than it does with discourse. It is a figure that *presents* itself rather than something that comes as a representation (Lyotard 1984). The representational work has to be done afterward by the subject who believes he or she has seen a ghost. The ghost usually appears as a sudden and unexpected rupture into the field of vision. The manner in which the figure speaks, then, is through *disclosure*. This word implies a paradoxical opening up and also a concealment at the same time: the conspiratorial revealing of some secret not accessible in obvious ways or to all. To disclose is to reveal, or to confess or confide, or to divulge or whisper.

Phantasmagoria, therefore, is a nineteenth-century neologism, invented for a form of popular entertainment but also for one of the first pre-discursive articulations of a new set of subject-object relations. It is in the space of illusion, of image and spectacle, that the ghost appears as if to speak. Phantasmagoria: the image that has a voice—a voice quite different than that of discourse. To be within a phantasmagoria is to encounter the figural outside of discourse. The effects are those of shock. As a member of the audience, no doubt there to be entertained, the image one sees is a supposedly truthful one, but one that is at the same time called into question the possibility that one can believe what one sees with one's eyes. If the principles of the camera obscura were more than a means of creating representations of the object world that might be used for science, art, or entertainment, but were a model for how people understood subject-object relations, then to expose people to those principles in form and to call them into doubt at the same time must begin to visibly challenge the model of both subjectivity and objectivity premised on those techniques. It was not that people necessarily believed what they saw in those shows—though there are contemporary accounts of startled audiences at phantasmagoria shows, nonetheless the suspension of disbelief was a well-practiced technique of theatre audiences that dates to long before this time (Agnew 1986)—but that their sense of themselves as subjects was made open to question by this process. It was, rather, the very fact that they could no longer believe what they saw with their own eyes, could no longer trust the object-effect established by the camera obscura projection of images that expressed and articulated the growing crisis of representation and challenged the classical idea of the subject.

It is around this theme that Marx's use of the metaphor of the phantasmagoria as a means of understanding the principles of fetishism is at its most problematic. In effect, he acknowledges the false image of reality that it, along with the camera obscura in general, creates. He is perhaps the first to recognize in his description of the commodity a new object-effect where all is not as it appears. The fundamental problem with his approach, however, is that he does not allow that the viewing subjects he constructs within this theory of fetishism might also recognize that too, that they are, in fact, *interpellated to do so by this viewing arrangement*. While he acknowledges a changing object-effect he does not allow the same for the changing subject-effect. Marx's capitalist subjects, those who live in the world of commodity fetishism, are alienated watchers of a phantasmagoria show who are unable to see the concealment, unable to suspend disbelief, who must really believe that they are seeing reality rather than an illusion. The absence of revolutionary class struggle is evidence enough of this for him and subsequent Marxists.

Marx's own Romanticism acknowledged a rejection of the camera obscura model of the subject and placed the creative laboring subject at the center of his worldview. That subject under ideal and free social conditions expresses him- or herself through creative productive work in which things are objectified and stand as external but not alien to the subject. The subject is able to recognize her- or himself in an undistorted way in the objects that have been created. In arguing this, and in explicitly critiquing Hegel's conflation of objectification with alienation in his approach, Marx directly challenges essentialist ideas of objectivity. He does so too, rightly, in his analysis of private property, which he sees as a subjective and not an objective creation. It is only under certain social conditions that the object of subjective work comes to seem as alienated, most strongly under capitalist conditions (Marx 1975b). Central to his attribution of fetishism to the creation of value in commodities is a challenge to capitalism's and its apologist's essentializing of the object as a creative and active force. That active force comes to appear as a ghostly figure, something conjured up to deceive. For Marx such a creative force can only reside in the subject within its material conditions of existence.

But that is not to say that Marx is a critic of all essentialisms. He certainly, and unquestioningly, essentializes the creative subject in labor. In his essentializing of human nature in labor (Homo Faber), he constructs a view of the subject who realizes him- or herself through labor alone. In doing this he constructs *a production view of the subject* (see Munro 1996) who stands as someone independent from the world in his essential and universal needs and then realizes himself in that world through laboring acts of mastery, craft, and control. He, and the gender assumptions about mastery might suggest that it is a he, is actualized as a subject through laboring to satisfy needs. Only under certain conditions (capitalism) is this subject thwarted in that activity (alienated) and unable to realize his species being.

The anthropological assumptions about essential needs that this view is premised on have been challenged since Marx was writing, not least through the argument that communication and symbolic exchange rather than production are more central to issues of subjective expressions and the formation of social relations (Sahlins 1972; Baudrillard 1975; Appadurai 1986; Birken 1988; Simmel 1990; Bataille 1991). Baudrillard, in particular, in *The Mirror of Production* provides a powerful critical engagement with Marx on this issue that suggests that the productivist assumptions about needs that Marx makes are in fact part of a productivist code created by capitalism itself and that Marx simply universalizes them in history and incorporates them into his own theory. As Baudrillard puts it, "man is not only quantitatively exploited as a productive force by the system of capitalist political economy, but is also metaphysically over-determined as a producer by the code of political economy" (1975, 31). In this respect, Marxist political economy can only know itself in the mirror of capitalism and the emphasis that it places on production. In this way Homo Faber is understood in Marx as a coherent subject position that is then alienated under conditions of capitalist production—whose phantasmagoric mask he seeks to unveil—rather than a more complex subject who realizes him- or herself through multifarious cultural and economic practices that center on forms of communication and exchange—conditions more readily associated with consumption than with production. To break the capitalist spell and its code of production requires that we focus more on subjectivity in this arena than the one that capitalist practices constitute discursively as its defining logic or code.

CONCLUSION

The commodity fetish is, for Marx, an alienated object of subjective activity that confronts the subject as a thing with image-like qualities—images of a particular ghost—the ghost of subjective activity that went into producing an object's value. But Marx's analysis of the subject is itself phantasmagoric but not in his sense of the term as a concealing illusion. It is a subject that produces the object-world through sensuous and figural understanding via the communicative world of consumption and exchange. The central problem in Marx's analysis of fetishism is that it freezes the encounter between the creative subject and the alienated object into a single moment in time beyond which that subject remains within the thrall of the object unable to act in the world. It is as if he or she is so stunned but the encounter with the ghost, an image of his or her own alienated labor power, that he or she is no longer capable of action in which he or she might engage with the fetish thereafter. It is almost as if Marx loses sight of his own understanding of the modern subject as a creative force in the world with a self-reflective consciousness and imagination and falls back on an earlier understanding of the pre-Romantic, pre-modern subject as his model for the subject in a modern capitalist world. For Marx, workers and capitalists alike are in effect depicted in the same manner as earlier Enlightenment writers had depicted African fetishists, as primitive and credulous. This was a view constructed at a time when the camera obscura model for subject-object relations still dominated. Subsequent Marxists too, with perhaps one notable, albeit qualified, exception (Benjamin), have continued to repeat this formulation in their adaptations of the theory of fetishism to the world of the commodity, not least Debord in his study of spectacle as we have seen. The only change has been to shift attention away from the fetishism associated with the production of commodities and onto that of their consumption.

Marx's view of the object-effect in his understanding of the phantasmagoric effects of the fetish is ultimately premised on a particular understanding of subjectivity that draws on the reception of fetishism during the Enlightenment and then fails to fully take into account the changing constitution of the subject that emerges during the early years of the nineteenth century. This is somewhat surprising given that Marx's own work can be seen as one of the preeminent examples that emerged from this particular humanist and Romantic discursive moment that challenged the de-corporealized rationalism of the Enlightenment (Gouldner 1973; Howes 2003). His early work on alienation, itself very much a product of this shifting discourse of the (Romantic) subject, offers an interesting take on understanding and questioning the material conditions of subject-object formation within capitalism (Avineri 1968; Mészáros 1970; Schacht 1971). While Marx makes much of the creative powers of the subject within a material environment of production, and makes a clear distinction between alienation and objectification in that analysis, he simplifies the ontology of the power effects of objects as fetishes upon alienated subjects in this process, naturalizing and essentializing subject-object relations in the process. It is this that leads to his emphasizing the importance of production (an alienated source of creative subject powers) and exchange value over consumption and use value (the realm of the object) in his analysis of capitalism (see also Baudrillard 1975; Howes 2003).

To return then to my main question: how should we understand consumption? Rather than reduce that mediation to a cinematic metaphor of spectacle, to the premise of a delusional screen in particular and to the sense of a separation between action and contemplation, we might do better to imagine it as a surrounding, a three-dimensional (perhaps four-dimensional) space through which we relate to one another though a multiplicity of forms of mediation. The idea of a surrounding found in the darkened phantasmagoria show better captures the reality of consumption than that of a spectacle; and rather than treat the spaces of consumption as spectacular, as much of the writing on consumption tends to do, we might do better to imagine it as a more heterogeneously mediated space. As such, its experiences are themselves likely to be heterogeneous, fragmented, partial, and uncertain. The possibility of resisting or rejecting such mediating forms of configuration or for constructing alternatives has the potential to leak back under such conditions. The subject that occupies this space is not a producing subject but a consuming subject (Munro 1996), and it is the implications of what that might imply that I wish to develop here.

Chapter Four

Memories of Capitalism

Only by approaching the subject from some distance and, initially, foregoing any view of the whole, can the mind be led, through a more or less ascetic apprenticeship, to a position of strength from which it is possible to take in the whole panorama and yet remain in control of oneself.

Walter Benjamin, Epistemo-Critical prologue[1]

PHANTASMAGORIA IN WESTERN MARXISM

The idea that a commodity as fetish be understood through a visual register of distortion was not one that remained with Marx and his concern with the exchange value of the commodity. While Marx's analysis of commodity fetishism was not central to the leading debates within the formation of Marxism after his death, it did figure prominently within the broader question of alienation that became central to the critical theory of Western Marxism that developed in Europe in the aftermath of the First World War (Arato and Breines 1979; Feenberg 1981; Jay 1978).[2] While Marx had been concerned with fetishism in relation to production and the abstraction of labor power, commodity fetishism subsequently came to be applied more widely to consumer relations and consumer culture in general and ultimately with all forms of experience, consciousness, and rationality within capitalism as a whole. That legacy is still with us. Beginning with Lukacs's seminal work on reification, critical theorists like Adorno and Benjamin were to see "mass" consumer culture (described as a culture industry; see Adorno and Horkheimer 1979) as inherently fetishistic. Most of the more recent work on consumer culture that makes the same argument draws on this tradition (Clark 1984; Saisselin 1985; Richards 1991; Friedberg 1993; Asendorf 1993; Maleuvre 1999). In doing this these writers pick up and develop Marx's use of the phantasmagoria metaphor as a key trope for their own understanding of how fetishism works (Adorno 1981; Benjamin 1999a, 1999b, 1999c).

Marx had had confidence in the processes of historical development and believed he was witnessing the final demise of capitalism. As we saw in Chapter 1, he believed the Great Exhibition to be its swan song. He concentrated on addressing issues of commodity fetishism in relation to the process and site of capitalist production—factories—believing them to be the key spaces of class struggle. Later Marxists could not be so certain or so confident. The persistence of capitalism, despite its many economic crises and social upheavals, did not seem to be giving way to a socialist society as Marxist theory had anticipated. Notwithstanding the Russian Revolution, Western Marxist intellectuals soon began to question the positivist orthodoxy and determinism of "dialectical materialism" and the productivist bias as set out in the later writings of Engels, Kautsky, Plekanov, Lenin, and others from soon after World War I (see Lichtheim 1961; Kolakowski 1981). Certainly by 1923, the year Lukacs published *History and Class Consciousness* (1971), and in light of the perceived crisis in revolutionary consciousness associated with the failed proletarian revolutions across central Europe in 1918–19, Marx's phantasmal image of capitalist social relations, supposedly easy to see through and change, could not inspire such an easy confidence as they had for Marx himself. The persistence of a fetishistic social reality and its reification of social relations more broadly came to be seen as one of the key obstacles to the development of revolutionary consciousness and the creation of communism. What marks out this Western Marxist writing from its orthodox and more determinist Soviet counterpart, therefore, is an emphasis on the themes of alienation and fetishism and their application to broader areas of social life.[3]

In this alternative emphasis we see a change also in the spatial location and application of theories of commodity fetishism to that set out by Marx. It moves from a focus on the place of production and wage labor, the idealized factory (Marx); to the rationalized, Fordist manufacturing plant with assembly-line manufacturing techniques (Lukacs); to sites of mass culture like the cinema (Adorno); to the whole of capitalist society that comes to be described as a consumer society, society of phantasmagoria, spectacle, or hyperreality (Benjamin, Debord, Baudrillard).

Here I want to address what happens to the idea of fetishism and the trope of the phantasmagoria in the work of Lukacs, Adorno, and particularly Benjamin.[4] Lukacs and Adorno offer a fairly orthodox interpretation of it that draws on what Marx understands by commodity fetishism. It is their application of the term to a broader field of social relations, and, in Adorno's case, his pessimism about the potential outcome, that differs from Marx. It is, however, Benjamin who offers us the most innovative, developed, and imaginative treatment of this term that I mostly want to concentrate on in this chapter. His syncretist, modernist, and theoretical position centers directly on an understanding of subject-object relations within capitalism in relation to matters of myth and phantasmagoria (1985a, 1999a, 1999b) that, through the influence of Jewish mysticism (Scholem 1954) and symbolist theories of language, take his approach some distance from Marxism in a search for a new conceptualization of experience within capitalist modernity (Lunn 1982; Wolin 1982; Frisby 1985; Agamben 1993; Cohen 1995; Tiedemann 1999; Lindroos 2001; Ziarek 2001).

While his contemporaries, notably Adorno, saw much of this approach as a misunderstanding of what Marx had said about commodity fetishism, we can today suggest that he had a much more nuanced and complex grasp of issues of subjectivity and objectivity and their underlying anthropology than these other writers. Certainly his work on the phantasmagoric character of capitalism retains many of the same problems as those found in Marx that I discussed in the previous chapter, but it also offers us the possibility of a richer view of the dynamics of consumer capitalism and of the place of the subject with the material culture of the modern world, not least because his theory of experience does not lead him to rely quite so unambiguously on a production-centered essentialist humanism found in the work of others within this Hegelian tradition.

REIFICATION, IMAGE, AND REALITY

If, for Marx, the commodity fetish is something that obscures but which in struggle becomes transparent, in Lukacs that veil of a false reality comes to be seen as having taken on an even more concrete and obfuscatory reality. He puts forward such a view in his most important work on fetishism, or reification as he terms it, in his essay "Reification and the Consciousness of the Proletariat" in his book *History and Class Consciousness* (1971). In that work he investigates the nature of proletarian consciousness under capitalism and offers a critique of the "unreason" that characterizes the reality of capitalist rationality. Rather than an alternative for fetishism, Lukacs conceives his study of reification as an extension of it under conditions in which capitalism has matured since the time of Marx's writing. To develop this argument he returns to Hegel's analysis of alienation and draws on non-Marxist sources, in particular, Weber's analysis of rationalization, as his basis for outlining the key changes that have come to define modern capitalism (Weber 1978). In particular, he applies this analysis to the conditions brought about within production processes by Fordism and Taylorism, notably in the mechanization and management of the factory system, and goes on to see the processes of rationalization in evidence there reflected in rationalized bourgeois thought and its ideological perspective on society. For Lukacs, this is a condition that does not remain within the sites of production but extends to a broader cultural outlook shaping society as a whole.

For Lukacs, the key problem to be investigated is how the proletariat can attain a consciousness aware of its own class interests and thereby the ability to overcome the false conditions created by capitalist social relations. While Marx's work is at the center of his analysis, he goes back to Hegel's work on subject-object identification to address this matter. For Hegel, alienation, akin to objectification, involves a separation between subject and object. Their ultimate unification in Spirit, which results in the overcoming of alienated conditions, is understood by Hegel as a the consequence of the dialectical overcoming of contradictions and the realization of reason in History. In drawing on this metaphysical argument, Lukacs seeks to give it a materialist basis by substituting the proletariat for Spirit in his reading and sees, in its coming to self-consciousness as a class through class struggle, that same realization of history for humanity and thereby the overcoming of all conditions of alienation. For Lukacs, reification, an expression of alienation in the social relations of capitalism, something that is articulated in the social and political thought of the bourgeoisie, stops this realization of subject-object identification in proletarian consciousness and leads to the ongoing survival of capitalism despite its crisis-ridden character.

For Lukacs, there are three phases in the development of reification in capitalist society: (i) the abstraction of labor power as a commodity, (ii) the reification of all social relations within capitalist society, and (iii) the reification of consciousness as a whole (Arato and Breines 1979, 115). His starting point in this analysis is Marx's understanding of commodity fetishism in *Capital*, which, he argues, describes the first of these phases, apparent during the development of capitalism in the nineteenth century. He reiterates Marx's position on the phantasmagoric character of commodity fetishism and makes it the starting point of his own analysis.

> The essence of the commodity-structure has often been pointed out. Its basis is that a relation between people takes on the character of a thing and thus acquires a "phantom-objectivity," an autonomy that seems so strictly rational and all-embracing as to conceal every trace of its fundamental nature: the relation between people. (Lukacs 1971, 83)

Lukacs's use of Marx's "phantasmagoria-as-visual-illusion" reference comes to assume a more concrete, instrumentally rational character than in Marx. His continual references in *History and Class Consciousness* to "illusion" (passim), "look[ing] on helplessly" (1971, 90), "distortion" (93), and "loss of vantage point" (95) have the idea of a phantasmagoric regime of curiosity as their central theme. Yet Lukacs's world is not only one of Marxian fetishism but also of Hegelian objectification-as-alienation and, importantly, of Weberian rationalization too. It is a world in which fetishism becomes total, a synonym for all forms of objectification (a position that Lukacs himself was later to repudiate in his preface, written in 1967, to the republication of *History and Class Consciousness* in 1971). This is a world where the human subject is in the process of becoming totally alienated, fragmented, separated, and constituted within the relations not only of production but also of culture as capitalism matures.

This totalizing trend that underpins the theory of reification comes not just from his Hegelian reading of Marx on capitalism but also from Weber on rationalization. In particular, he follows Weber in arguing that we are witness to the ongoing unfolding of rationalization within Western society to the point where an abstracted instrumental rationality, divorced from the embodied conditions of social life that have been based originally in custom, tradition, and affect and later expressed in ethical forms of value rationality (such as that associated with religion), has become total and inescapable.

In modernity, instrumental rationality, in this Weberian understanding, comes to dominate social life through the separation of different spheres of life (law, politics, religion, culture, education, and so on, overturning earlier societal unity) and through the emphasis on formal considerations in social conduct, rules, and a bureaucratic outlook on social organization more generally (Whimster and Lash 1990). In the workplace, this process of rationalization is found most acutely, for Lukacs, in the conditions described as Fordism and Taylorism, but he believes these principles are moving beyond there to all areas of capitalist social life and more broadly to the dominant rational and scientific consciousness of the bourgeoisie whose views are reflected in these social relations.

This extension and generalization of commodity fetishism in the abstraction of labor power as a commodity to reification associated with all forms of capitalist rationality marks an important if subtle shift in the way that the false reality of capitalism is understood. That shift has to do with the relationship between materiality and image. If Marx conceives fetishism as a process where social relations (associated with the production of exchange value) become image-like, in Lukacs those relations become much more thing-like in this totalizing move. In effect, for Marx a fetish (commodity) is a thing that acts like an image of social relations; in Lukacs and subsequent Western Marxist approaches to commodity fetishism (we have already seen this in Debord), a fetish is seen as an image or representation that acts like a thing.[5]

And here begins a shift in the theory of commodity fetishism: from a theory of the fetish-like quality of things that act like images that obscure the reality of particular social relations (Marx) to a theory of the image that becomes thing-like, in the concept of reification (and spectacle), that obscures social reality as a totality (Lukacs) (see Pels et al. 2002).[6] Both are still concerned with the illusory character of the figure but in Lukacs's case, the model of a false reality created by conditions of reification becomes more total, all encompassing, and increasingly inescapable. Even more than Marx, Lukacs adheres to, and compounds, a model of subjectivity in capitalism in which the image is understood as a product of a form of reception modeled on the camera obscura regime of curiosity: the subject is confronted by a reified image of social relations detached from the material conditions of production and he or she believes in the truth content of that image because he or she can know no other, except in revolutionary struggle.

If Marx had understood the phantasmagoria as a different figuring device, a model in which there was no longer a clear separation between subject and object, but a constitution of the subject within the surrounding material world that they were able to engage with, then this might have led him and his successors to a quite different understanding of fetishism. Such an understanding of fetishism might have led to a different conception of the relations between the subject- and the object-world of the commodity also. It might have led also to different and more fruitful views on issues of consciousness and social change as well in which the theme of totality might not have been granted such an overdetermining position.

Lukacs partly acknowledges the limitations of Marx's approach in his quest to find a route to the development of revolutionary consciousness. But he does not do this by questioning the production view of the subject that underpins the theory of fetishism; rather, he simply looks for its alienation in other spaces of society.[7] However, while he notes that reification is in the process of coming to define the conditions of capitalist rationality in their totality, he does not follow Weber in see- ing such conditions as an inescapable iron cage. The conditions of lived reality for proletarians, Lukacs believes, follow a different, less instrumental form of rational- ity, which will, as bourgeois instrumentalism encroaches on their lives more and more, he believes, lead to conflict and class struggle rather than quiescence. And because Lukacs equates the proletariat with the Hegelian subject-object identifica- tion in Spirit, he sees in such struggles the potential culmination of History and the demise of capitalism. When workers begin to recognize in these struggles that they are reduced to their commodity status, that capitalist relations come increasingly to dominate all areas of their social lives, that consciousness itself is imbued with a reifying calculus and that they have no other being in capitalism than as a thing that can be bought and sold as labor power, Lukacs believes they will attain the consciousness that will allow them to see the false reality of commodity fetishism and to change it.

Yet, for Lukacs, while the move to consider matters of totality is central (see Jay 1978), he does not follow this analysis through to its conclusion by broadening the scope of his own analysis. Although the theme of totality is apparent, he largely remains with the site of production, the mass-production factory, as the locus for this class struggle. Lukacs believes that the processes of assembly-line mechaniza- tion (Fordism) and rationalization (Taylorism) found in the modern manufacturing plant, the embodiment of bourgeois instrumental rationality, were enough to lead to an intensification of alienation and thereby its overturning in those sites by class struggle.

Certainly his analysis implies an extension and intensification of the condi- tions of alienation in capitalist society and the tendency for the development of an outlook that is the product of reified consciousness unless checked by struggle, but it was left to later writers to analyze how the commodification of the lives of workers outside of the place of work was developing, not least in the realms of entertain- ment, consumption, and culture. Lukacs's own extensive analysis in the cultural realm does not do this. What he offers, rather, is a defense of realism against all forms of illusory technique and abstraction in cultural form. He sees in realism the potential for struggle against all forms of mystification. His critiques of modernism, and of Brecht in particular, are developed in this light (see Adorno et al. 2002). Lukacs is also mainly interested with the products of bourgeois high culture in this respect, the theatre and the novel in particular, and he pays little attention himself to culture as a general site of struggle. His analysis does not really extend to popular culture—the culture of the everyday lives of workers—and does not address that culture either through analysis of its commodification as later writers, drawing on his work, were to do.[8] It was left to those who followed his analysis of commodity fetishism as reification to take his arguments into this arena.

ALIENATED EARS, EXCHANGE VALUE, AND THE CULTURE INDUSTRY

Adorno's treatment of the phantasmagoria metaphor for fetishism, and for understanding the culture industry based on it, follows many of the principles identified by Lukacs but makes this move to analyze reified social relations beyond the factory gates (Adorno and Horkheimer 1979; Adorno 1981, 1999b). Situated within a broad account of the commodification of culture but retaining something of the productivist slant, emphasizing its transformation into an alienated and alienating "culture industry" (with Hollywood film and jazz in the 1930s serving as the key models), Adorno sets out to explore the cultural as opposed to purely economic effects of fetishism in modern capitalist societies. He highlights music, in particular, when developing this analysis, but his interests are broader (1981, 1999a). His main concern is not revolutionary consciousness—in the age of totalitarianism he almost accepts that this has been defeated by capitalism—but to develop an understanding of capitalism by focusing on the triumph of exchange value over use value in the field of cultural consumption/reception and the effects of this on issues of individuality and critical judgment. The trope of the phantasmagoria remains central to this approach.

For Adorno, capitalist social relations are no longer concentrated at the point of production. The development of a culture industry from the mid-nineteenth century has led to the extension of capitalist social relations into other spheres, notably those of consumption and popular entertainment. He singles out sports, film, and music as key sites of this culture industry (1999a, 41). As a musicologist, he is particularly interested in analyzing the effects of capitalism on the latter (1981, 1999a). For Adorno, serious autonomous art, by which he means art that is not subject to the conditions of fetishism, places the individual in a relation with a cultural object such that the subject is able to critically reflect upon it as an individual. Its effects present a viewer/listener with the opportunity for understanding and enlightenment. This conception of the subject as creatively engaged with the work of art through reception is, as we saw in the previous chapter on Marx, a central preoccupation of German Romanticism. For Adorno, such a form of subjectivity is undermined by the fetishistic relations of capitalism that tend toward promoting mass forms of cultural and artistic reception as passive rather than active productive contemplation (what he calls, in the context of music, "regressive hearing") and a disempowered, unreflective pseudo-individuality as a consequence (Adorno and Horkheimer 1979).

While highly critical of theorists of mass culture who denigrate its popular appeal solely on grounds of bad taste, Adorno, nonetheless, adheres to a critique not only of the forms of popular culture prominent in his day, notably Hollywood film, jazz, and other forms of popular music, but also to their reception. Individuals, for Adorno, have become isolated from their class while at the same time becoming part of a broad mass audience through the facility of technology (film and radio) and are no longer capable of appreciating autonomous art or challenging the fetish character of popular consumer culture through their reception of its products.

It is easy to dismiss Adorno as just an elitist snob who did not like popular culture.[9] Notwithstanding that he probably was, and that the critical judging bourgeois individual is his idealized model of the rational subject (he is like the bewildered Dickens in that respect), he does not make taste a central theme in his analysis of the culture industry. Instead, he makes commodity fetishism, and its phantasmagoric effects, central. A major point in Adorno's critique of the culture industry has to do with the shifting relationship between exchange value and use value associated with its products. Whereas for Marx the fetish character of the exchange value of a commodity relies on the preservation, at least in residual form, that it has some sort of use as a thing and therefore an appeal to potential consumers, for Adorno this position is increasingly eroded by the extension of commodification within all areas of mass culture. Initially in capitalism, for Adorno, use value becomes a phantasmagoria of the commodification of things; latterly, exchange value alone becomes the phantasmagoria and use value is all but made redundant in consumer practices.

> If the commodity in general combines exchange value and use value, then the pure use value, whose illusion the cultural goods must preserve in a completely capitalist society, must be replaced by pure exchange value, which precisely in its capacity as exchange value deceptively takes over the function of use value…. The more inexorably the principle of exchange value destroys use value for human beings, the more deeply does exchange value disguise itself as the object of enjoyment. (1999a, 34)

In effect: people buy things because they are worth money; they value things because of how much they cost and the prestige associated with that; because they are rare and exclusive and so on. In this argument people want things because of the image of value associated with them rather than for their actual practical use. Adorno is effectively arguing that exchange value, in appropriating the function of use value to itself, becomes a sign that can be consumed in itself. More recently analysis of the purchase of things as signs or as brands with distinctive logos rather than as objects with a use appears to fulfill this function most clearly and to develop a similar line of argument (see Baudrillard 1981, 1983; for a discussion on this, see Lury 1996, 2004).

Adorno applies this argument particularly to the capitalist transformation of music—not the production of music by artists-as-workers who have to sell their works as commodities in the marketplace—but its consumption by a mass audience. It is in this work that he most clearly develops an understanding of the phantasmagoric character of commodity fetishism that he associates with this changing relationship between exchange and use value (1981, 1999a). While all forms of music, classical and popular, are subject to this analysis, he singles out the encroachment that exchange value has on use value in this field: the celebration of the aura of the star performance; highlighting musical arrangement over composition; the emphasis given to the commercial hit as a way of judging the success of a work; the emphasis on famous and popular sections of a composition to the detriment of the more challenging sections, and so on. All these effects are seen by Adorno to disempower the listener and produce what he calls a fetishised "regressive listening" (1999a).

Notwithstanding his trenchant critiques of the popular in music, it is the late Romantic music of the "serious" composer Wagner who is the subject of Adorno's most biting criticisms (1981). It is also in his analysis of Wagner that he develops most clearly his discussion of phantasmagoria as a way of understanding the commercialization of listening and consuming. For Adorno, Wagner's music represents the culmination of a fetishistic bourgeois culture associated with what he calls the "occultation of production by means of the outward appearance of the product" (1981, 85). Drawing on Marx and also on his discussions with Benjamin (Rose 1978), Adorno deploys the trope of the phantasmagoria to analyze key elements in Wagner's music (1981, 85–96). In the use he makes of sound for magical or delusional effect (sound from afar, diminishing sound, and so on), Adorno sees Wagner making use of phantasmagoric effects in the construction of his music.[10] In subjecting this to critical analysis he not only tells us something about what he thinks of Wagner and his music but also, through him, of cultural production within a capitalist society in general. While embedded in Marx's analysis of fetishism he also moves beyond it. Notably, what is central to this move is Adorno's understanding of the role of the phatasmagoric in the appropriation of the function of use value by exchange value.

> [P]hantasmagoria [is]…the point at which aesthetic appearance becomes a function of the character of the commodity. As a commodity it purveys illusions. The absolute reality of the unreal is nothing but the reality of a phenomenon that not only strives unceasingly to spirit away its own origins in human labour, but also, inseparably from this process and in thrall to exchange value, assiduously emphasises its use value, stressing that this is its authentic reality,

that it is "no imitation"—and all this in order to further the cause of exchange value. (1981, 90)

No longer is fetishism just concerned with how the production of value within a commodity is hidden; for Adorno, in the consumer context, a commodity becomes desirable by presenting an exchange value as a use value through image.

If the principles of commodity fetishism were set down by Marx and extended to all areas of capitalist society by Lukacs, then Adorno seeks to investigate how it operates in the broad cultural sphere, in the areas of social life we now associate with consumer culture. As with Lukacs, Adorno shifts the emphasis away from the materiality of the commodity-object and onto its thing-like effect as an image. He then goes on to analyze that effect within the culture industries. A consequence of doing this is to detach the phantasmagoric image from the actual materiality of the thing being consumed (and the practices associated with it) and to treat that image as if it were the thing being consumed (see also Baudrillard's later approach to the consumption of sign value, 1981). If Marx can be criticized for presenting the object as an alienated thing with illusory qualities, positioning the subject as a powerless spectator, then Adorno (and Lukacs) compound this point by divorcing the image of the thing from its materiality altogether. The subject becomes an object—an object of passivity, so distracted as to be unable to do anything to challenge this positioning. This is why Adorno is dismissive of early forms of audience reception study that might suggest multiple readings of cultural works by audiences (1991a, 40). In his own terms, for Adorno, no matter how imaginatively consumers interpret the cultural product they are confronted with, they cannot ever escape its fetish character because their subjectivity as producing agents is alienated within these conditions. His argument does not give them scope to see through the illusion. Interpretation, for Adorno, is not a matter of subjective and individual consciousness but of the material conditions of social existence, as it was for Marx, and those conditions have become all determining. However consumers decode cultural products (see S. Hall 1992), for Adorno, their decoding will always be phantasmagoric even if they are oppositional. For Adorno, consumers are trapped inside the phantasmagoric relations of a false reality of capitalism's making, and without the possibility of appealing to a space outside (created by class struggle), they are unable to do anything about it. Class struggle is a receding possibility for Adorno because the phantasmagoric effects of capitalism have become total, no longer allowing workers to compare experiences that once existed outside of capitalist social relation (forms of cultural life) with those that they cannot avoid (work) in the way that Lukacs imagined as a hope for change. They only know a fetishistic reality and nothing outside of it. The scope for resistance in this argument dwindles almost to nothing. For Adorno, only through skilled understanding (creative contemplation conceived as a productive act by the autonomous subject) of the cultural products of a tiny minority of artists still producing genuinely autonomous and non-fetishistic art (Kafka, Schonberg, etc.) can a person still retain the possibility of a view outside of the phantasmagoria of capitalism to a de-fetishized reality beyond. This opportunity is open to a dwindling few in this analysis.

If we want to challenge Adorno's argument we cannot do so simply in terms of skilled audience reception and consumer creativity per se. It is not at all my intention to adopt a postmodern argument that all consumption should be seen as creative and expressive of individual agency outside of any social constraints (see, for instance, Fiske 1989; Willis 1991). Rather, the argument has to address how Adorno understands phantasmagoria to operate, notably by considering and contesting the relationship he establishes between image, materiality, and reception within his approach to it. The issue is not one of interpretation as such but of engagement with the material world that is also a social world. In the appropriation of the function of use value by exchange value in Adorno's analysis, materiality—the stuff of which useful things are made—is disappeared into the realm of the visual (and aural) illusion. The main problem for Adorno's analysis is that he does not provide us with any scope to consider the ongoing (fetishistic) effects of materiality in a consumer context because he simply conjures the material out of existence. Yet even the most fashionable branded objects have a use and that use has its reception. Designer clothes, fine wines, country houses, antiques, and so on can indeed be consumed because consumers are attracted by their exchange value (or as a sign; see Baudrillard 1981). This is not just a point made by Adorno. There is a longstanding sociological tradition from Veblen (1987) [1899] to Bourdieu (1984) that characterizes consumption as principally an agonistic struggle for distinction and taste that is reflected in the potlatch effect of spending money on unnecessary things (vicarious consumption) (see also Mauss 1990; Bataille 1991; Baudrillard 1981, 1996). It may well be that, but it is also more than that. Consumption as an expression of an engagement with social relations, including those of (class) membership, is not just about this struggle for distinction. Rather, all social relations can be expressed through the practice of consumption (Douglas and Isherwood 1986). Clothes can be worn as an expression of self-worth, a subcultural uniform, or just to garden in and not just to show off at parties. Fine wines can be an investment and a status symbol but they can also be drunk and their flavors enjoyed; houses are not just an investment but also places to live in and to bring up children; and antiques can be appreciated for their aesthetic value or their sentimental value just as much as for how much they are worth on the open market or in being passed on to future generations. This is not saying that exchange value does not appropriate the function of use value within these or any other fields within consumer society, but it is saying that consumer society should not be reduced to this alone, as Adorno seems to do. People engage with things in all sorts of ways as consuming subjects and not as alienated producing subjects. The phantasmagoric/fetishistic effects of consumption are broader but also weaker in their hold than Adorno suggests. To see how this might be the case we should turn to Adorno's friend and contemporary, Walter Benjamin, especially in his unfinished *Arcades Project* for an alternative, if ambiguous, approach to phantasmagoria that might provide us with a more fruitful line of analysis of consumer culture than that encountered so far.

THE MATERIAL EXPERIENCE OF CAPITALISM

Unlike Adorno, Benjamin came to the analysis of commodity fetishism through a rather less certain and more indirect route, largely because his critique of the mythic character of capitalism that is at the center of his analysis began in an understanding based on non-Marxist arguments and influences early in his career (Wolin 1982). He never broke with these early influences as clearly and irrevocably as Lukacs did with his (Lunn 1982). Yet, during the 1930s, the issue of commodity fetishism within a Marxist framework increasingly came to dominate his thought. And what he did was to reinterpret this (not always coherently) through his earlier understanding of the power and the potential of myth.

The key texts in Benjamin's analysis of commodity fetishism that highlight its importance to his view of the development of capitalism in the nineteenth century are those associated with his unfinished *Arcades Project (Passagen-werk)*: the collection of convolutes that make up that work (1999a) and the two exposé he wrote as outlines for the project in 1935 (1999b) and 1939 (1999c). We can also associate with this his essays on surrealism (1985a), the impact of mechanical reproduction on the auratic quality of art (1973a), and his work on Baudelaire that came out of the arcades research as a separate but also unfinished book project (1973c).

I don't intend to offer a full account of all Benjamin's writings mentioned here and how they relate to his understanding of capitalism, exemplified by the development of bourgeois life in Paris during the Second Empire (around the same time as the Great Exhibition in Britain). That task has now been undertaken on a number of occasions to good effect (see Buck-Morss 1989; Cohen 1995; Gilloch 1995). What I want to do in a more limited way is highlight the central importance that the theme of phantasmagoria has in his approach to commodity fetishism (see also Cohen 1989, 1995) and relate that to what he has to say about the changing character of modern experience involving the shift from *Erfahrung*, a coherent, distanced and reflective understanding of one's position in time and space, to *Erlebnis*, a fragmented experience of the lived moment, which I outlined briefly in Chapter 1 (for discussions of this issue, see in particular Wolin 1989b; Agamben 1993; Cohen 1995; Lindroos 2001; Ziarek 2001; Koselleck 2004).

For Benjamin, the main task of *The Arcades Project* is a bold one: to reveal a way of awakening the mass in a capitalist society from its mythic, fetishistic, and dream-like mode of experiencing the lived present into a historically aware and active class consciousness. Following in the Lukacian tradition of identifying reified consciousness within capitalist society as a totality and not just with the abstraction of labor power, he seeks to address the problem of consciousness in a rather more unorthodox and theoretically syncretist manner than that of either Lukacs or Adorno, which draws, above all, on the methodological principle of montage. Benjamin's theoretical aim is inherently modernist before it is Marxist (see Lunn 1982), not least in his recasting of the issue of consciousness as one of experience (*Erfahrung/Erlebnis*). Marx, Lukacs, and Adorno can all be seen in some respects as "realists" in their approach to garnering a true picture of capitalist reality through theory building (Lukacs explicitly so); but Benjamin, in his adoption of the modernist/surrealist technique of montage, something that deals in uncertain juxtapositions and fragmented images and a kairological sense of time (Lindroos, 1998), challenges the simple dichotomy between a picture of a truthful reality and a fetishistic illusion that these other writers tend to assume in their theoretical models of fetishism. The implications that this has for the question of subject-position is significant.

Benjamin's aim in *The Arcades Project* is to write a book made up almost entirely of a montage of quotations from historical sources with as little interpretive commentary as possible. His method is to use those sources to create a figural constellation that would be self-revealing of the historical reality of capitalism—something that capitalism seeks to spirit away in its creation of mythic phantasmagoria. Awakening to history, Benjamin believes, will come through experiencing the shock effect and the right timing (*Kairos*) of these juxtaposed sources, brought together as a constellation, in which what is revealed is what lies behind the phantasmagoric image-world that capitalism creates. It is almost as if he wants this technique to pull away the screen to reveal what lies behind the ghostly image that capitalism relies upon in creating the world of consumption. Revelation, recognition, and awakening are the main methodological aims of this project rather than outright critique. For Benjamin, only an awakening from the dream-state of a mythic understanding of capitalism can possibly challenge the phantasmagoric effect.

The project remained unfinished at his tragic death in 1940. The extensive notes for it were left in the charge of Georges Bataille for hiding in the Bibliotheque Nationale during the Nazi occupation of France. Benjamin had organized these notes into *Convolutes* (thematic sections of quotes with some of his own commentary added to them in note form). Although unfinished, that form conveys at least something of the method and style that he would have wanted to retain for the finished work (see Tiedemann 1999). That said, the two exposé he wrote for them and the correspondence he had with Adorno over the project, as well as the fact that he spent thirteen years on this project, all suggest he was still struggling unsuccessfully to find the best way to express this methodological approach in a written form. In effect, he was grappling with how to express the figural experience of the commodity world in discursive form without betraying the radical qualities that it had.

The aim of bringing together such a montage of contemporary sources from the nineteenth century, centered on Second Empire Paris, is to induce in the reader a sense of shock and also of recognition of what lay behind the myth-laden phantasmagoria of the cultural products of that time. This shock effect is intended to act, for Benjamin, in the same manner as an involuntary memory as when we encounter something half forgotten from our past as evoked by Proust, or like something emergent from a strange surrealist juxtaposition in which people might see their longings and wish images revealed as loss, but not just in the case of their own lives but that of humanity as a whole. Conveyed in the material culture, the images, the packaging, and the techniques used for selling commodities in the past, is a true utopian wish for happiness, Benjamin believes, premised on the dream of a classless society; a wish image that capitalism, moreover, makes its own and turns into a deceiving phantasmagoria in the expression, above all, of *progress*. For Benjamin, capitalist progress is really catastrophe for humanity (1973b); the phantasmagoric image of a utopian heaven it presents is really that of the hell of capitalist social relations, and he wants people to be able to see that and to be able to change it.

Inspired by a symbolist theory of language—most notably influenced by his reading of Baudelaire and Mallarmé (see Lunn 1982)—the Jewish mystical tradition associated with the Kabbala (see Scholem 1954), and with the sense of the Intervention of the messianic event as a right-time or *Kairos* mainly from Paul Tillich (see Lindroos 1998), he seeks out, through such a montage principle, the means for revealing the correspondences hidden within the language of material culture of the past and its aesthetic presentation, something that is not communicated by subjective or intersubjective interpretation alone; he is after that ghostly language of the figure that has been suppressed by the emphasis on discursive visibility and knowability created by a logocentric Western culture focused on the transcendental signified since the Renaissance (see Bann 1995). That figure, constituted in the montage of bringing things together, reveals, names, and translates a hidden truth and a hidden past. For Benjamin, that language could be found in the utopian wish-images of many media—text, architecture, and material culture of a particular time—by creating what he calls "dialectics at a standstill" or "dialectical images" through the techniques of montage (see Wolin 1982). Benjamin understands dialectics at a standstill as a monadological figural expression rather than a discursive one, which brings the material culture of the past and the present together as a constellation in which the act of past creation is recognized as a product of history (sensuous human activity) rather than of capital and in so doing is thereby de-fetishized. He presents the idea of dialectics at a standstill as a form of figural knowledge, thus:

> It's not that what is past casts light on what is present, or what is present its light
> on what it past; rather image is that wherein what has been comes together in
> a flash with the now to form a constellation. In other words: image is dialectics
> at a standstill. For while the relation of the present to the past is purely tem-
> poral, the relation to what-has-been to the now is dialectical: not temporal in
> nature but figural. Only dialectical images are genuinely historical—that is,
> not archaic—images. The image that is read—which is to say, the image in
> the now of its recognisability—bears to the highest degree the imprint of the
> perilous critical moment on which all reading is founded. (Benjamin 1999a,
> 462 [N3, 1])

Through the methodological technique of bringing together as a constellation a
range of contemporary and historical sources on each of the key motifs of bourgeois
culture, its fetishistic character is to be subject to the redemptive criticism of dialectics at a standstill.

> Ambiguity is the manifest imaging of dialectic, the law of dialectics at a standstill.
> The standstill is utopia and the dialectical image, therefore, a dream image. Such
> an image is afforded per se: as fetish. (Benjamin 1999b, 10)

Benjamin understands fetish, expressed in the writing, pictures, and material culture of the nineteenth century (such as that encountered in the Crystal Palace), as a
set of phantasmagoric figures that both deceive as a false reality (pace Marx) but also
allow for the possibility of revealing a hidden utopian wish-image truly worthy of
redemption within that false reality. This is more than simply recognizing that use
value has been co-opted by exchange value, as Adorno argues. What is at stake here
is not the recognition of use values but *the transfiguration of values through the practices associated with reception*. Benjamin uses the Parisian arcades as a major figure
through which to explore a wide range of elements of bourgeois capitalist culture
and suggests a more complex reading of the manner in which fetishism operates
that that offered by Marx or other later Marxist writers. In his approach the fetish/
phantasmagoria is not only that which obscures but also the way to Truth. This is a
both/and approach rather than an either/or one that we might learn from.

FETISHISM AND THE ARCADE

The arcades were glass-roofed spaces, capitalist ventures intended as shopping spaces
for luxury consumption. Influenced by the exoticized Orientalism of the Middle
Eastern bazaar in the eighteenth-century imagination, they were developed initially
in Paris in the galleries found in the Palais Royal in the 1780s. There, they became
sites associated with the exoticized consumerism of luxuries but also with theatrical
spectacle and other pleasures, notably food, drink, gambling, and sexual encounter
(Geist 1985; Hetherington 1997). Their popularity soon led to the development

of purpose-built arcades being constructed in upmarket parts of town all across Europe in the first half of the nineteenth century by capitalist speculators who saw them as a potentially highly profitable enterprise. They were filled with shops selling the latest fashions in luxury items and trinkets: clothing, porcelain, antiques, artworks, lace, jewelry, snuffboxes, scent bottles, "toys," and so on, in a tranquil space, often also used for promenading by the well-to-do in a display of themselves to one another, away from the associations of the class-mixing bustle of the street (Aldburgham 1964, 107ff.; Morrison 2003, 99ff.). In effect, they were the epitome at that time of consumer associations with the material culture of elegance, luxury, and status in early bourgeois culture. The reason the arcades are so important for Benjamin is because they were not only the first spaces to be given over entirely to modern consumer culture, but were also the first to fall into decline and to thereby reveal the dialectical image of progress as ruin that he saw behind the mythic and fetishistic character of capitalism.

Benjamin initially comes to recognize the significance of the arcades as a once new luxury space now turned to ruin through his reading of the novel *Le Paysan de Paris* [Paris Peasant] by the Surrealist writer Louis Aragon (1987). In that book, seen as a revelation for Benjamin that opened up his whole thinking on bourgeois culture, Aragon seeks out in the arcades of the early twentieth century—by then run-down and decayed, given over to junk shops and street walkers, with just a few remaining out-of-fashion luxury shops—a "mythology of the modern" in the detritus, scraps, and ruins left over from the culture of the previous century. Hidden in the montage of rubbish are the now outmoded dreams and fantasies of earlier generations turned into junk. Benjamin seeks to turn this insight into a methodology for excavating the hidden wish-images behind the capitalist phantasmagoria of one-directional progress and improvement that had been expressed in the original conception of the arcade.[11] Although the arcades are only one of a whole series of fetishistic space (what he also calls "dream-houses of the collective," referring also to department stores, world fairs, bourgeois interiors, and modern cities in general) through which he aims to construct these dialectical images, in effect, they stand for all of the commodity spaces and artifacts of industrial capitalism that can be subjected to this form of methodological enquiry.

For Benjamin, everything in an industrial capitalist (and thereby also a consumer) society presented as new, fashionable, and desirable—as progressive—reveals the ever-same character of the commodity form. One fashion replaces the next in a seemingly endless succession of the new coming into being for the first time. Yet what is new one day becomes outmoded the next, though its material detritus has the tendency to linger on discarded and disregarded as a ghostly trace. For Benjamin, this fantasy of the new and fashionable as an expression of progress reveals the inevitable betrayal of the dreams of happiness of consumers encouraged to endlessly pursue, in a futile manner, what is deemed to be desirable and fashionable. Only when such commoditized expressions of the idea of progress fall into inevitable ruin as they are replaced by something else does their initial promise reveal its phantasmagoric and illusory character: through the juxtaposition of the new and old in the creation of a dialectical image as in the arcades a century after their heyday.

It is not only the products found in these spaces that undergo this process of ruination over time; the same can be said for the "progress" of the spaces themselves. The arcades had their heyday after about 1790 and they remained as the leading spaces devoted to consumer luxury until around the mid-nineteenth century, when they were superseded by department stores like the Bon Marché in Paris (Miller 1981).[12] Likewise department stores, once the height of shopping fashion, look dated compared to out-of-town shopping malls (Shields 1989, 1992); and they, in turn, will be replaced by something else.

Yet, for Benjamin, the arcades are more than just shopping spaces in which commodity fetishism is given full reign; they are a monadological figure, a dialectical image, for everything associated with industrial capitalism and consumer culture. He recognizes the idea of progress as a myth but a powerful one that has come to define the outlook of producers and consumers alike in capitalist societies. As he puts it, "Capitalism was a natural phenomenon with which a new dream-filled sleep came over Europe, and, through it, a reactivation of mythic forces" (Benjamin 1999a, 391 [K1a, 7]). Yet that idea of progress that is so central to bourgeois culture is always already, Benjamin suggests, in a state of catastrophe, its dreams in need of rescue. For Benjamin that is something Marxists, too, have to recognize as well as bourgeois consumers. For him, historical materialism has uncritically absorbed the bourgeois idea of temporal progress in an un-dialectical and overly chronological, or historicist, manner (1973b; Lindroos, 1998). An important part of his project is that he seeks to challenge the taken-for-granted notion of progress as a linear, one-directional condition in which society in moving in all its guises, including that of Marxist theory. Progress is foremost, therefore, among the phantasmagorias that capitalism creates in its alliance with mythic thinking.

Benjamin first introduces the trope of the phantasmagoria in his 1935 précis-like exposé to *The Arcades Project*, written for the Frankfurt Institute of Social Research in that year (1999b). In that exposé he introduces the theme of phantasmagoria in a rather unsystematic way in the latter sections of the essay, after which it comes to dominate the analysis he offers. In the process of being worked out, perhaps consciously for the first time since Marx used it his discussion of commodity fetishism, it comes to dominate *The Arcades Project* thereafter (see Buck-Morss 1989).

As is well known, the exposé is organized into a series of themed sections headed by a name of a leading Parisian figure from the nineteenth century alongside one of its most significant cultural spaces, the suggestion at work being that the work of one is addressed by the corresponding (phantasmagoric) space. Thus: Fourier/arcade; Daguerre/panorama; Grandville/world exhibition; Louis Philippe/

interior; Baudelaire/street; Haussmann/barricade. The theme of the phantasmagoria as a space is not addressed directly[13] (just as there is no convolute on phantasmagoria in *The Arcades Project* itself, though there is one on the panorama); rather,
Benjamin first mentions it in the section on Grandville/world fairs. However, it
becomes apparent that he is suggesting that each of these spaces corresponds to one
of the central phantasmagoria of industrial capitalism, something that is reflected in
the "work" of the person named in each section.

In the section on Grandville/world fairs (he has the Paris exhibition of 1867,
in particular, in mind) he sees the fair as a pilgrimage to the commodity fetish where
workers as customers are presented with the phantasmagoria of exchange value their
own labor power has created, presented as a thing embodied in the multitude of
commodities they see displayed before them.

> World Exhibitions glorify the exchange value of the commodity. They create
> a framework in which its use value recedes into the background. They open
> a phantasmagoria which a person enters in order to be distracted. The enter-
> tainment industry makes this easier by elevating the person to the level of the
> commodity. He surrenders to its manipulations while enjoying his alienation
> from himself and others.—The enthronement of the commodity with its luster
> of distraction, is the secret then of Grandville's art. (1999b, 7)

It was such a view of the phantasmagoria and its relation to exchange value, in
particular, which was to so influence Adorno's adoption of the term.[14] In this light,
Benjamin goes on to speak of fashion, a product of the commodity world, as the "sex
appeal of the inorganic" (1999b, 8) worshipped as a fetish.

In the section on Louis Philippe/interior, the bourgeois interior is treated as a
phantasmagoria of the bourgeois universe, a seeming totality where the parlor and
the world are understood to be reflections of each other in the bourgeois imagination. In the section on Baudelaire/street, it is the crowd that is the phantasmagoria
to the flâneur (idler/stroller). Benjamin also discusses what he calls the phantasmagoria of cultural history (1999b, 9). This important section is at the center of this
1935 exposé and was to change somewhat with the later exposé of 1939. Central to
the bourgeois understanding of cultural history, Benjamin suggests here, are the
themes of novelty and fashion. Novelty, for Benjamin, is the central feature of commodity fetishism, deriving as it does from exchange value rather than use value.

> Newness is a quality independent of the use value of the commodity. It is the
> origin of the illusory appearance that belongs inalienable to images produced
> by the collective unconscious. It is the quintessence of that false consciousness
> whose indefatigable agent is fashion. The semblance of the now is reflected, like
> one mirror in another, in the semblance of the ever recurrent. The product of
> this reflection is the phantasmagoria of "cultural history" in which the bour-
> geoisie enjoys its false consciousness to the full. (1999b, 9)

Notwithstanding the influence of his ideas on the consumption of exchange value in itself, it is the suggestion of a collective unconscious in this passage and the somewhat subjectivist view of commodity fetishism that was famously to draw Adorno's ire (discussed below) and subsequently lead to something of a rethink on Benjamin's part and a turn to a more recognizably Marxist approach to fetishism in the later 1939 exposé. Nonetheless, the Nietzschean theme of eternal recurrence, of the new, the fashionable, being, in fact, the same old thing dressed up in new clothes, remained crucial to his understanding of the nature of the commodity within a consumer society (for an overview and extended discussion of this, see Frisby 1985).

The section on Haussmann/barricades suggests two further phantasmagorias. He mentions that the phantasmagoria of space for the flâneur is something that corresponds to the phantasmagoria of time for the gambler. He then goes on to suggest that the Paris Commune of 1871 dispelled the phantasmagoria of 1789, which had suggested to the French political imagination throughout the nineteenth century that the bourgeoisie and the proletariat could work together to create a new and better society.

Emphasizing the way in which Benjamin understands these phantasmagorias sums up his approach in the 1935 exposé: as an illusory collective dream under capitalist conditions that we can only wake from through a recognition of dialectical images.

> From this epoch derive the arcades and interiors, the exhibition halls and panoramas. They are residues of a dream world. The realization of dream elements, in the course of waking up, is the paradigm of dialectical thinking. Thus, dialectical thinking is the organ of historical awakening. Every epoch not only dreams the one to follow but, in dreaming, precipitates its awakening. It bears its end within itself and unfolds it—as Hegel already noticed—by cunning. With the destabilising of the market economy, we begin to recognise the monuments of the bourgeoisie as ruins even before they have crumbled. (1999b, 13)

Adorno's well-known criticisms of this approach were trenchant. They can be found in a lengthy letter to Benjamin written in August 1935 (2002, 111–120). There, Adorno questions Benjamin's association of fetishism with a collective unconscious. For Adorno, as for Marx, fetishism is not a product of the flawed consciousness of the bourgeoisie; rather, fetishism objectively produces their consciousness, and therefore cannot be understood with reference to a subjectivist understanding of dreaming applied to a collective, something he sees a profoundly wrong (fetishistic) in Benjamin's expose (1977, 111). He also challenges Benjamin's conception of the dialectical image as something found in consciousness as a dream awaiting awakening and suggests instead that Benjamin de-psychologize "dream" when he talks about human hopes. He goes on, furthermore, to challenge Benjamin's reference to a collective unconscious as the place where those dreams are located. This would lead him, Adorno believes, close to the conservative and mythic approach to dreams found in the irrationalist work of a writer like Carl Jung—precisely the kind of mythological and phantasmagoric imaginings that Benjamin's project was seeking to challenge in the first place (1977, 113).

That Benjamin took note of these criticisms is reflected in the fact that the main definition he subsequently gives to phantasmagoria in *The Arcades Project* comes through a direct reference to Adorno.

> The property appertaining to the commodity as its fetish character attaches as well to the commodity-producing society—not as in itself, to be sure, but more as it represents itself and thinks to understand itself whenever it abstracts from the fact that it produces precisely commodities. The image that it produces of itself in this way, and that customarily labels as its culture, corresponds to the concept of phantasmagoria. The latter is defined by Wiesengrund "as a consumer item in which there is no longer anything that is supposed to remind us how it came into being. It becomes a magical object, insofar as the labor stored up in it come to seem supernatural and sacred at the very moment when it can no longer be recognised as labour." (Benjamin 1999a, 669 [X, 13a])[15]

This really just takes us back to Marx's use of phantasmagoria in *Capital* and the question one has to ask is whether, notwithstanding acknowledging the importance of Adorno's criticisms of mythic thinking and subjectivism in Benjamin's 1935 exposé, something isn't lost from the creative approach he adopts there to phantasmagoria in this more orthodox, productivist Marxist approach. It is a debatable point, and the evidence is by no means clear, but one could argue that *The Arcades Project* remained unfinished at least partly because Benjamin was wrestling unsuccessfully with reconciling his criticized mythic approach to fetishism that had been rejected by Adorno on the one hand with a more reductionist Marxist one that he could not fully believe in on the other, and that he was not able to resolve the tension between them in his project.

In the exposé of 1939, Benjamin drops the reference to collective dreaming and to subjective understanding of commodities, preferring, instead, this more orthodox Marxist understanding. He is also now more systematic in his treatment of phantasmagoria than he had been in the earlier exposé. In this new exposé, Benjamin more clearly than anywhere else in his writings tries to summarize the intentions of *The Arcades Project* as a whole, by placing the idea of the phantasmagoria at the center of his analysis much more clearly than he had done previously.

> Our investigation proposes to show how, as a consequence of this reifying representation of civilization, the new forms of behaviour and the new economically and technologically based creations we owe to the nineteenth century enter the universe as a phantasmagoria. (1999c, 14)

Most of the rest of the exposé is much the same as in the earlier one. While there are some changes to subheadings (the panorama section disappears—perhaps because it might create confusion now with phantasmagoria as the key visual display trope in his analysis?), the examples of phantasmagoria that Benjamin gives remain much the same. The one further change is in the concluding section where Benjamin discusses a little-known text by the revolutionary Auguste Blanqui, *L'Eternité par les Astres* [Eternity via the Stars] written in 1872 while Blanqui was in prison following the Paris Commune. Discovering this text in 1937 was a revelation for Benjamin (see Buck-Morss 1989, 106). In its wild cosmological speculations he found two related themes that he had been struggling with all along in his own work: a critique of the nineteenth-century fascination with the idea of progress as phantasmagoria (as with Benjamin, modernity is seen as a hell that is presented as heaven by Blanqui too; see Buck-Morss 1989) and related to that the doctrine of history as eternal recurrence, written some ten years before the concept was seemingly introduced to the world by Nietzsche in *Thus Spake Zarathustra* (1961). Benjamin says of Blanqui's text, "The book completes the century's phantasmagoria with one last, cosmic phantasmagoria which implicitly comprehends the severest critique of all the others" (1999c, 25). While, for Benjamin, Blanqui does not see the source of this phantasmagoria as capitalism, he does acknowledge Blanqui's understanding of "history as catastrophe presented as progress," an important insight for his own project. He ends his own piece by recognizing this and sums up what he sees as the consequences of the phantasmagoric character of capitalist society.

> The century was incapable of responding to the new technological possibility with a new social order. That is why the last word was left to the errant negotiators between old and new who are at the heart of these phantasmagorias. The world dominated by its phantasmagorias—this to make use of Baudelaire's term is "modernity." Blanqui's vision has the entire universe entering the modernity at which Baudelaire's seven old men are the heralds. In the end, Blanqui views novelty as an attribute of all that is under the sentence of damnation. Likewise in Ciel en Enfer, a vaudeville piece that slightly predates the book: in this piece the torments of hell figure as the latest novelty of all time, as "pains eternal and always new." The people of the nineteenth century, whom Blanqui addresses as if they were apparitions, are natives of this region. (1999c, 26)

This last quote encapsulates Benjamin's vision of capitalist modernity as hell and catastrophe for humanity. This is a world where everything appears as new and progressive but is in fact old, myth ridden, alienated, and the ever same of the endlessly deceiving, fetishized commodity form. Like Lukacs before him and Adorno, his contemporary, this is something that comes to characterize the whole of capitalist society and not just the alienated labor process. It comes to produce not only consciousness, for Benjamin, but also the whole realm of human experience.

On this reading one might be led to believe that Benjamin's analysis is even more pessimistic about the consequences than Adorno, but this is not the case. Unlike Lukacs and Adorno, who both used the notion of a phantasmagoria in their work in a manner more directly related to Marx's use of the term as a figure for an illusory fetishistic reality, Benjamin is subtler in his usage. Certainly he treats the notion of phantasmagoria as another word for commodity fetishism but he also believes there is another form of experience, expressed as a utopian wish-image, that is contained in what he describes as phantasmagoric. Benjamin does not want to simply subject phantasmagoria to critique. Rather, and this is what singles him out from the Marxist tradition, he wants to construct these phantasmagoria as dialectical images in order to reveal, and thereby redeem from capitalism, the genuine utopian quest for an experience of the world that humanity has which is expressed in such ideals as luxury, comfort, abundance, and ease.

The wishes and dreams of a capitalist culture, always suggestive of duration but inevitably premised as fashionable, fleeting, transitory, and in need of repeat, are expressed, for Benjamin, in concrete and material form in such a space as the arcade. He seeks to construct dialectical images out of the writings but also the artifacts, fashions, architecture, technological apparatus, pictures, illustrations, old adverts, signs, and brands of the nineteenth century—each of which presents the myth that it will be the best and will last forever, whereas most will become outmoded in a very short time. In effect, he seeks in his dialectics at a standstill to construct the space of the dream-like phantasmagoric figure in order not only to make it visible as something produced but also to give it a voice; an awkward, ghostly voice that could not be described from within capitalist discourse and could only be redeemed outside of it. In taking possession of things (commodities) through our consumer activity, we are ourselves possessed by the ghostly figure or mythic form of our betrayed dreams of happiness.

Notwithstanding his 1939 nod to Adorno's more orthodox understanding of fetishism, Benjamin makes a big point of the dream-like quality of capitalism's phantasmagorias. The dreams and wish-images Benjamin seeks to recover from within this culture are not revealed by such artifacts standing on their own but through his intervention in bringing them into contact with the present in the manner of a montage. In this way they are figures of *Kairos* that rupture the hermetic story of History as a chronology of progress. The resulting dialectical images are treated like ghosts—phantasms in this capitalist agora—as figures not just of the past and present brought into contact with one another with unsettling effects but of different expressions of time (Lindroos, 1998).

Benjamin's reading of surrealism and incorporation of some of its ideas is central to his approach (1985a). Montage, as a surrealist technique, works on the principles of shock and revelation. The shock-effect of juxtaposition, of bringing incongruous things together, bringing fantasy into contact with reality, will act, Benjamin believes, as a source of "profane illumination…a materialist, anthropological inspiration" (1985a, 227). This is an idea Benjamin develops from his reading of Breton (1960) and Aragon (1987). He goes on to suggest that this is what the Surrealists had revealed in their fascination with the (ruined) object in their sojourns around Paris in the 1920s. Commenting on Breton's pursuit of the ghostly figure of Nadja through Paris in his novel of that name (1960), Benjamin says:

> He [Breton] was the first to perceive the revolutionary energies that appeared in the "outmoded".... No one before these visionaries and augurs perceived how destitution—not only social but architectonic, the poverty of interiors, enslaved and enslaving objects—can be suddenly transformed into revolutionary nihilism.... They bring the immense forces of "atmosphere" concealed in these things to the point of explosion. (1985a, 229)

He goes on:

> The Surrealists' Paris, too, is a "little universe." That is to say, in the larger one, the cosmos, things look different. There too, are crossroads where ghostly signals flash from the traffic, and inconceivable analogies and connections between events are the order of the day. It is in the region from which the lyric poetry of Surrealism reports. (231)

Most perceptive of all, though, is what Benjamin recognizes in these "ghostly signals," these phantasms, these fetishes; their disclosed message is the expression of a figural language not contained within any rational bourgeois discourse. In fact, they stand in opposition to discourse, most especially the discourse of progress. The truth of disclosure resides not in the appearance of the outmoded object in itself, even though that is what we see, but the shock effect it creates when it is brought into contact with the present. As Benjamin famously puts it:

> Language takes precedence. Not only before meaning. Also before the self. In the world's structure dream loosens individuality like a bad tooth. This loosening of the self by intoxication is, at the same time, precisely the fruitful, living experience that allowed these people to step outside the domain of intoxication. (1985a, 227)

For Benjamin, the language of "ghosts" is the potentially redemptive language of the figure revealed not in words but through images and material artifacts left behind by progress or improvement; images that we find in the not fully disposed of, the ruin, whose juxtapositions are encountered in the anachronism of mixed-up temporal sequences as the past is brought together with a new context. It is this figural language that his methodology of dialectics at a standstill seeks to address.

This is clearly not the language of the subject. No one is supposing that ghosts, the figural, or the once new but now discarded objects in which this is manifest, actually speak. The issue is not one of parole. Rather, in his *Arcades Project*, the essay on surrealism just quoted, and in his studies on Baudelaire, Benjamin develops a materialist approach to this question of the disclosure of language through the figure. The wish-image is the language of the ghost of humanity's past dreams (and labor) manifest in material form betrayed, and, for Benjamin, we encounter them in the objects and images of commodity culture and our engagement with it. What the surrealists suggest, and Benjamin too in following them, is that we need to suspend disbelief that there could be a language outside of the subject, a language of the figural object, a language of time outside of historicism and the phantasmagoria of progress.

MODERNITY AND EXPERIENCE

Benjamin's methodology seeks to engage not simply with matters of consciousness in the way that Lukacs does but more broadly with the character of experience, with the subject as an embodied and active person as historical subject in a world of material things. It is his approach to the question of experience that marks out his understanding of fetishism and phantasmagoria from these other Marxist interpretations. His sources, in opening up this way of addressing the issue of experience, come from outside Marxism. In particular, he seeks to explore and also to challenge the category of experience as lived present that had become a prominent issue within German neo-Kantian philosophy at the end of the nineteenth century (see Lindroos 2001; Koselleck 2004) and also in the emergence of modern art from a few decades before. Such an approach can be found clearly in some of Benjamin's key influences; Georg Simmel, Charles Baudelaire, Marcel Proust, and André Breton (see Frisby 1985; Cohen 1995).

Benjamin acknowledges that metropolitan life, and that of capitalism in general, has changed the character of human experience. This, for him, is a defining feature of modernity; a mode of experience first described by Baudelaire and later by Proust, theorized by Simmel (1971b; 1990), and an alternative to it sought by Breton (1960) are some of his key sources in his analysis. Since Goethe, poets and artists have been struggling with what modernity does to experience (*Erfahrung*). In particular, a theme that emanated from Romantic thought has been to address how, in modernity, we witness the decline of an archaic form of experience (*Erfahrung*) where people are able to situate themselves in the continuity of cultural tradition, through custom, narrative, and shared communal values (see Berman 1982; Koselleck 2004). A central theme of this Romantic outlook after Goethe, an outlook that Benjamin, like the early Marx, is very much immersed within, has been to address the question of *how to forge a subjectivity in the face of the modern world* *in which experience (*Erfahrung*) associated with tradition, continuity, narrative, and memory is principally felt as loss,* without simply retreating into a reactionary, mythic, and conservative nostalgia for the past (see Gouldner 1973; Berman 1982; Koselleck 2004). What modernity brings in its place, a modernity in which capitalist social relations are based on the phantasmagoria of commodity fetishism, is, in effect, alienation in the form of the fragmentation of experience and an endless experience of the now as a lived moment detached from the continuity of natural time (*Erlebnis*). Perhaps Benjamin's major contribution to Marxism is to address this issue of alienation through experience rather than consciousness as Lukacs and others had done.

The moment that one lives through, bombarded by consumer stimuli, the reified urban reserve and blasé attitude cultivated as a defense (pace Simmel), leads the modern subject to know experience not as *Erfahrung* but as *Erlebnis*—as the fragmentary set of moments in which the subject becomes detached and isolated from any locatedness within a broader understanding of the continuities and realities of social life. This is a central concern of the turn-of-the-century Lebensphilosophie of which Simmel was a leading figure (see Frisby 1981). Benjamin acknowledges this as a key theme too for neo-Kantian philosophers like Dilthey (1973a; see also Gadamer 1975), and also for the vitalism of Bergson, and it is, significantly, a key question for both Proust and surrealism as well (see Wolin 1989b; Cohen 1995). *Erlebnis* in this tradition suggests not only disorientation (what I called in Chapter 1, bewilderment) but a fragmented, distracted outlook on the world that, for Benjamin, leads to a susceptibility to the powers of phantasmagoric impression and myth that provide a false sense of identity, *Erfahrung*, lived reality, and consciousness. This was especially evident for him at the time he was writing in the Nazi co-opting of phantasmagoric illusions of Volk, Gemeinschaft, and *Erfahrung* in its propaganda during the 1930s.

Benjamin was never a conservative defender of the aura of tradition, nor did he believe it was possible to return to a now lost form of experience that capitalism had melted away. However, he did want to redeem tradition, for him, expressed in the wishes of the past, all the same because of the utopian impulse that he believed lay behind all human history. Jewish themes of redemption in the material and human world and bearing witness were always prominent in his work. However, he was also a believer in the Marxist idea of praxis, and his *Arcades Project* was intended foremost as a contribution, if a tragic one, to that. Out of it he wanted to awaken, through the techniques of shock and revelation, a sense of the impoverishment of *Erlebnis* within modernity and an awareness of the utopian traces and memories of a fuller form of experience that were latent in the phantasmagoria that crystallized in the material culture of capitalism and which one day might be brought into existence in a new way.

Benjamin does not clearly give us an answer to how this might be achieved, though evidently his approach is dialectical: a novel synthesis emerging from the contradictions between the ideology of *Erfahrung* and the actual reality of *Erlebnis*. It is certainly an issue he had grappled with for many years, and the fact that *The Arcades Project*, begun in 1927, remained unfinished at his death some thirteen years later, reflects the argument that he had not fully worked out all the answers he wanted on the issue of experience (see Wolin 1989b). Nonetheless his work does present a glimpse of the ways in which he believes the phantasmagoric character of capitalist society might be used in this process.

We find him at his most optimistic on such an issue in his well-known essay *The Work of Art in the Age of Mechanical Reproduction* (1973a) and the distinction he makes there between contemplation and distraction in the face of a work of art. Each of these modes of attention might be seen to correspond to a different form of experience: *Erfahrung*/contemplation and *Erlebnis*/distraction and, we might add, different conceptions of the subject: *the producing subject in the former case and the consuming subject in the latter*. However, recognizing that Benjamin is not simply saying that the former is good and needs to be recovered and the latter is bad and needs to be done away with, but that a dialectical realization is needed that will create a new mode of experience out of the contradictions between them, we can begin to see something of the redemptive capacity of reception and practice within consumer culture that Benjamin seeks to expose from behind the phantasmagoric veil.

Benjamin's mechanical reproduction essay is often read as a contrast to Adorno's pessimism in the face of the culture industry to suggest a way in which popular culture might provide a source of critical opposition to the dominant cultural motifs of the time (Hollywood escapism and fascism)—most famously, Benjamin's celebration in that essay of the undermining of the conservative hold than an artwork's aura of uniqueness has on its viewers by mechanical reproducibility. This is singled out as a way of recognizing that audiences are now much more free to interpret and appropriate an artwork in ways that challenge that dominant culture: "[W]hen the age of mechanical reproduction separated art from its base in cult, the semblance of its autonomy disappeared forever" (Benjamin 1973a, 220). While twentieth-century cinema is the example often cited as the harbinger of mechanical reproduction and the decline of aura, five centuries of mechanical reproducibility of images (etchings, lithographs, photographs, etc.), as Benjamin was well aware, had also been part of this tradition (see also Ivins 1953; Malraux 1978).[16] It is, however, what Benjamin says about film that is central to how he addresses the relationship between reception and experience. It is not just images that have aura but experience (*Erfahrung*) too. In the key section (1973a, 222–24), Benjamin argues that film presents the experiences of the actor as *Erlebnis* to the watching audience for the first time. The auratic quality of experience (*Erfahrung*) is no longer present—as it had been in theater (1973a, 223).

While at first glance this seems rather questionable, to say the least, given the aura that continues to be associated with movie stars in our age of celebrity, Benjamin does acknowledge the continuing possibility for aura to be attributed to actors (1973a, 224). However, he suggests that that is created as another phantasmagoria in the marketing of films and not in the watching of the performance itself. What the filmgoing audience sees that the theatre audience does not is experience presented as *Erlebnis* rather than *Erfahrung*. Film audiences are presented with an image of their own reality, a fractured, disjointed set of lived moments (scenes) that they have little control over rather than a self-reflective understanding of their position in the world. An awareness of this is only possible because of the loss of presence and the undermining of aura made possible by mechanical reproduction. Audiences have to construct their own interpretation of what they see rather than accept one presented to them as if given and unchanging.

Benjamin is well aware of the ongoing phantasmagoric effects of film, just as he is of its position within consumer culture in general, and he does not uncritically celebrate it as a liberating force for radical change as some recent commentators appear to believe. What he does suggest is that film has the power to shock in the same way that dialectical images shock—as a source of awakening—and that audiences retain the possibility to be attentive to this because of the mode of reception they adopt. The key issue in his essay on mechanical reproduction is not that of what happens to aura per se but what he has to say about reception. Linked to the undermining of aura and the development of experience as *Erlebnis*, reception, in Benjamin's view, is changing from one based on absorbed contemplation in which the reader is a producer of what he or she sees (the gaze, in other terminology) to that of distraction where he or she consumes (or the glance).

Theater audiences and audiences of auratic art engage in acts of concentrated contemplation—they stand outside the work of art and view it through an act of *productive* mastery over it. It is as much a reflection of their own mode of experience (*Erfahrung*) as the nature of the art they encounter. The pure gaze of the Kantian aesthetic (see Kant 1957; Bourdieu 1984) can be seen as the epitome of this mode of emotionally disinterested yet cognitively attentive aesthetic reception in which the individual in isolation contemplates and judges a work of art. Such a mode of reception—absorption—was indeed promoted in the beginnings of bourgeois art in the French academy in the late eighteenth century (also in the Royal Academy in Britain) where salon painting encouraged such a mode of reception in the way images were depicted (see Fried 1980). Yet, for Benjamin, mechanical reproduction not only undermines the aura of such art but also the contemplative form of reception by singular individuals, encouraging in its place a distracted mass audience reception instead (1973a, 232–34).

> Distraction and contemplation form polar opposites which may be stated as follows: A man who concentrates before a work of art is absorbed by it…. In contrast, the distracted mass absorbs the work of art. (232)

For Benjamin, distraction allows people to develop habits of seeing that are in part shaped by what a person sees. A culture where there has been a shift from contemplation to distraction as the main way of seeing is a culture in which the key mode of apperception has changed. This is something he believes has now happened and is reflected in the importance of cinema: "[R]eception in a state of distraction, which is increasingly noticeable in all fields of art and is symptomatic of profound changes in apperception, finds in the film its true means of exercise" (233).

Distraction, for Benjamin, equates to *Erlebnis* and a *consuming* rather than producing mode of reception; to a mode of experience as something modern and fragmented, something that is lived in the present, consumed, and detached from any sense of continuity with the past. Unlike Adorno, perhaps the last true defender of bourgeois art and its contemplative mode of apperception and critical judgment, who sees mass distraction as a source of passive contemplation in an entirely negative manner, Benjamin is more ambiguous and sees both danger and promise in such distracted reception.[17] On the one hand, he is suggesting that absorbing art rather than being absorbed by it—or being a consumer of experience rather than a producer of experience—reflects the destruction of aura and allows for new ways of critically engaging with the world as it is experienced. Yet he is also suggesting, on the other, that reactionary forces in capitalism (fascism is the most extreme) have been able to co-opt such a mode of reception and offer a distorted illusion of experience as *Erfahrung*, filling in for any sense of loss. For Benjamin, there is nothing intrinsically liberating about *Erlebnis* and its distracted, consuming mode of reception; it is highly susceptible to being captivated by the illusion of what it sees—phantasmagoria. The phantasmagoria can take possession of one. Yet only this modern form of experience and its distracted reception of the social world, under the right conditions, is capable of recognizing the phantasmagoria for what they are and thereby rejecting them by taking possession of them. For Benjamin, a contemplative mode of reception is always absorbed in the aura of the image and cannot stand outside it. In effect, *a distracted reception and fragmented form of experience are, for Benjamin, necessary conditions of possibility needed for revolutionary action to occur.* Such action cannot take place outside these conditions. He is not saying that such an experience will inevitably lead to such action, or that distraction cannot be prey to reactionary diversions, but that *only such a fragmented (alienated) outlook is capable of responding to the shock-effect of dialectical images and the possibility of awakening to the moment of Kairos where the past enters into contact with the present and in which are found the real human concerns for happiness and fellowship that they afford.*

CONCLUSION

What is a phantasmagoria if not a device for the mechanical reproduction of images? It is a device that stands midway between the camera obscura and cinema both historically and figuratively. We can agree with Benjamin that it is the key trope for understanding consumer culture and capitalism in the period from the latter half of the nineteenth century to the present. And that indeed, Benjamin rather than Lukacs, Adorno, or Debord is the key interpreter of Marx's analysis of commodity fetishism through this metaphor. Yet, in many ways, he stands too firmly in the Marxist tradition to fully allow us to use his work unquestioningly to understand the genesis of consumer culture in total. Most notably his understanding of culture under capitalism is too closely defined by seeking answers to the problem of revolutionary action. His treatment of consumer culture through themes of fragmented experience and distracted reception are fruitful for thinking about issues of subject formation and people's relationship to the material world of commodities, but in his hands they are too closely tied to the methodology of dialectics at a standstill and the problem of awakening to real interests. Ultimately *The Arcades Project*, despite its defenders' claims, remains an incomplete, even if brilliantly insightful, approach to cultural analysis. Benjamin is much less optimistic in outlook there than he is in the earlier essay on mechanical reproduction, perhaps because of the way he absorbed Adorno's criticisms of it in the early stages. The Marxist tradition that he aligns himself with—Marx, Lukacs, Adorno—will have nothing to do with the idea that the kairological figure can be a potential source for challenging capitalism's false reality. Realists that they are, they see nothing potentially redemptive in that. He was always going to be on difficult ground. What they all do that Benjamin does not in their understanding of commodity fetishism through the trope of phantasmagoria is construct the viewer as an absorbed subject who is thereby deluded by what he or she sees. For Benjamin their distraction is a source of energy and change. It should be our starting point too for considering a consumption view of the subject. Whereas Western Marxism constructs the mode of reception associated with the phantasmagoria as one of passive contemplation, just as earlier writers constructed the fetish-worshipping African, for Benjamin, a distractive mode of reception is a more active and engaged one than this tradition will allow for. It is this wonderfully perceptive, counterintuitive move on distraction as an active rather than passive form of agency that lifts Benjamin's work out of this tradition and its pessimism. He points us in the direction of a much richer analysis of subject formation within capitalism even if that is not his key problematic and not an issue he follows through to its conclusion with any success. We might say that in the end he became rather too *absorbed* by Marxism by the time of the 1939 exposé, whereas he might have done better to have remained *distracted* by it as he was in 1935. That, in sum, is how we should address this Marxist approach to commodity fetishism. In the analysis of consumer culture, we still need to be distracted by Marxist concepts and arguments but should not ourselves become fully absorbed contemplators of them. Distraction, after all, is a means to détournement. People do certainly make their own lives under conditions that they do not choose themselves (Marx 1978), and they often make that life by responding to the conjured-up ghosts and creating phantasmagoria that get taken for reality, but they are also easily distracted in those conditions, able to make judgments about the validity or otherwise of what they see. It is true that the phantasmagoria still has a trace of the theatrical construction of contemplative reception about it, more than twentieth-century cinema does certainly, but as a transitional device (not only between theater and cinema but also between different epistemic constructions of the subject) that presents images rather than actual appearances; it positions its viewing subjects in an uncertain space between these two modes of reception—contemplation and distraction—and perhaps two modes of experience as well. If people confront the material world of commodities through images and scenes and receive those through a distracted rather than a contemplative mode of reception, they may well see the world in a different light than the one suggested by Marxist fetish theory. We should take a look at the phantasmagorias, spaces, and materials that went into the making of some of Benjamin's "dreamhouses" and consider the type of subject that they afforded—shop, house, museum. The aim is to think about how subjects get constituted within capitalism as active and distracted agents in figural spaces of uncertainty.

Chapter Five
The Distracted Flâneuse

We are not able to stand against the overwhelming temptations which besiege us at every turn.... We go to purchase something we want; but when we get to our shop there are so many more things that we never thought of till they presented their obtrusive fascination on every side. We look for a ribbon, a flower, a chiffon of some sort or other, and we find ourselves in a Paradise of ribbons, flowers, chiffons, without which our life becomes impossible and our gown unwearable. There are many shops in London into which one cannot safely trust oneself.... There are two important changes which have contributed to the temptation of spending money nowadays. One is the gathering together under one roof of all kinds of goods—clothing, millinery, groceries, furniture, in fact all the necessities of life.... The other reason for the increased temptation to spend money is the larger numbers of women which are now employed.... Women are so much quicker than men, and they understand so much more readily what other women want.

Lady Jeune, "The Ethics of Shopping," *The Fortnightly Review*, **January 1896 (quoted in Adburgham 1964, 235–36)**

In the first four chapters of this book, I explored the ways in which the analysis of consumer activity in capitalist societies has been shaped by an overdetermining approach to commodity fetishism. Following a critical discussion of the fetishist character of consumer society as a society of spectacle, I looked at the genealogy of this idea in that of fetishism and the trope of phantasmagoria, first used by Marx in his conceptualization of fetishism (1938), and then developed subsequently by Lukacs, Adorno, and Benjamin, who placed the term at the center of their analysis of capitalism in a post-productivist era of mass consumption. This type of approach has now become something of a commonplace for understanding the character of consumer society and the seemingly manipulated false consciousness associated with the subjectivity of consumers even in studies that are not obviously Marxist, and that is the main reason why we still need to address it (see Baudrillard 1981;

1983; Williams 1982; Clark 1984; Bowlby 1985; Crary 1990, Richards 1991; Asendorf 1993; Friedberg 1993).

My aim has been to question some of the assumptions made about the character of subjectivity within these approaches by returning to it within the field of political economy and opening it up to scrutiny. While it should be clear from Chapter 2 that I am somewhat critical of the theorization of spectacle that currently has a prominent position within this area of research, my aim has in no way been a simplistic liberal defense of capitalism against Marxist and post-Marxist criticisms, nor has it simply sought to offer an unquestioning valorization of the playful and creative consumer as a skilled individual agent. Consumers are indeed constituted as skilled *social* agents (see Douglas and Isherwood 1986; Campbell 1987; McCracken 1988; Lury 1996) but that does not mean one defends the idea of consumer culture or ignores the issues of power, inequality, impoverishment, injustice, environmental impact, and resource depletion that emanate from this area of social life.

I want to understand better how capitalism operates in people's lives and how their subjectivity is constituted within the parameters of a market society where consumption rather than production is the most significant force. We need a better understanding of fetishism than that offered within the Marxist tradition, but rather than turn to another field, such as psychoanalysis, for the answers, I have sought to remain within the field of political—or perhaps now better called cultural—economy in order to do this (on cultural economy, see Du Gay and Pryke 2003).

I have taken Benjamin as my lead in this because of all the writers within this tradition, his emphasis on the issue of the changing character of experience, and understanding of consumer distraction as practice, allows him to develop, albeit in an incomplete manner, a better understanding of the powers of capitalism that are expressed through consumption rather than production and the ways in which they position people as subjects.

In what follows over the next three chapters, I want to explore and develop some of these concerns within the context of some of the key social spaces in which mass consumer culture developed in the nineteenth century—all of which remain significant today in order that we might develop what I call a consumption rather than a production view of the subject (see also Munro 1996). The spaces I have chosen to concentrate on should come as little surprise, as there has already been much analysis of each:

- The *department store* that emerged during the 1860s as a site of mass consumption (see Porter Benson 1979; Miller 1981; Chaney 1983; Williams 1982; Bowlby 1985; Abelson 1989; Leach 1993; Lancaster 1995; Crossick and Jaumain 1999; Rappaport 2000)

- The *parlor/interior* as a key space for the private life of the bourgeoisie (Calder 1977; Saisselin 1985; Sennett 1977; Loeb 1994; Nunokawa 1994; Bryden and Floyd 1999; Logan 2001)
- The *museum* as a site for the singularization of commodities and the transformation of their value within a narrative of history (see also Harris 1990; Hooper-Greenhill 1992; Bennett 1995; Maleuvre 1999; Cummings and Lewandowska 2000; Fyfe 2000).

Through an investigation of each and the overlaps and links between them we can address different moments of consumption and their dynamics—(i) acquisition, (ii) use, and (iii) disposal—and the ways that those dynamics intersect with subject formation.

It is inevitable that in presenting the argument in this way, the narrative constructs a simplifying chronological model for understanding production-consumption-disposal. I would not want this to be the case and argue that we need to recognize the more complex interrelationship and enfolded character of these different processes (see Hetherington 2004). I organize the following three chapters in this way to address these moments in consumer culture in turn for the sake of clarity of argument and not for any other reason.

In this chapter I analyze the department store as a space primarily associated with the acquisition of commodities and the process of subject formation associated with it. This was an important cultural space for Benjamin too, in large part because its emergence in the 1860s was the major reason for the ruin of the earlier form of consumer space, the arcade, which was so much an emblem for his interests in the trajectory of capitalism in the nineteenth century. For Benjamin, the main example of the subject found in such a space is the much vaunted flâneur (stroller) who appeared in the arcades of Paris in the early years of the nineteenth century and became the model for the modern subject's visual and aesthetic outlook on the city of consumption after Baudelaire's appropriation of him (and he is gendered as male) as the key figure for understanding the modern artistic reception of that city in the 1860s (see Benjamin 1999a; Buck-Morss 1989; Tester 1994; Gilloch 1995). Important as it is to consider this figure and his relationship to the spaces of consumption, more recent analysis has challenged the emphasis given to him, notably because of the unacknowledged assumptions made about the gendered nature of his gaze upon the modern capitalist city (see Pollock 1988; Wolff 1990). Others, following on from these early critiques and refusing to accept women's status as a victim of the male gaze of the flâneur (as passanté—the "passed by" who is constituted as a subject by being gazed upon as an object by the male flâneur), have sought to bring to the fore the female subject equivalent instead—the flâneuse—as a subject who was not to be found in the arcades but in the department stores and the suburban shopping streets that replaced them in the second half of the nineteenth century (see Wilson 1991; 2001; Friedberg 1993; Nava 1997; Vickery 1998; Rappaport 2000; Parsons 2003). I take my lead here from this work. If we are to understand the fetish character of shopping and the phantasmagoric space of the department store in which it occurred then we need to center it on the place of the subject that was primarily constituted by that space and has been described thus as a flâneuse.

The significance that women played within this new space across Europe and North America during the latter part of the nineteenth and into the twentieth century raises important issues about the relationship between the commodity, gendered subjectivity, and spatiality that I want to investigate in this chapter. The old simplified idea that women were subject to a rigidly enforced ideology of domesticity and confined to the private sphere of the home is no longer accepted without considerable qualification by feminist historians (see, for example, Bowlby 1985; Wilson 1991; Walkowitz 1992; Nava 1997; Nead 2000; Parsons 2003). No one is denying that such a discursive formation surrounding issues of femininity and the domestic sphere prevailed within Victorian society (see Davidoff and Hall 1987; C. Hall 1992), but the idea that there was a straightforward spatial separation of public/private spheres with the location of men in the former and women in the latter has proven to be too simple a formula. The department store does much to confound that spatial formula. The situation was more complex and the position of women, in particular, much less certain and more paradoxical within such space, leading to its conceptualization as also more paradoxical (see Rose 1993). It has been the investigation of the department store as a public space for women that has allowed it to become one of the main social spaces that has been used to challenge this earlier argument about private sphere confinement (see Porter Benson 1988; Abelson 1989; Rappaport 2000).

I develop the argument here that the figure of the flâneuse occupied the space called the department store in a paradoxical manner. Her subjectivity and the character of the store as a social space were coproduced as positions of consumer desire within the consumer culture of the late nineteenth century (see also Rappaport 2000).[1] It is often argued, following Benjamin, that that space be described as phantasmagoric—that it was a key space of the commodity fetish. Given that I have sought to problematize rather than reject that term in the preceding chapters, my task here is to explore some of the consequences of utilizing that term in other than a taken-for-granted Marxian way. The central theme that I shall explore here is that of paradox and undecidability in relation to fetishism. As suggested in Chapter 3, phantasmagoric space is deeply paradoxical with regard to how subjects are constituted in relation to the visual world of things. In terms of both subject formation and the making of social space, paradox is a key term (see Rose 1993). The figure of the flâneuse is important because it is she, more than her ironic and distanced male counterpart, and from practice as much shaped by gender as class, from whom we can trace a genealogical start for the modern consuming subject.[2] It is around such a subject that we can explore the shaping of experience (*Erlebnis*) that is at the center of a consumer society and the uncertainties that surround it.

I would suggest that one of the main problems with theories of commodity fetishism is that they locate the subject within the (seemingly non-paradoxical) terrain of production and dwell nostalgically on the demise of experience as a totality centered in the creative or laboring subject (*Erfahrung*). That model of the subject and of fetishistic seeing is then applied, after Lukacs, to the world of consumption with little reflection and little change in analysis—except somewhat ambiguously in Benjamin's work. In the paradoxical space of the department store we can see in the display of things for the flâneuse, the constitution of her desire to look at them and to consume them visually as well as sometimes to acquire them for use, the development of the modern consuming subject.[3] I will suggest that this space of gender not only constitutes the female subject in a paradoxical manner but that it constitutes, through its promotion of the fetishism of display and the techniques for selling, consumption in a paradoxical way too and that the two are intertwined in ways that cannot be separated or treated differently. While issues of gender must be at the center of this analysis (class too, though there is less paradox in that respect as this is preeminently a space for the middle-class consumer during the period in question), they are issues that involve modern subjectivity and vision in a broader and more general manner as well.

THE SPACE OF THE DEPARTMENT STORE

The history of the department store as a space for selling things is now well known (for overviews, see Ferry 1960; Porter Benson 1988; Leach 1993; Lancaster 1995). In addition to general studies, there have also been a large number of works on the histories of particular stores such as the Bon Marché in Paris—often seen to be the original purpose-built department store (see Miller 1981).[4] Department stores developed from the 1860s onward and dominated the retail scene in Europe and North America for about a century thereafter until being superseded in influence by the shopping mall from the 1970s onward (see Shields 1989).

The department store played a significant part in *The Arcades Project* for Benjamin too, for it was their emergence in the Haussmannized Paris of the 1860s that brought about the decline of the once-fashionable arcades with their luxury shops and strolling pedestrians (flâneur) and with it the first example of how capitalism creates ruins out of commercial activity as ever-more profitable ventures are sought in a process of eternal recurrence that he sees at the heart of consumer culture. In effect, for Benjamin, in the shift from the arcade to the department store, one phantasmagoria replaced another in a seemingly endless succession of forms of selling commodities all expressed under the sign of progress. In practice, the department stores did not literally emerge as a direct successor to the arcades in quite as straightforward a way as he imagined, though one cannot deny that the latter went into decline as a form, albeit gradually, after the introduction of this new, grander, and more profitable space for selling.

Some department stores were purpose-built ventures by capitalist entrepreneurs seeking to harness the effects of change brought about by industrial mass production and the expansion of the consumer market beyond that of luxuries for the well-off. The Bon Marché in Paris is the typical example here. Other stores, especially in Britain and the United States, emerged more piecemeal out of pre-established indoor bazaars and markets that had many stalls run by different proprietors, and others developed from existing successful shops, notably dry good stores and drapers or, in the case of Harrods in London, from a grocery store (see Lancaster 1995). Indeed, the arcades continued to be built well into the late nineteenth century (see Geist 1985) and while many undoubtedly went into decline and became the seedy leftovers of a forgotten age in the manner that Benjamin suggests, others were able to survive by maintaining a niche at the top end of the market by providing wealthy clientele in upmarket parts of town with a place for luxury shopping, often selling high-status handmade goods. A few are still there today, thriving in the twenty-first century selling the same kinds of good that they had done originally, and others now survive in a different guise as part of the heritage regeneration of many city centers.[5]

Nonetheless, the department store was the new and fashionable place to shop in the second half of the nineteenth century rather than the arcade. These stores no longer simply brought together a range of different retailing outlets as in the case of a market, bazaar, or arcade but now housed, under one roof, a single retailing outlet with many different departments selling an unprecedented range of goods all in one place. They were organized spatially into ordered departments selling specific classes of goods and were aimed at a wide cross-section of the market but with an emphasis on marketing goods to the growing middle class. In many cases, world expositions like the Great Exhibition were the model for how they displayed their goods (see Richards 1991; Cummings and Lewandowska 2000).

As in the past, luxury still led the way in shaping market trends in what was put on sale though department stores were not just concerned with selling luxury items but more everyday useful items too (see Harrods 1972 [1895]).[6] In these early days department stores became the setters of fashion and taste. Yet something happened to the idea of luxury within these new spaces. The idea that one consumed luxury was central to the aura of the department store. This emphasis on luxury in influencing fashion had been the case at least since the early modern period when luxury goods shaped tastes in courtly circles, and then typically spread to others (see Sombart 1967; Simmel 1971c; Williams 1982). Through this the appeal of the commodity that had once been the preserve largely of the luxury goods market became more widespread and began to attract a bigger audience.

The growth of the middle class across Western countries and their demand for the trappings of civility that had previously been associated with the aristocratic elite had been fueling the development of a consumer society since at least the second half of the eighteenth century (see McKendrick et al. 1982; Campbell 1987; Benson, 1994). Indeed, most historians now accept that it was increased consumer demand rather than changes in agriculture or developments in machine technology per se that fueled the development of industrialism after about 1750.[7] This challenges the productivism that was at the heat of classical economic theory (Smith, Ricardo, Marx) but does not deny that changes in production are not also strongly implicated in the development of consumer markets.

Consumer demand alone, though, is not the full story here. It was only possible because of: increased availability of raw materials from various sources within expanding and exploited empires (and the use of slave labor); the introduction of steam power and machinofacture in factories that facilitated mass production to meet a high demand; the development of the railways as a cheap and quick means for transporting large volumes of standardized goods; and the expansion of middle-class markets that began in the previous century. These changes from after the 1860s that led to the emergence of the department store as the means for selling large volumes of commodities are associated with the fields of both production and consumption that come with an industrial society. All these factors combined led to the possibility for larger retail outlets to succeed because they could respond to both a bigger market and to the growing volume of goods. The new techniques of mass production did not just generate economies of scale. In order for manufacturers to succeed they required a fast turnover, ever expanding markets, and a proliferation of commodities in the marketplace to appeal to a large consuming public. Old traditional shops, arcades, and bazaars were more suited to craft and proto-industrial production than to factory production and mass consumption.

Clearly department stores could not sell luxury items in the same way that the arcades had done previously and meet these demands for high turnover. Luxury goods had always been the exclusive privilege of the wealthy elite. That was too small a market for capitalists able to make use of the opportunities of mass production and consumption. Certainly the demand for luxury was there from a growing middle class wanting to express their newly acquired wealth, status, and taste in material goods but that had to be served through mass-produced goods instead. Notwithstanding the selling of a few genuine luxury items as loss leaders, in order to meet these demands, as well as that of producers and their own need for profit, the department stores had to tie the idea or the aura of luxury to goods made in an industrial rather than craft production system.

While in practice, therefore, the true luxury market of non-mass-produced but craft-made items remained largely the preserve of the upper classes and was to be found elsewhere, department stores presented to their ever-expanding clientele the idea of luxury.[8] The key to the success of the department store was to sell the *idea* or aura of luxury to an expanding middle-class market. That was its phantasmagoria. In other words, they were engaged in the promotion of what Rosalind Williams has called "the democratisation of luxury" (1982, 96). To sell the idea that one was buying luxury required a selling space fit for that purpose and goods that could be associated with it. They did that through opulent, phantasmagoric displays, use of glass and mirrors and lighting, and by creating lavish "stage sets" for their departments in which goods were displayed. An exoticized Orientalism was a common theme for presenting the aura of luxury in this way (see Williams 1982).

Department stores were intended to be inviting places where people would come in and browse and be able to handle produce (something often not allowed in a traditional shop), and where new fashions and new tastes would be on display with fixed prices that were visible to all. Some allowed credit or payment by installment and promoted the idea of a service culture where customers would be treated by staff who acted more like servants (see Miller 1981). Most department stores also had restrooms; they offered refreshments and some had restaurants, aiding them in their appeal to a middle-class clientele. In all, the aim was to create an ambience of luxury, comfort, and ease and to amuse and cultivate the senses in such a way that people would want to buy things on a regular basis.

In particular, therefore, the ideals associated with aristocratic luxury consumption were translated into a bourgeois space for a bourgeois class. Indeed, class was often used in the spatial ordering of the stores themselves with the working class catered for in the (bargain) basement where the cheap goods were located and each floor above that catering to a greater degree of luxury and higher class position (see Leach 1993, 78).[9] The emphasis throughout was on abundance and opulence, luxury and fashion, daydream and indulgence.

The way in which this space of fantasy and luxury has been understood in most recent analysis has been through the theme of spectacle, or the idea of a "dream-world" produced by the visual display of an abundance of commodities for sale; what I have discussed here under the theme of phantasmagoria (see Williams 1982; Bowlby 1985; Richards 1991; Leach 1993). Rosalind Williams's analysis of French department stores is typical: "If the use of commodities to create a dream world was not a late nineteenth century innovation, what was new in that era was the great increase in the varieties of dreams appealed to by commerce" (1982, 109). Similarly, William Leach, in his analysis of the rise of the department store in the United States, places an emphasis on their role in democratizing desires and the idea of creating an aura of luxury particularly through the use of appealing window display (1993). The world fairs, like the Great Exhibition, while having an ambiguous relationship to the ideals of commerce, nevertheless introduced some of the key ideas behind the department store: they were given over to the display of an abundance of things, often ordered around a particular theme (see Richards 1991).[10] Department stores were well lit, making use of new technologies like gas (and later electric) lighting (see Schivelbusch 1988) and the development of plate glass in the display of artifacts both in window displays onto the street and within the stores themselves (see Leach 1993).

This, then, is how recent work, often following a loosely Marxian commodity fetish line of argument, has come to understand the department store.[11] For Richards, department stores were spaces of distraction (1991, 31); for Bowlby a spectacle of luxury consumption (1985); for Williams (1982), who draws as much on Elias's analysis of the civilizing process (1978) as she does on Marx,[12] as creating a spectacle of luxury that lured people into buying things, of creating wants rather than satisfying needs and presenting that through a hypnotic allure.

> As environments of mass consumption, department stores were, and still are, places where consumers are an audience to be entertained by commodities, where selling is mingled with amusement, where arousal of free-floating desires is as important as immediate purchase of particular items. Other examples of such environments are expositions, trade fairs, amusement parks, and (to cite more contemporary examples) shopping malls and large new airports or even subway stations. The *numbed hypnosis* induced by these places is a form of sociability as typical of modern mass consumption as the sociability of the salon was typical of pre-Revolutionary upper-class consumption. (Williams 1982, 67, emphasis added)

William Leach, too, though in a less obviously Marxian-influenced analysis, sees one of the main effects of the department store as taking the commodity as a thing out of the world of commerce and relocating it in a space of fantasy (1993, 66). It is quite clear that the idea of mass consumption in the department store as taking place in a phantasmagoric space is pervasive in how the department store has come to be understood over the past three decades.

I have not tried to deny the significance of this concept in the analysis of consumption in the previous chapters. Rather, I have tried to question the understanding of the subject related to this space that informs much of this analysis under this theme. Cruder versions of the fetishism thesis treat consumers as little more than cultural dopes who are unable to escape the fetishized vision presented in such spaces. In such analysis the department store, like the Universal Exhibition, becomes such a space in which they are captured and their subjectivity manipulated. I have argued that we should not accept such a view at face value because of its productivist understandings of the subject that are not appropriate for understanding how the subject of consumption is constituted within capitalist societies. I would add that here, in the context of the department store, if we want to challenge this kind of approach, we need to return to thinking more closely about how the experience of the subject is formed within such a (phantasmagoric) space.

There is one further, and perhaps crucial, issue that we need to address in doing this. This subject was not an unmarked gender-neutral subject but one that was predominantly gendered female by the department stores and in the associated advertising and marketing. As all studies of the department store tell us, their main customers were women and they were created as spaces that it was thought (often correctly) would appeal especially to women. The department store was a phantasmagoria of distracted consumption for women that played an important part in shaping their subjectivity in a bourgeois society. But we should not treat that subjectivity under the sign of a manipulated cultural dope or even the alienated producing subject. We should look instead at the much less certain and often ambiguous character that it took. In doing that we might start to see that the space of the department store was also more ambiguous and paradoxical than much of the recent literature has suggested.[13]

THE DEPARTMENT STORE AND THE FLÂNEUSE

While Benjamin's analysis of fetishism and experience can still be useful because, unlike the analysis offered by, say, Lukacs or Adorno, it is more ambiguous and nuanced in its approach to subjectivity, one of its major failings is undoubtedly that of its gender-blind character. Benjamin's analysis of the figure of the consumer, if not of particular consumers, is of a male subject and is understood though the figure of the flâneur (the urban stroller) who he locates in the Paris of the mid-nineteenth century. Benjamin's emphasis on this figure comes, in particular, from his reading of Baudelaire (1964, 1970), and he locates that figure at the center of his analysis of the arcades and therefore of consumer capitalism (see Buck-Morss 1989; Tester 1994).

For Baudelaire, the flâneur is a bohemian artist who is immersed in the everyday life of the changing city of the 1860s (1964). Detached, disillusioned, yet interested in the changing world around him, Baudelaire attributes to him a heroic quality of being able to create a degree of distance from the everyday into which he is submerged. He is a special kind of character who is able to live in a conscious and self-reflective way with a new mode of experience: modernité (see Frisby 1985, 1994) or what has become known as *Erlebnis*. This is important for Benjamin, who is preoccupied with the changing character of experience in the nineteenth-century city. The flâneur, for him, becomes the archetypal urban resident, a casually strolling observer of urban life who is able to treat what he sees with a degree of interested detachment.[14] He famously describes the flâneur as a kind of collector who goes "botanising on the asphalt" (1973c, 36). The arcades are his abode, a space of the interior, albeit a part of the public life of the city at the same time. The flâneur, for Benjamin, is also a detective of modern life as he was for Baudelaire too. He is conceived as someone to whom the city discloses its secrets after careful investigation. But the flâneur is no mere voyeur; in both Baudelaire and Benjamin, the flâneur is imagined as a *producing* subject rather than a consuming subject per se. He produces the scene through his dissecting vision, his (bohemian) conversation and writing, or through his (Impressionist) art.

The influence for both Benjamin and Baudelaire in focusing on the anonymous stroller in the city as their figure for the modern subject is Edgar Allen Poe. For Benjamin, and for Baudelaire likewise, Poe best captures the spirit and the interest of the flâneur in his short piece *The Man of the Crowd* (1938). In Poe's story, the anonymous narrator, a convalescent sitting in a London coffeehouse observing recognizable city types—clerks, gentlemen, pickpockets, prostitutes, and so on—move about in the street in front of his gaze, lights upon a man who does not fit any obvious classification. Intrigued, he decides to follow him through the evening and night as he traverses the gaslit city, merging in and out of the crowd and the shadows as he goes about his uncertain business. Unable to ascertain the purpose or the identity of the man he is following, he continues to follow him into the next day but eventually gives up, realizing in the process that the man is in fact a new type of subject, not just an urban stranger who "comes today and stays tomorrow" (see Simmel 1971a, 143), not a man in the crowd, but a man *of* the crowd, a figure of the anonymous city itself who "does not permit himself to be read" (Poe 1938, 475). This world of bewilderment, the world of London for Poe, and Paris for Baudelaire, the world of the flâneur is more generally the world of the commodity. As Benjamin puts it:

> The flâneur is someone abandoned in the crowd. In this he shares the situation of the commodity. He is not aware of this special situation, but this does not diminish its effects on him and it permeates him blissfully like a narcotic that can compensate him for many humiliations. The intoxication to which the flâneur surrenders is the intoxication of the commodity around which surges the stream of customers. If the soul of the commodity which Marx occasionally mentions in jest existed, it would be the most empathic ever encountered in the realm of souls, for it would have to see in everyone the buyer in whose hands and houses it wants to nestle. Empathy is the nature of the intoxication to which the flâneur abandons himself in the crowd. (1973c, 55)

We know that Benjamin's starting point is the Marxist theory of commodity fetishism. He generally accepts Marx's reading of commodity fetishism and its model of the subject. Yet unlike other writers in the Western Marxist tradition, his work also opens up a space for another view of the subject. How the bourgeoisie came to be allured by the promise of the commodity, the collective dream that makes capitalism appear to be a society of promise, prosperity, and abundance rather than one founded on immiseration and insecurity—potentially even for the prosperous—is one that he hopes to reveal by studying the material cultural forms left behind by capitalist forms of progress. In the flâneur, we find a figure that is not at home in the world, *unheimlich* (unhomely); his world is uncanny (Freud 1958; Castle 1995). Like Freud, like the man of the crowd, the flâneur feels compelled again and again to return to a scene to re-view it and to comprehend himself in the *productive act* of making sense of what he sees. In such a case, a sense of bewilderment and of an uncertain and mobile view onto that world prevails. All he can do is abandon himself to his bewilderment. And yet this is ultimately something he cannot do because he comes into being as a subject who tries to produce sense out of the uncertainties of *Erlebnis*. In this he is a tragic character, one doomed to fail in his purpose. The question, then, is how are we to relate all this with the act of shopping?

By the 1860s, when the department stores were beginning to find their place within the metropolitan scene, the flâneur was already an outmoded figure. Baudelaire's focus on this figure as a hero of modern life took as his model the young bourgeois man with bohemian tendencies from the 1830s rather than his own time and relocated him in the 1860s as the prototypical Impressionist artist who sought to capture the changing character of modernité that characterized the modern Haussmannized city. Baudelaire reinvented an already established, yet by then outmoded, figure from popular commentary and literature and gave him a new twist (see Parkhurst Ferguson 1994; Gluck 2003).

As a historical figure, the flâneur was born in the arcades of the Palais Royal in the revolutionary ferment of the 1780s, came to prominence in France around 1830, and was acclaimed as a figure of fascination in the popular literature of the day and died with the barricades of 1848. He was a figure from popular French novels and stories of the 1830s, a young, dissolute figure not quite at home in the world of the bourgeoisie—an early casualty of anomie we might say—from which he came, and, like the arcades, already outmoded and passé by the 1860s when Baudelaire sought to give him a second birth. While the figure of the flâneur might work well with thinking about the arcades of the 1830s, he does not sit easily with the department store of the 1860s and especially not with the world of consumption after about 1890 when those stores had become fully established across the Western world and beyond. This is not a space for his heroic, yet troubled, male gaze. Rather, it is his female counterpart and successor who made her home in that space.

Feminist writers have long been suspicious of the flâneur, indeed, in some cases, openly hostile to all that he stands for in the Baudelaire/Benjamin tradition. In two important essays written in the 1980s, he came in for critical scrutiny for the first time and was rightly shown to be wanting as a typical representative figure for the modern subject (see Wolff 1990[15]; Pollock 1988). Both Janet Wolff and Griselda Pollock focus on women's exclusion from these studies of modernity—in Wolff's case focusing on sociological writings about the city, and, for Pollock, in the understanding of modernity through the male canon of modern art established in the nineteenth century.

Wolff adopts a "separate spheres" argument that was common among feminist theorists and historians during the 1970s and 1980s. She sees women confined to the private sphere of the home and men occupying the public sphere of the city. It is this masculine public realm, she argues, that has been treated as the sphere for defining the character of modernity in general—by Baudelaire, Simmel, and Benjamin in particular—and by subsequent writers who have taken their lead from them. She sees the flâneur as the male figure who occupies, in this analysis, a position of mastery within this sphere, and whose vision comes to define the city and modern experience associated with it.

> The flâneur is the modern hero; his experience…is that of a freedom to move about in the city, observing and being observed, but never interacting with others…. These heroes of modernity thus share the possibility and the prospect of lone travel, of voluntary uprooting, of anonymous arrival at a new place. They are, of course, all men. (Wolff 1990, 39)

For Wolff, women occupy a decidedly marginal position within the public sphere in this literature—as prostitutes, victims, widows, lesbians, and old women (these are all Baudelaire's female passanté figures of the city). They are gazed upon by the male flâneur, whose gaze, in turn, produces and masters this space that does not belong to them. Where women do appear in the public realm it is as consumed subjects of this gaze, their experience counting for little or nothing in the analysis of modernity. Interestingly, Wolff does single out the department store as a female space in the city but she does not see it as countering or challenging this dominant gaze in any significant way.

> The establishment of the department store in the 1850s and 1860s provided an important new arena for the legitimate public appearance of middle-class women. However, although consumerism is a central aspect of modernity, and moreover mediated the public/private division, the peculiar characteristic of "the modern" which I have been considering—the fleeting, anonymous encounter and the purposeless strolling—does not apply to shopping, or to women's activities either as public signs of their husband's wealth or as consumers. (1990, 46)

Wolff does not go on to say why not; rather, she argues that there cannot be a female equivalent to the flâneur—the flâneuse—because such a position is "rendered impossible by the sexual divisions of the nineteenth century city" (1990, 47). She does not elaborate this point either. Rather, what is needed, she argues instead, is that we take account of women's lives in the place where they were most confined—the private sphere—in our understanding of modernity. While this last point is important, Wolff draws too rigid a line between these different spheres in her analysis. Not only does she see the flâneur as the master of the experience of public space (something that is debatable because of his uncertain social and historical position), she does not allow that we might think about social space in less definite and less regionally defined terms. Another criticism that might be made of her argument is that she reproduces in her critique a production view of the (male) subject that is at the center of the patriarchal analysis she is challenging. Women simply do not fit this model so they cannot assume a counter-hegemonic role within it. While we might agree with this general position, what Wolff does not do is consider the alternative—that women's position in society was the basis for a consumption view of the subject that is quite different to her male counterpart and that she might, therefore, in the guise of the flâneuse, be an alternative model for thinking about the subject in modernity. Wolff is simply too quick to dismiss the significance of consumption and the consuming subject in her approach to reevaluating modernity.

Similar arguments are put forward in Griselda Pollock's analysis of these issues, and similar criticisms can be applied to it. Pollock's interest is with understandings of modernity expressed through the reception of impressionist art—notably in Clark's influential work *The Painting of Modern Life* (1984) that I discussed briefly in Chapter 2. This, she acknowledges, brings an important class perspective to the understanding of the experience of the modern city—expressed by Impressionism—but, Pollock argues, ignores the whole issue of gender. For Pollock, modernism in the nineteenth and twentieth centuries is engaging in the normalizing of not only a modern but also a distinctly masculinist way of seeing that is concerned with mastery in ways that ignores or marginalizes women and subjects them to that gaze at the same time. The flâneur figure, for Pollock, typifies this gaze, in which the woman becomes the passerby or passanté who is gazed upon. Her aim in this critique is twofold. First, she aims to make women artists visible and to recognize their understanding of modern life (she discusses, in particular, the art of the private sphere of modernity by Mary Cassatt and Berthe Morisot), and second, she seeks to deconstruct the masculinist discourse about modern art (1988, 56ff).

> The spaces of femininity operated not only at the level of what is represented, the drawing room, the sewing room. The spaces of femininity are those from which femininity is lived as a positionality in discourse and social practice. They are the products of a lived sense of social locatedness, mobility and visibility, in the social relations of seeing and being seen. (1988, 66)

She also points out the differential access that men and women had to social space and how women's vision is largely confined to the private sphere. For Pollock, the male gaze of the flâneur is one of mastery over social space, a gaze that not only excludes women but challenges the validity of their more partial and complex perspective on the everyday. As with Wolff, there is a tendency to see women as overdetermined by a demarcation between public and private space in this conceptualization of the flâneur and to accept the production view of the subject on which this figure is founded in the Baudelaire/Benjamin tradition. This is clearly not Pollock's overall

intention, as a large part of her argument has to do with also attempting to deconstruct this public/private distinction. She suggests, though does not fully develop
the idea, that we consider some kind of third space argument. However, she does not
do this in terms of gender but only by introducing the complicating factor of class.

> These territories of the bourgeois city were however not only gendered on a
> male/female polarity. They became sites for the negotiation of gendered class
> identities and class gender positions. The spaces of modernity are where class
> and gender interface in critical ways, in that they are the spaces of sexual
> exchange. The significant spaces of modernity are neither simply those of
> masculinity, nor are they those of femininity which are as much the spaces
> of modernity for being the negative of the streets and bars. They are, as the
> canonical works indicate, the marginal or interstitial spaces where the fields
> of the masculine and the feminine intersect and structure sexuality within a
> classed order. (1988, 70)

Pollock does not use the department store as an example here but she could have.
Indeed, if she had considered women's consumerist vision of the public sphere rather
than of the private sphere then she might have come to a different analysis of the
character of social space and some of its gender implications that she clearly wants
to suggest in her argument. As with Wolff, she rejects the idea of a female equivalent
of the flâneur—the flâneuse—because such a figure would simply replicate a male
vision of mastering social space. It would only do so, I would argue, if it were modeled on a productivist way of seeing.

   Feminist social theorists and historians have challenged some of the key
assumptions in these early critiques of the flâneur over the past few years (see Wilson
1991; Walkowitz 1992; Ryan 1994; Nava 1997; Rappaport 2000; Parsons 2003).
This work has been part of a broader feminist move during the 1990s that has seen a
shift away from a concern with describing women as oppressed victims of patriarchal
society and emphasizing the need for making their once-hidden lives visible, to a
position that instead recognizes women's marginal status in society but treats that as
a position for recognizing resistance and transgressive social practice that can be associated with the making of classed and gendered identities (see also Vickery 1998).

   One of the first to develop this line of argument was Elizabeth Wilson (1991,
2001). While acknowledging that women are treated as marginal within the public
life of the city in the nineteenth century and thereby subject to restrictions and
regulations, they are not completely passive and accepting of this position. Wilson's
main concern is to affirm women's agency within a patriarchal society rather than to
see women as victims of that society with no opportunity for resistance. The way she
does this is to seek out, in the nineteenth-century context, examples of women who
act like flâneur (George Sand, George Eliot) as well as the public spaces that women
made their own such as the theater, department store, and hotel (1991, 52ff.). She

looks at how such spaces provided women with the potential for a sense of pleasure, eroticism, and danger that they found affirming and exciting even if it went against established social conventions. Social space, for Wilson, is not something that is already regulated and mapped out in advance but something that is negotiated and contested through social practice. She also rejects the earlier feminist understanding of the flâneur as a figure who masters social space through his gaze. Instead, she argues that his gaze—while certainly male—is in practice much less certain than either Pollock or Wolff suggest. The flâneur was himself a marginal figure, a bohemian among the bourgeoisie, who was insecure economically as well as in his sexual identity. As she says, "he is a figure to be deconstructed, a shifting projection of the angst of modernity rather than a solid embodiment of male bourgeois power.... The flâneur therefore represents not the triumph of masculine power but its attenuation" (2001, 87). She goes on to argue, in contrast to both Wolff and Pollock, that it is he rather than his female counterpart—the flâneuse—who is the real marginal figure. She participates in the public life of the city through its dominant code, consumption, whereas he has a much more marginal and precarious position as observer rather than consumer.

Significantly, this begins to move us in the direction of placing consumption rather than production at the center of modern experience and subject formation. We can now see that the male flâneur's precarious position arose because of the ambiguous situation he held toward production. In large part, his subjectivity was constituted as a *failed producer*, an idler, who could not quite turn his hand to consumption either. Rather than serving as an archetype for the modern male subject, he simply shows up its limitations. He is the deconstructor of that gaze and reveals some of the limitations of trying to think of consumption through a production view of the subject.

Most recent feminist historical research on the theme of the flâneuse has not been particularly kind to the position adopted early on by both Pollock and Wolff. It takes its lead more from Wilson's position and seeks to affirm women's position and significance within the gendered space of the capitalist city rather than see her as outside of that space, confined to the domestic sphere (see Walkowitz 1992; Nava 1997; Nead 2000; Rappaport 2000; Parsons 1999). Women become shoppers who challenge the gendering of space in a counter-hegemonic manner through their shopping practice (see Ryan 1994; Nava 1997; Parsons 1999; Rappaport 2000); they become philanthropists who explore the city in order to try and reform it (Walkowitz 1992); and they become writers who describe the city from a woman's perspective (Parsons 1999; Harvey 2003; Nesci 2001). The emphasis in all this work has been to highlight the ways in which women resist dominant discourses about their place in society, find pleasure in public activities such as socializing and shopping, and in general are not confined by their constitution as passanté, caught in the flâneur's mastering gaze, but actually look back in ways that are defiant of masculinist social conventions. *They do not produce through their gaze, they consume—not for any biologically essentialist reasons but because of their paradoxical subject positioning.*

In the context of the department store, women were the main customers and the stores knew that and catered to their interests and wants. As Rappaport points out, nineteenth-century shopping was more than just about buying. For her, it is a way in which women created their own pleasurable activity (2000, 5). In the new spaces of the department stores and the upmarket or "West End" districts of cities (such as London), they went to browse, to buy, to socialize with female friends in a highly fetishized space given over to the visual aura of the commodity as an object of desire. Acquisition was a part of this set of practices but it was not carried out in a wholly functional or utilitarian manner. Just as it isn't today. Rather, acquisition of commodities took place in spaces that were constitutive—of a particular female way of looking—the distracted, desiring, and consuming gaze of the flâneuse. That this was a fetishized gaze of a modern kind of urban experience is without doubt true. She was interested by the figural qualities of the commodities on sale (see Campbell 1987). The flâneur could never be at home in such a place as the department store but it helped to create the flâneuse, and that subject position is an archetype for the modern consumer.

Department stores changed the character of shopping and thereby the shopper. In shops found earlier in the eighteenth and early nineteenth centuries, one engaged in an interaction with a store worker or owner who advised on what was available, was measured up for clothes, looked at pattern books, saw sample objects, and placed an order, usually on credit. The item would then be delivered and accounts subsequently settled (see Adburgham 1964). There were showrooms in the eighteenth century that allowed a certain amount of browsing and looking at things on sale but it was really only top-end luxury goods that were displayed in such a manner (porcelain, silver, paintings, and so on)—the enterprising and forward-thinking Josiah Wedgwood, for example, opened such a showroom in London during the 1780s to sell his ceramics (see Kowaleski-Wallace 1997). Even then, these were just as commonly sold from pattern books or at auction as they were from showrooms where one could see the goods and place an order (see Young 1999). Before the arrival of the department store, the idea that one would simply visit a shop, see what one liked, and then buy it would have only been associated with goods sold at markets (basic provisions or everyday essentials). Such places were not associated with shopping as a pleasurable social activity, but as a necessity to be done by the poor and one's servants.

The department store did not change everything overnight. People had to learn how to consume in this new way. While items were put on open display and not kept behind counters, department stores still employed many counter staff and floor-walkers who were there to help and advise customers in potential purchases. At home, women's magazines were full of articles and adverts concerning shopping and the products one could buy (see Gruber Garvey 1996). These helped to familiarize women readers in the techniques of consuming; they contained, as Garvey has pointed out, the same kind of ordered miscellany of things as the stores themselves (1996). As in the catalogues for the Great Exhibition, these magazines and advertisements as well as visits to the stores themselves, encouraged a browsing mode of activity in a world of cluttered abundance and a (bewildered) distracted, glancing, and desiring way of seeing, rather than a contemplative, gazing, and producing mode of looking at that world. This distracted way of seeing was facilitated by this new mode of shopping and created the subject position of the flâneuse as a desiring subject who realized herself through consumption and saw the modern world in those terms. The space that she occupied is an important matter for us to consider in this regard.

DESIRE AND EXPERIENCE IN PARADOXICAL SPACE

I have argued in the previous chapters that the bewildering space of phantasmagoric vision was shifting and uncertain, and it was around that that the subject of consumption was constituted and the means through which fetishism operated, challenging more definite understandings of both subjectivity and spatiality found in established theories of commodity fetishism. Through the department store we can see parallels between women's subject positioning within the city and the consumer's subject positioning within capitalism more generally. The figure of the flâneuse is the link between the two.

Feminist geographers, notably Gillian Rose, have done much to highlight women's paradoxical positioning in and view on social space (1993). Challenging male geographers' approaches to space and gender—which either ignore women's perspective in general or reproduce the dominant ideology of a dualistic separation: male/female, superior/inferior (i.e., public/private)—she seeks to show that women are positioned in multiple ways within social space and that such space is experienced in a paradoxical manner that imposes constraints while at the same time affording opportunities for women.

> These [feminist] notions of space, location, place, position, mapping and land-scape imply radically heterogeneous geometries. They are lived, experienced and felt. And they also articulate specific arguments about power and iden-tity. Their complex and contradictory spatialities are a "precarious conceptual geometry of the non-Euclidean type" which speaks of power, resistance and the acknowledgment of difference. So I argue that this paradoxical sense of space can challenge the exclusions of masculinist geography. (1993, 140–41)

Women are objects within male space, they are subject to and defined by a male gaze (i.e., the Baudelairean passante). Their subjectivity and their experience is con-stituted within such constraining and controlling strategies—or as Rose puts it, women are Other in the terrain of the Same (1993, 149). What is important about

Rose's argument is not her recognition of these dimensions of patriarchal power but her *both/and* rather than *either/or* treatment of these issues alongside those of challenge and resistance, what she calls, quoting Braidotti, the "positivity of Otherness" (1993, 150; see also Braidotti 1991) in which women can be seen to be in two places at once (the places of Same and Other), dispersed, fragmented, complex, uncertain, undecidable, and challenging in their paradoxical position. In such ways, she believes, women make power visible through their social practices.

There are a variety of ways in which the figure of the flâneuse is positioned within the department store in such a paradoxical manner.

Flâneur/passanté

The flâneuse is both the stroller who looks (at commodities and their surroundings) but also the one who is looked upon as a woman out of place—as challenging and out of place within the male-defined public space of the city. She has little social power in this context but is at the same time center stage within the increasingly important world of mass consumption. Her subjectivity is defined as someone who is observed by the male gaze and yet through engaging in the practices of consumption she looks back at that disembodied gaze, albeit through gendered social conventions. As Friedberg puts it:

> The flâneuse appeared in the public spaces—department stores—made possible by the new configurations of consumer culture. The flâneuse was empowered in a paradoxical sense: new freedoms of lifestyle and "choice" were available, but, as feminist theorists have amply illustrated, women were addressed as consumers in ways that played on deeply rooted cultural constructions of gender. (1993, 36)

That look back, a kind of gaze, is not a defining, ordering, producing, and mastering gaze; rather, it is, as Friedberg suggests, a gaze of choice (1993, 34). That gaze is a distracted and consuming one, bewildered in the sense that it does not fix on any one thing and seek to master it and yet is also desiring, subject to the phantasmagoric allure of the figural qualities of luxury, exoticism, abundance, and diversity offered by the department store. Those stores did not tell her what to buy, though advice was on offer at the stores as well as in the consumer magazines that she read; they positioned her with the opportunity to choose and in so doing to express her desires and tastes. In establishing this, they encouraged a distracted, glancing, roving way of seeing that wanted to take everything in without mastering it, a way of seeing that was fascinated by details, in order that multiple purchases might be made on impulse or through browsing (on detail and the female gaze in art, see Schor 1987). Such looking facilitated daydreaming and fantasy as an expression of desire. It promoted the idea of the constitution of self through the construction of imaginary worlds of the commodity (on daydream and consumption, see Campbell 1987).

Public/Private

The department store was both a public place and a private space. It was a place associated with the public life of the city—the street—but was also an interior to the street, plaza, or square. The window displays in department stores were designed to entice the customer in from the street. Shoppers were allowed to browse in a space that presented an interior world of luxury and fantasy—a space of indulgence, opulence, and excess. One went there to engage in the public act of shopping but also to indulge in private fantasies that suggested one might express one's taste, social standing, or family position in the eyes of others through one's consuming activities. The woman who went to shop there had to make her way across town, sometimes with a friend or servant, often unaccompanied in her carriage or by omnibus or metropolitan railway. She was on public display and yet the popularity of such places and their marketing as safe for the unchaperoned women all conveyed a sense that she was also engaging with the ideals of the private sphere in a public place. Typically she would be buying for herself as well as for her children and her household—all important elements in the ideology of domesticity that then prevailed in a powerful way. In shopping in department stores, she both challenged the rigid demarcation and ideological construction of the public and the private while at the same time reproducing elements of that division through her social practice.

Included/Excluded

I have argued that department stores saw their main customers as women and provided for their wishes (Bowlby 1985; Rappaport 2000). They came to be seen as women's spaces within the public sphere—safe, dependable, and, by and large, respectable. Women's inclusion, therefore, was positively invited by proprietors, and they developed a service culture among their staff in order to try and maintain this position (Miller 1981). Women were encouraged to shop in department stores, spend money, browse, come and see the latest fashions for themselves and their households. The department stores played an important role in the shaping of women's subjectivity as active consumers, notably among the middle class. They conveyed a woman's freedom and her autonomy to make a space for herself and through her female social interactions. Department stores became spaces that shaped and were shaped by women's consumer desires.

At the same time department stores reproduced a woman's exclusion within Victorian society. If she bought on credit, it was her husband's creditworthiness that mattered. Similarly, if she bought using cash, unless she was very wealthy and had her own money, it was her husband's or father's cash that provided her with spending power (Rappaport 1996, 2000). Women, especially married women, occupied a position outside of the marketplace. They were consumers but only with the illusion of spending power. To be a consumer is to be able to freely act within the realm of economic exchange. But most women could not do this. While some exploited this to their own advantage (refusing to pay their credit bills, for instance), for all women, department stores reinforced women's position as surrogate consumers, buying either on behalf of their families/households or for themselves but with the tacit (financial) agreement of their husbands or fathers. To have an allowance, after all, connotes "to be granted permission" by patriarchal authority as much as it means having money in your purse. While creating the phantasmagoria of inclusion, which we can only imagine was experienced as a genuine freedom for many middle-class Victorian women, department stores also reinforced existing gender positions and assumptions at the same time.

Gratification/Utility

Victorian consumerism did not exist in a "throw-away" consumer society as has been suggested now characterizes our time. This was a society in which women still made things such as clothing, where old and worn-out artifacts were mended, darned, or repaired rather than thrown out, and where thrift and utility were important social values (Strasser 1999). Every household would typically have a sewing machine, for example, and sewing, embroidery, and darning were seen as important social skills for a middle-class woman to have. It was just as likely, therefore, that the woman on a shopping trip to a department store would be going to buy fabrics and perhaps patterns in order that she might be able to make her own clothes as she would be going to buy something off the rack. In other words, while department stores were constituted as dream houses of desire and wish fulfillment, filled with the aura of luxury, they also catered to more down-to-earth utilitarian values such as hard work, thrift, and what we would call today "do-it-yourself" or bricolage (Strasser 1999).

Department stores, therefore, can also be seen as paradoxical in relation to the distinction between need and desire. In effect, they did much to blur the boundaries between these two social categories in a time of changing discourses. They were filled with an abundance of desirable artifacts, they encouraged, through their window displays and in-store displays, such practices as impulse buying or buying more things than were actually needed (and consequently shoplifting was born) (Abelson 1989). Yet at the same time they encouraged the idea that what they had on offer was what was needed by a woman if she wanted to remain fashionable, keep a good up-to-date home, maintain her social standing, please her husband, and so on. The flâneuse was constituted paradoxically as a desiring subject who was encouraged to act on an impulse or a whim but who at the same time often had to justify her desires (and purchases) in terms of utility or need, either for herself or her household.

There are other ways in which we might elaborate on these paradoxes that center on the figure of the flâneuse: she was active/passive, she was consumer/consumed, for instance. Department stores were seen by some as spaces of necessity/

vice, they promoted proximity/distance to the goods on display, goods that were available/unavailable to some, perhaps because of cost, and that encouraged immediate purchase/deferred gratification. She viewed the world of consumption while at the same time she was a central part of it, unable to detach herself from it through the kind of mastering ironic distance associated with the flâneur. As such, it is she and not the flâneur who is the real model for the modern consumer subject. It is this positioning within such a paradoxical space that most characterizes her experience of consumption in spaces like the department store.

One of the things that we can draw from this is that the experience of social spaces and practices, such as consumption as paradoxical and uncertain in these ways, typifies the nature of modern experience as *Erlebnis*. It is not just that modern experience is fragmented, changing, and ephemeral. as the Baudelaire/Benjamin tradition would have it, it is also paradoxical, undecidable, and felt most acutely by women in their subject position as desiring consumers in and of a social space that places their position there in question. Modern subjectivity is characterized by being put into question in all manner of ways—and consumption is one of the most important of them. Experience as *Erfahrung* can be associated with the eighteenth-century model of the possessive individual and with a productivist discourse of need. Experience as *Erlebnis*, in contrast, is associated with the desiring rather than the producing individual and with the discourse of wants and tastes.

There is a further dimension to this story that we need to address. What is important to all these different forms of paradox is the central place given to the object—the commodified artifact—that was available to be viewed, desired, and purchased by the consumer. The phantasmagoria of the department store can be summarized as being all about an encouragement of the idea of *taking possession* of the artifact through desire rather than need (Nunokawa 1994, 20). It is in such a context that we must look at the relationship among fetishism, subjectivity, and experience that surrounds the figure of the flâneuse.

THE CONSUMPTION VIEW OF THE SUBJECT

We can argue that this subject position developed as part of a broader shift in discourse and social practices that was ongoing then that challenged the old productivist question of need with a new consumerist question of desire. Without doubt this caused much anxiety at the time (Williams 1982) and did much to position women in a paradoxical and uncertain way. The main issue, therefore, is to think about how subjectivity came to be constituted within these new practices and spaces. We need to acknowledge, I suggest, the emergence of what might be called a *consumption view of the subject* in the later years of the nineteenth century.

I adapt this term from Munro's discussion of what he calls a "consumption view of the self" (1996). Through a critical analysis of recent anthropological work on consumption (such as Douglas and Isherwood 1986), Munro suggests that what this work challenges is a production view of the self that still prevails in most economic thought on consumption. This production view, Munro suggests, begins from an essentialized notion of the self in the rational person who then "builds" himself, through extension-as-prosthesis, into the material world through productive activity (1996, 249ff.). Marx's idea of Man as Homo Faber discussed in Chapter 3 would be the typical example of a production view of the self. A consumption view, in contrast, is one that does not acknowledge an essentialized self in the rational person but starts from seeing the self as something that is constituted through the act of extension into the world of goods (through consuming the material world). In a sense the producing self does work in changing the world through actions (including vision), whereas the consuming self comes into being through that world. If the former is concerned with actualization, especially through need (pace Marx's emphasis on species being), then the latter is actualized, instead, through desire.

A similar argument is made in an important yet rather overlooked work by Lawrence Birken, where he also suggests that consumption should be seen, not just as an act, but as a way of seeing (1988). For Birken, this emphasis on consumption and desire first comes to prominence in scientific discourse in the mid-nineteenth century, notably after the publication of Darwin's *Origin of the Species* in 1859, which places desire at the center of the theory of biological development (Birken 1988, 7) and begins to redefine modern society, not without contest, thereafter.

> [T]he emergence of Darwinism and its conception of what was nothing less than a genderless state of nature inhabited by transsexual organisms marked the beginning of the erosion of the sex-caste and thus the appearance of a concept of universal citizenship based on desire. (1988, 10)

Thereafter desire (which is strongly associated with consumption), rather than the eighteenth-century idea of property (which is associated with production), comes to the fore in other scientific discourses associated with subjectivity too; in particular, in sexology, where it is associated with the idea that people are polymorphously perverse and place desire at the center of their ideas about self-realization through sex.

> Against this background, the work begun by Darwin and elaborated by Krafft-Ebing, Havelock Ellis, and Freud more or less centred on the formulation of a natural law of sex. If classical political economy argued that the self-determination of the possessive individual was compatible with a self-renewing (masculine) productive order, the sexual sciences that emerged after Darwin implied that the self-determination of the genderless consuming individual was compatible with a self-renewing reproductive order that embraces both sexes. (1988, 13)

We can agree that it does but that it was often expressed in practice through the marginal figure of the female consumer rather than through a genderless figure, even if the implications went wider to modernity as a whole.

Likewise, for Birken, a similar discursive move is made in neoclassical economics, where centrality was given to the issue of desire through the argument that it is desire rather than labor that is the creator of exchange value (i.e., that value is established in the marketplace through people desiring to possess things rather than in the factory where they are made). Commodities become desired objects rather than just abstract material goods, as Marx so often seems to see them in his productivist terms (Birken 1988, 28ff.; see also Baudrillard 1975).

The practices of desiring things associated with this discourse of self-realization through desire do not just happen through consumption in general, as both Munro and Birken suggest, but find their actualization, perhaps initially, in department store shopping. There, perhaps for the first time for the mass of people, need is increasingly replaced by taste as the legitimating reason for wanting something. In the panoramic surrounding of the department store, in that glittering world of luxury and abundance, the consumer's wants are constructed as endless and never capable of being fully satisfied. They simply multiply as desire multiplies. And yet the society in which these discourses developed and the consumerist social practices associated with them that began to emerge after 1860 did so at first in a paradoxical and uncertain manner. As Birken suggests, this was still largely a society that was defined through a dominant discourse of the productivist concern with hard work, utility, and thrift. It was those who were marginal or excluded from these positions that defined the public life of Victorian society—most notably women—who were the first to convey these new consumer values and orientations in their practice.

> It would seem that a genderless and gendered conception of human life dwell together in the same ideology. Women were simultaneously included and excluded from the realm of consumption and citizenship. (1988, 55)

In effect, the flâneuse was a blank figure, a trickster-like figure, whose paradoxical social position allowed her to become the vehicle for changing values to develop, and a new way of seeing and desiring to be expressed (on blanks, see Hetherington and Lee 2000).[16]

She would visit a store and browse, sometimes she would buy on impulse, sometimes buy many things. She would meet up with friends and take tea or perhaps have lunch. Shopping became an extremely popular social activity among middle-class women. It was their way of gaining access to the public life of the city. And it was not without its risks and uncertainties. Many upstanding women found that they could not control these desires and were tempted into the act of shoplifting. The aspirational character of browsing and desiring things that the stores promoted led some women into the temptation to steal (Abelson 1989). Others bought but did so on their husband's credit and then never got around to paying. Ironically, because of patriarchal laws in countries such as Britain that stated that a married woman had no property and everything she had belonged to her husband, stores could not take a woman to court and recover the money for goods acquired. There were numerous unsuccessful attempts to prosecute husbands for their wives' nonpayment for goods, but these usually failed as the husband could usually plead that he was not responsible for his wife's actions (Rappaport 1996, 2000). This was a major reason why department stores eventually stopped giving credit and demanded cash at the time of purchase.

At the time these "problems" were constructed not as changes within social attitudes but as failings in the female character and were often addressed through a medicalized discourse about women's nature and character (Abelson 1989). She was constituted as a figure of desire by the space of the department store. The law and the medical profession still largely thought of and judged people in productivist terms, but society was changing nonetheless.[17] The department store came to be seen not only as a space for purchasing mass-produced goods as if they were to be found in a world of luxury, but this space could become one of obsession and addiction. But capitalist society was changing and the desiring subject became a necessary precondition to any success in the development of a consumer culture. The more we consider the figure of the flâneuse, the more we see her novel paradoxical character and her importance within the world of a nascent form of mass consumption. That paradoxical position and the paradoxical space that it was associated with were inherently fetishistic and phantasmagoric. We can now consider what these terms might come to mean in relation to the practices of the consuming rather than the producing subject.

I have argued in the earlier chapters of this book, following William Pietz's historical analysis of the discourse of fetishism (1985, 1987, 1988), that the fetish as artifact exists and is made sense of in a space of cultural exchange or betweenness. In the Western Marxist tradition that space has been conceived (but often misunderstood) through the term phantasmagoria. Here, I have accepted the Benjaminian approach to that term but have added the suggestion that such a space be seen as inherently paradoxical—especially for the subject—as all spaces of the fetish are paradoxical.[18] The position that most typifies the subject in this case can be described through the figure of the flâneuse. She is foremost the figure for the female shopper in the department store during the nineteenth century and thereafter the figure for the modern consumer in general.

What makes the space of the fetish inherently paradoxical is its unstable position that derives from its multivalent character within forms of cultural and symbolic exchange. It is the space not of a binary *either/or* type of situation but of a *both/and* one. It is not just an uncertain space (where images of ghosts swirl about) but is an undecidable space that cannot be fully resolved in any particular manner. It is a space where tangible objects and the immateriality of the desiring imagination mingle and coalesce through the discourse of desire. The fetish-object facilitates the conditions of paradox, undecidability, and exchange that take place in this space.

CONCLUSION: THE SUBJECT AND CONSUMPTION

We can now begin to summarize the differences between the type of subject position expressed within established theories of commodity fetishism (what I call the production model) and those offered here (the consumption model). I draw on and adapt Birken's argument (1988) to develop this distinction:

Production View of the Subject
> Possessive individual
> Gendered as male
> Subject actualized through production/labor
> Coherent subject position grounded in class
> Experience as *Erfahrung*
> Character
> Contemplative gaze—the big picture
> Worker alienated through fetishism

Consumption View of the Subject
> Desiring individual
> Gendered as female
> Subject actualized through consumption/pleasure
> Dispersed/paradoxical subject position
> Experience as *Erlebnis*
> Personality[19]
> Distracted "gaze"—attention to detail
> Consumer Realized Through Fetishism

In the first case, where society is defined in terms of the relations of production, the subject produces values that are then alienated and represented to that subject as created elsewhere (in the market). In the second, where that society is defined by the market and the circulation of goods, it is the subject that produces values in the acts of desiring and acquiring things—not exchange values per se but symbolic values as a translation of exchange values, whose translations are articulated through fetish objects (see also Appadurai 1986; Simmel 1990). In the first case, fetishism creates an illusory world (social space) that obscures reality and presents that illusion as reality; in the second, the fetish facilitates access to a cultural reality that can only exist in the imaginary realm. But that realm is not an illusory one, it is one where all that is seemingly alienated in the first model can be accessed and made real for people—albeit only indirectly. Yet this is not the stuff of individual desires and self-expression that characterizes a postmodern argument about consumption; it is, rather, the stuff of significant social relations.

We should not deny that the department store was a space of the phantasmagoric and that it was constituted as a phantasmagoria for the female shopper in the nineteenth century. The real issue is how we understand these terms to operate. In offering a positive rather than a negative view of the fetish, I have tried to develop a model of fetishism here that develops out of assumptions about consumption rather than one that develops out of assumptions about production that are then applied to consumption as if the same conditions prevail. The model here is not one of *being possessed* by the ghosts of the phantasmagoria (pace Marx) but of *taking possession* of those immaterial ghosts through the acquired artifacts found on display. In this chapter the subject that engages in such acts of taking possession can best be captured through the figure of the flâneuse—the female shopper of the nineteenth century who can be seen as the model for all consuming subjects thereafter. But this is only part of the story—one bit of the process of consumption, if you will. In the next two chapters I aim to develop these arguments further by looking at different spaces: the home/interior and the museum.

Chapter Six
At Home in the World

Picture puzzles, as schemata of dreamwork, were long ago discovered by psychoanalysis. We, however, with a similar conviction, are less on the trail of the psyche than on the track of things. We seek the totemic tree of objects within the thicket of primal history. The very last—the topmost—face on the totem pole is that of kitsch.

Benjamin 1999a, 212 [I1, 3]

THE DOMESTIC INTERIOR

If the department store opened up a space for a woman in the nineteenth century, albeit in a paradoxical manner, then the space of the home was seemingly one associated, in contrast, with her confinement. At least that is the established argument that underpins the notion of an ideology of domesticity that is thought to be at the heart of Victorian society. Perhaps more than any other space, the domestic interior has come to be seen as signifying the core values of that culture but also some of its core contradictions. How those values interacted with the culture of the commodity, at first glance as far removed from the ideals of this private space as it is possible to be, is the central paradox of this space and one that I want to address in this chapter. I want to explore the fetishized relationship between the meanings that we might group together under the heading of *interiority* and the consumer culture that was both inside and outside of the spaces constituted around an imaginary set of principles that can go under that heading. I will look at these issues through the space of the domestic interior, in particular through the public/private space of the Victorian parlor, as that is the space most defined by this paradoxical position—at once the space most removed from the capitalist marketplace—a supposed moral haven of peace and stability and yet at the same time deeply imbricated in its enduring and transforming commodity logic.

Like the department stores and the arcades of the era, the interior was an important bourgeois phantasmagoria that Benjamin identified in his arcades study. He devotes a section to it in both the 1935 and 1939 exposé to *The Arcades Project* and addresses it in a number of the convolutes in what has become the main text (1999a [H, I, K]). In the first exposé, he notes how capitalism, for the first time in history, separates the spheres of work and dwelling (public/private) from each other. The bourgeoisie seek principally to understand this ideologically as a separation of the amoral social world of the market from that of the moral life of the individual and the family (1999b, 9). As a class, they were the main beneficiaries of capitalist society and yet the condition of permanent change and erosion of certainties by market forces lead to the ever-present risk of debt, financial ruin, and subsequent social disgrace for the bourgeoisie. The culture of the bourgeoisie can in large part, then, be read as an anxious reflection of this dual position of prosperity and insecurity (see also Sennett 1977; Stallybrass and White 1986; Nunokawa 1994). A particular consequence is that the idea of the interior, the private space removed from the public world of capitalism, becomes a space defined as one of retreat and refuge from the world that makes it. Interiority in this context might be seen as the cultural expression of how the bourgeoisie relate to the outside capitalist world from this private sphere, by constructing, Benjamin believes, a phantasmagoria of the interior as the whole world in which one dwells as its defining central point of subjectivity. In effect, the cultural preoccupation of Victorian society with panorama and totality, found in public exhibition spaces like the Great Exhibition or the department store, is translated into miniature form in the parlor of the house as a representation of a total worldview (see also Stewart 1993).

The home dweller in this space is, for Benjamin, represented in his or her purest form by the collector of things whose accumulation of artifacts aims to strip them of their commodity status and their usefulness and to assign to them some other kind of cultural value instead within a total world that makes up a collection.

> The interior is the asylum of art. The collector is the true resident of the interior. He makes his concern the transfiguration of things. To him falls the Sisyphean task of divesting things of their commodity character by *taking possession* of them. (1999b, 9, emphasis added)

I want to develop the argument that this idea of *taking possession* is the governing trope not just of collecting, but also of the idea of interiority that marks out the space of the Victorian home. To take possession of something is not merely to own it but to transfigure its value through the various acts of possession: display, ordering, and arrangement, or more specifically through acts of care such as dusting, polishing, and so on—in a word, one takes possession of something through the acts of bricolage.[1] This is something that we witness not only in those engaged in the deliberate act of collecting, the most explicit form of taking possession of a multitude of different things (and bringing them together into an ordered homology) while at the same time being possessed by them, but in the accumulation of things that is involved in homemaking more generally.

In the second exposé of 1939, Benjamin makes this relationship between the interior and the outside world more explicit. The public sphere of the capitalist city is a space in which experience (*Erfahrung*) is most obviously lacking, and the bourgeois seeks to compensate for that lack by turning the space of the interior into a (phantasmagoric) space of total experience instead.

> The interior is not just the universe of the private individual: it is also his étui. Ever since the time of Louis Philippe, the bourgeois has shown a tendency to compensate for the absence of any trace of private life in the big city. He tries to do this within the four walls of his apartment. It is as if he had made it a point of honor not to allow the traces of his everyday objects and accessories to get lost. Indefatigably, he takes the impression of a host of objects; for his slippers and his watches, his blankets and his umbrellas, he devises coverlets and cases. He has a marked preference for velour and plush, which preserve the imprint of all contact. (1999c, 20)

What goes into the making of the interior as a space enriched with a culturally relevant form of experience for the bourgeoisie, Benjamin believes, is that that culture is expressed through the desire to separate artifacts from their commodity function. This desire to take possession is expressed through the idea of the interior as a totality that constitutes bourgeois cultural vision. The drive to panoramic completeness, to overwhelming abundance, and to order and classification of the whole is one we have already seen in exhibitions and department stores and it is also found in the cluttered Victorian interior as well (see Maleuvre 1999). The bourgeois interior, for Benjamin, is constituted through "dream house" ideas of coziness, protection, and security from the uncertainties of the commodified outside, and this is done by creating a surrounding full of things that have significance beyond mere use or their exchange value. This distinguishes Benjamin's argument from that of the leading theorist of bourgeois culture prior to his work, Thorstein Veblen, for whom the display of wealth, or conspicuous consumption, appears to be the sole raison d'être of bourgeois culture (1987 [1899]) rather than just one of its cultural manifestations (see Lears 1989). In Benjamin's approach, the interior becomes like a shell, a space of plush and contrived luxury, overstuffed with things, artworks, and useless knick-knacks alike. In its response to the alienating and experience-fragmenting world of capitalism (1999c; see also Bachelard 1969), the interior world of sentiment and kitsch becomes the totality of culture for the bourgeoisie.

There is much to commend in Benjamin's critical analysis of the interior (an analysis that has been rather overlooked by many of the recent specialist historical works on the Victorian domestic interior).[2] In it, as in his discussion of fetishism and phantasmagoric projections in general, he offers a powerful critique of capitalist culture while at the same time acknowledging that it contains within it kairological moments within the sphere of consumption for such things as comfort, ease, and security—important dimensions of experience—that are worth redeeming and the creation of consuming subjects susceptible to both the false reality of commodity fetishism and the possibility of awakening from the false promises of capitalism. Yet, as with the department store, there is one important shortcoming that again repeats itself in his analysis: his gender-blind treatment of the space of the interior and the subject who comes to be defined by it as its principle character. That character, in this case, is the housewife, and she has an important place in the intersection between the world of the commodity and that of the home (on the cultural significance of the housewife, see also D. Miller 1995).

It is not just that Benjamin should be given a "ticking-off" for ignoring the significant position of women within the Victorian home but that the absence of a gender awareness in his analysis of the relationship between the market and the interior in his understanding of phantasmagoria misses a crucial dimension. Above all, I want to argue that the constitution of the housewife is the key figure of the sort of value transfiguration that he hints at taking place in this space through his notion of taking possession. It is she who is positioned as subject in this space in such a way as to be used to facilitate the transformation of the commodity status of artifacts within the home and to give them a different significance associated with the high ideals and displaced meanings of bourgeois culture that focus on the idea of interiority (see McCracken 1988). It is predominantly she who, in this process, is the home's chief bricoleur too. Yet we should not to overstate this as a position of a woman's power in the home or celebrate her creative agency without acknowledging the broader issues of power within the social composition of this space and the subject that it constitutes. Neither should we ignore the very definite patriarchal character of the space of the domestic interior. Just as the department store was a paradoxical space for women in this respect, so too is the interior. Rather, it is her underdetermined position in relation to the paradoxical combination of home/market that is the source of her possession-taking subjectivity.

Like the department store, the spaces of the bourgeois house, while all firmly existing within the defining terrain of patriarchal authority, were distinctly gendered—some spaces were constituted as male (e.g., library, dining room, study) and some female (e.g., parlors and drawing rooms, bedrooms, nursery, kitchen) (see Calder 1977; Logan 2001; Flanders 2004); all of this was done in a broader patriarchal constitution of social space itself divided into clearly defined regions, in this case, rooms. If, in the now extensive literature on Victorian society and Victorian consumer culture, the department store has come to be seen as a space of relative public freedom for women to develop their identities within a patriarchal society

(Williams 1982; Bowlby 1985; Wilson 1991; Rappaport 2000), the interior is still largely seen as a space of male dominance and female subjection within a defining patriarchal ideology of domesticity (Calder 1977; Davidoff and Hall 1987).

The now many studies of the Victorian interior, varied as they have been in their particular focus (for instance, Calder 1977; Davidoff and Hall 1987; Thompson 1988; Vickery 1998; Logan 2001), have all rightly placed gender issues at the center of their analysis, focusing on middle-class women's position within the home in particular. However, this has sometimes been done at the expense of looking at issues of consumption and to a lesser degree of class. We need to bring the analysis of gender together, therefore, with these questions about the (paradoxical) development of capitalist culture within the home that Benjamin identifies so well.

The emphasis made in early, second-wave feminist writings about the separation of spheres in Victorian society into (i) public/work/market/men and (ii) private/home/family/women, as work and home life became separated within capitalism, has been shown to be too limited and too involved in replicating, albeit in a critical way, the spatial assumptions of the patriarchal discourse of separate spheres that was constituted during the late eighteenth and nineteenth centuries (Vickery 1998). Not only was the home often a space of work, for women and especially for female and male working-class servants (Langland 1995; Donald 1999 [in Bryden and Floyd]), it was also a space as much defined by the marketplace and by the commodity culture of the "public sphere" as by the withdrawal from it (Saisselin 1985; Agnew 1989; Asendorf 1993; Loeb 1994; Nunokawa 1994; Benjamin 1999a; Vickery 1998). It is not just a matter of describing the interior world that Victorian women were expected to live in on its own terms but of analyzing how that female-constituted world intersected with that of a broader consumer culture of capitalist society. As with the department store, we should again think topologically about this social space rather than regionally, deploying the idea of paradoxical space to consider the constitution of the interior and its subjects (Rose 1993). The space of the parlor may have been imagined as a distinct region within the layout of the house and may have been constituted through the material culture of the house, from the walls and doors inward, but it was connected to other spaces and to an imaginary of space in ways defined other than by those walls and doors. Issues of gender are, therefore, central to this investigation of the bourgeois interior, but they are caught up in a less certain understanding of the constitution of social space than was perhaps once assumed. In this chapter I want to look at the Victorian interior through the uncertain figure of the housewife and the paradoxical space she occupies. I want to explore how this subject-as-housewife is figured within this space of possession and through her explore further the ways in which consumer subjectivity comes to be constituted through such a process.

THE FLÂNEUSE AT HOME

The general picture that has emerged of the analysis of the home interior and of women's position associated with it is a similar one to that associated with the department store: it was largely ignored by (male) academics more interested in the public world of work and politics rather than that of the private sphere for many years (see Oakley 1974; Calder 1977); became a subject of feminist historical analysis during the 1970s and 1980s where it came to be seen as the space that epitomized patriarchy in practice (Calder 1977; Schwartz Cowan 1983; Davidoff and Hall 1987; Sparke 1995); and has recently been treated as a space where the effects of patriarchal authority are qualified by recognizing women's creative agency and resistance from within (Hayden 1981; Gruber Garvey 1996; Vickery 1998; Logan 2001). However, where we saw in the previous chapter that now a number of feminist writers acknowledge the department store as a space where women's subjectivity was expressed in ways that challenged the dominant discourse, the domestic interior is still primarily seen as a space associated with the confinement of women within the ideological construction of femininity, domesticity, and the idea of a moral private sphere—with limited resistance occurring within that world but not really challenging it.

This ideology of domesticity (associated with ideologies of masculinity and femininity, family, beauty, etc.) is a set of discourses that emerged in the late eighteenth century that promoted the idea that women be seen as virtuous moral guardians of society's values. For this view to be maintained required the promotion of the idea that women's virtues came from their association with the private sphere of home and family. Such a view increasingly led to women being excluded from the public realm and being defined as subjects solely in relation to the private (except through the uncertain sphere of consumption as we saw in the previous chapters). This ideology emerges in the late eighteenth century out of a complex mix of discourses composed of Christian beliefs on the essential nature of sexual difference and female inferiority, liberal ideology associated with property rights that asserted the rights of bourgeois men but not their wives, a cultural acceptance of the virtues of hard work and thrift (Protestant work ethic), and a desire to separate the practices of paid work from the space of the home (for a detailed analysis, see Davidoff and Hall 1987). The development of the factory system, not an overnight process by any means, saw the gradual removal of much of the productive function of the household as a maker of goods of one kind or another and its development in other spaces given over exclusively to this function, such as workshops and factories. This allowed for the bourgeois home to be seen as a separate private space that was removed from the practices of work, if not the Protestant values associated with labor. That public world of work and of the market associated with it in the capitalist economy came to be seen as an uncertain and ever changing place where fortunes could be made and lost in equal measure. The home was an imaginary construction removed from all that, became associated with the idea of a haven of bourgeois security, and was symbolically structured and ordered thus as a total universe that made up for the lack of security in society as a whole (Calder 1977, 115; Logan 2001). The ideology of domesticity and this cultural idea of interiority and retreat from the market go hand in hand. The domestic interior became a space where cultural values associated with moral upbringing; stable, hierarchical, and settled gender divisions; recognized social status and rank and moral order and propriety were articulated through not only the texts and social practices associated with homemaking but also through the very architecture and material culture of the space as well.

Early in the nineteenth century, the home came to be imagined as a space of virtue and the moral improvement of character befitting a virtuous family.

> Between the Home set up in Eden and the Home before us in Eternity, stand the Homes of Earth in a long succession. It is therefore important that our Homes should be brought up to a standard in harmony with their origin and destiny. Here are "Empire's primal Springs;" here are the Church and State in embryo; here all improvements and reforms must rise. For national and social disasters, for moral and financial evils, the cure begins in the Household. (McNair Wright 1884, 3)

In addition to being seen as an ordered space with clearly defined and demarcated functions, the figure of the productively idle yet hardworking and dutiful wife was central to representing the values of this space. Her subjectivity was constituted in that space. Ideas of virtue, once associated with conduct in public life (Sennett 1977; Habermas 1989), had, by the mid-nineteenth century, come to be associated ever more with conduct within marriage, family life, and the private world of the home and less with public activity, except, perhaps, where philanthropic work was the expression of a person's private standing.

The role of the wife and mother within Victorian society was imagined through associations with the protection of the values of a morally upstanding family in a world of social change and opportunity. Associated with the private sphere, she was supposedly removed from change and uncertainty and became a figure of stability and security—in effect, a figure of Christian virtue and an imagined experience (*Erfahrung*)—a stable and grounded experience in a known totality. To achieve this position, her role had to be continually performed as one separated as much as possible from the potentially contaminating associations with public life, paid work, and the market. The middle-class wife was not expected to engage in paid work outside of the home but to become responsible for the daily running of the household, its servants, and its economy (both moral and financial economy). It was generally the husband who provided the money for the setting up of a household and its annual income, either through his own paid work, inherited wealth, successful investments, or because he had become the owner of any assets his wife might have brought with her as part of the marriage settlement. He might have had overall control of the household finances but she was expected to manage the books and to be the moral guardian of the family's financial position though her homemaking conduct.

In addition to her various tasks in household management she was expected to engage in virtuous and largely economically useless gendered activities such as sewing, embroidery, reading, drawing and painting, gardening, and home decoration. While some of this no doubt conformed to the prevailing productivist values of a work ethic and thrift within the household—making new things, mending, and recycling old things rather than just acquiring new things in an extravagant way by buying them in the shops (Strasser 1999), this was primarily a cultural rather than economic activity aimed and reproducing this ideology of domesticity. The husband's standing defined the space of the home and it was the wife's role to act as protector and guardian of that role; to perform it as manager of household and servants (and later as houseworker herself); as mother to the children, responsible for their correct upbringing; and as the embodiment of bourgeois virtues against the moral turpitude of the outside (Calder 1977; Flanders 2004).

The Victorian home of the 1850s and 1860s was primarily a space of the projection of moral character of the family unit, and women's central position within that home was that they were expected to have withdrawn from the world of paid work as the guardians of the attributions of character. We can say that this ideal of character was both patriarchal and productivist in nature. The cultural historian Warren Susman has shown how important this idea of character was to the shaping of nineteenth-century society, certainly until the 1880s. As he suggests, based on his reading of nineteenth-century popular self-help pamphlets, books, sermons, and manuals through which this discourse of character in home life was articulated:

> A review of over two hundred such items reveals the words most frequently related to the notion of character: citizenship, duty, democracy, work, building, golden deeds, outdoor life, conquest, honor, reputation, morals, manners, integrity, and above all, manhood. The stress was clearly moral and the interest was almost always in some sort of higher moral law. The most popular quotation—it appeared in dozen's of works—was Emerson's definition of character: "Moral order through the medium of individual nature." (2003, 274)[3]

A man's character was reflected in his home and, because she was the guardian of that space, through the conduct of his wife. What was key to this discourse of character was that it allowed two of the central values of the middle-class life to come together: character was a reflection of one's social position and character was the means to self-realization within society in which older forms of recognition, position, and the means for betterment through established power networks were unavailable, at lest initially, to this newly arrived bourgeois class.[4]

The early and mid-Victorian home interior became a reflection of this pre-occupation with character, reflected in how the house was laid out, the use of its different rooms, and the ways in which those rooms were decorated and used for displaying the family's wealth. Women were positioned within this space as subjects there to reflect a virtuous Christian life and to reflect the standing and character of the family—defined in terms of social position or class. This space of character was a private space no doubt but one that had a very public face. The private sphere became a domestic haven from the uncertainties of the capitalist world of work and was gendered as a female space, but it was also often on public display to others through a series of social conventions in which status and position were managed through their display to others. The Victorian parlor of the period up to the 1870s was primarily a space of presentation and display of character to others.

The rules of conduct and successful management associated with the home were not something that a newly married wife could be expected to know all about in advance, despite whatever advice her mother and other female relatives might have given her. Instead, she had to be taught how to become a successful bricoleur in making this space. To aid her in this role there was a continual succession of domestic economy guides published during the nineteenth century that aimed to inform women of their roles and duties and to guide them in their correct performance of them. Such manuals, written by both men and women, also reproduced this domestic ideology. The best known of these in Britain was perhaps Isabella Beeton's guide to domestic management (1968 [1861]), better known today as a cookery book that more or less single-handedly murdered English cuisine; in practice it covered a wide range of issues in domestic economy well beyond those of food preparation (see also, among many others, Walsh 1874; McNair Wright 1884; Watson 1897). The form of these guides was invariably encyclopedic and concerned with the cultural preoccupation with totality. The parallel with the catalog for the Great Exhibition is again apparent. Typically running to several hundred pages on all topics imaginable, and nearly always addressed to an imaginary woman reader, these guides speak at length and in a highly didactic and often condescending tone about such things as: the setting up of a household after marriage, its successful financial management, decorating its various rooms in the latest fashions, rules for entertaining guests, the arrangement of ornaments and pot plants, how to nurse sick children, how to make a sorbet or syllabub, how to hire and fire servants, how to clean silver, and so on. It is easy to be cynical about the legislative tone of all this but the compendious nature of these volumes and the overbearing moral tone in which the reader is addressed (and which grates with our contemporary view) are important in the context of aiding people in the rules of establishing their character through their domestic interior.[5]

In general, these guidebooks to the virtues of bricolage set out with the starting belief that if the household were not managed properly across the range of all eventualities it would bring both financial and moral ruin on the family that occupied it.

In other words, their character would be spoilt by not running a proper home. Their compendious detail aims to help the woman of the house with advice on all possible eventualities from the most mundane and everyday ("boiling vegetables," "use of flannel") to the most potentially calamitous ("dealing with poison," "debt") and all categories in between ("purchase of a horse," "maiden aunts"). The home is constituted not simply as a haven of rest and peace from the public world of work and city life but as a space beset with uncertainty and risk if not properly managed: observing the rules of display, the presentation of one's taste to others, one's social position, cultured civility, and popularity—all important social conventions of Victorian society and reflected in the display functions of the house—all cost money and need to be carefully managed if they are not to bring financial and social ruin. In effect, character has to be bought; it is commodified, but it has to appear as natural if at all possible and one has to avoid stepping beyond one's station and risking social opprobrium and possibly the consequences of debt.

Ideas about character were not only expressed in these latter-day books of manners and etiquette but were reflected in the makeup of the parlor room as well.[6] Today we would typically call this room a living room (or, in the British context, a lounge), and it is and was the main reception room in the house. Not only was it the space where the family socialized with one another and engaged in all manner of pastimes and entertainments like music, singing, and parlor games, it was also a rather formal room used for receiving and entertaining guests.

This emphasis on character was important in the early part of the Victorian era and remained unchanged until the 1870s when it began to be transformed into something else, a concern more with personality and individual taste.[7] Susman's work discusses these terms together as a pairing (albeit in a somewhat cursory manner) in his study of the changing culture of American society in the twentieth century (2003). He argues that nineteenth-century society was based on a cultural preoccupation with character and moral conduct that produced a certain type of individual, and twentieth-century society with personality and self-expression that produced another. Significantly for our purposes, this shift from character to personality, he suggests, is related to the move from a society defined by production to one defined by consumption (2003, 275).

Susman's argument follows in the "culture and personality" tradition of American cultural sociology that developed in the 1950s in the context of investigating the impacts that postwar consumerism and suburbanization were having on individuals within society (see Riesman 1950). In such approaches, an ideal type of the hardworking and morally upstanding American individual is set up as the archetype from earlier times. Such a model is defined, in particular, with reference to an idealization of Protestant individualism (coupled to the republican values enshrined in the constitution) that is associated with an upstanding moral character, deferred gratification, individual self-sufficiency, and hard work. Such an ideal type was first described by Max Weber in 1904 in reference to the relationship, or elective affinity, between Protestantism and the development of a spirit of capitalism in seventeenth-century Europe (and, notably, after he spent a year traveling in the United States where he witnessed the Protestant individual from his ideal type in its closest empirical form; 1985). In this sociological tradition, such an individual, a self-directed individual who is typically, if unreflectively, conceived as male, and is imagined as a personality type being undermined or eroded by changes within society, most notably associated with the forces of consumption. This personality type is replaced by a weaker alternative, an other-directed personality, more susceptible to outside cultural pressures and the need for recognition by others, and, implicitly at least, gendered as a female subject.[8]

Susman argues that from the 1880s the concern with the acquisition and expressions of culture as a sign of one's character and moral standing begins to change into a more individualized form of self-realization. He uses the discourse of self-help manuals over the period as evidence for this. In the period prior to 1880, these books were concerned with displays of culture as a display of character. From after that date they become preoccupied in guiding people in ways that they can realize themselves as persons through the display of culture. This is the kind of concern with personality that we know today—spaces like the home are seen as extensions of ourselves and how we want to be seen by others and less about conforming to social conventions associated with the moral character associated with class and status position. For Susman, this is the product of a mass consumer society that begins to develop after 1880 in the United States (later in Europe—probably not until the "decadent" 1890s), a society defined increasingly by consumer rather than producer values. In effect, what marks this transition in ideas about the space of the interior are the advent of the department store and mail order catalogues and the shift to shopping as a cultural and leisure activity by women. During this time how and what one consumes becomes less a badge of rank and more a means of individual self-expression (Susman 2003, 279; see also Campbell 1987).

In the context of the domestic interior, this argument has parallels with that developed by Richard Sennett in his highly influential study of the rise of the private sphere and its social-psychological significance within industrial capitalism, *The Fall of Public Man* (1977). While he does not discuss Susman's thesis, nor suggest a clear shift from character to personality, Sennett's discussion of the nineteenth century describes precisely this rise of a culture of personality and locates it firmly within the private sphere of the home. For Sennett, the contrast is not so much between different moments in the private sphere as the retreat from the public by the bourgeoisie to the private as the space in which their class identity is established. Where once people had expressed their personality through their public roles, he argues, as the nineteenth century moved on, this became ever more a preoccupation associated with the private sphere (1977).

In the context of the changing forms of the domestic interior in the nineteenth century, Karen Halttunen has taken up Susman's argument (1989). She reads this shift from character to personality within the space of the interior of the home and sees it reflected in the shift from the mid-century idea of the parlor to the 1890s development of the idea of the living room. The parlor, she argues, was a space of character, whereas the living room is a space of personality. In many ways the cluttered interior of the 1870s and 1880s marks the moment of transition. Ideas of moral virtue and character expressed through the productivist sentiments of thrift and hard work and reflected in the pious and worthy space of the parlor gradually give way to a concern with coziness, comfort, and, above all, self-realization, personal touch, and individual taste reflected in the modern interior. In the parlor, objects, displays, and decorations are an expression of moral values, whereas in the living room they become an expression of self (1989, 189). While Halttunen's reading of domestic interior manuals and magazines across the period charts this transition, she is less clear on its reason and does not spell out all of its consequences. She simply echoes Susman's argument and agrees with his position.

These rooms would have been filled with things in the way Benjamin describes: full, cluttered, eclectic in their stylistic mix, and redolent with the symbolism of sentiment and comfort (see also Steegman 1987; Briggs 1990). In terms of their furnishing, there would typically be a fireplace below a mantlepiece as the focal point of the room. Around that there would be a variety of chairs and sofas, low tables, and sometimes, if the room was large enough, a more central table with chairs, a piano, display cabinets, and sideboards (Newton 1999; Osband 2001). In addition to the furniture, this room would be highly decorated with paintings and pictures, often hung from a picture rail near the ceiling. There would also be gilt mirrors; ceramic, glass, or Parian ornaments and vases (in other words, a wide variety of bibelot and knickknacks); potted plants; fire screens; plush curtains with pelmets and tie backs; carpets or floor rugs; and rich, elaborately patterned wallpaper (Greysmith 1976; Saunders 2001). In some cases there might be elaborate displays of ferns or stuffed animals or birds in glass cases (Saisselin 1985; Olalquiaga 1999; Logan 2001). Exotic shells were popular ornaments for a time too, as were tourist souvenirs (Stewart 1993). There might be embroidery or scrapbooks and later on photographs of family members on display. While the early Victorian home would probably have been lit with candles or oil lamps, later on gaslights might have been installed and toward the end of the nineteenth century the adventurous and wealthy were just beginning to introduce electricity into their homes (Asendorf 1993). Keeping this space in good decorative order and keeping it clean and tidy was a source of much anxiety and housework, usually involving a number of servants waging war on dust (Langland 1995; Amato 2001).

While there were continual campaigns by nineteenth-century designers and design reformers from the proponents of the Gothic revival in the 1840s and 1850s

(Clark 1962) to writers like Charles Eastlake who sought to improve and educate the taste of the middle classes (1969) through to William Morris and other members of the arts and crafts movement who sought to bring craft and tradition back into the home but through modern styles, the parlor that had developed by the 1870s was, above all, full of an eclectic mix of different aesthetic styles and objects that were often an expression of sentiment and kitsch (Olalquiaga 1999). It was through sentimental display that the virtues and character of the Victorian family were put on display. This was not something that they only did for themselves. Visiting or "calling" on friends and acquaintances within one's circle was a very important form of sociality, one beset by rituals of various kinds. Most would have had *carte de visite* made up with details of who they were, sometimes with a photograph of themselves added, that they handed in when they called on someone. One's position within society was often measured by such visits and through dinners and other entertainments associated with them that one might be invited to. The reason why the cookery sections of most domestic economy books tends to be the largest section reflects the importance of being able to entertain successfully as a display of position in front of one's peers.

This is not the frugal space of thrift and utility that might be associated with early bourgeois homes where a concern to project one's character was in play. But neither is it the modern living room where our main concern is with expressing our own personal taste in the furnishings. One can detect elements of both. As a space of transition, this paradoxical situation can be seen as one where concerns for character and personality mingle. How this cluttered space has been read, however, has often been without that sense of uncertainty.

THE CLUTTER OF THINGS

There have been many attempts to read the Victorian parlor. The conventional art history approach, focusing on aesthetics, has often seen it as little more than an expression of bad taste: eclectic in style with little knowledge of different periods and styles, often using mass-produced "luxuries" or items of sentimental value to display a weak aesthetic sensibility (see, for example, Pevsner 1951). Indeed, until quite recently, high-Victorian design prior to the design reform movement and arts and crafts style of the late nineteenth century was seen as anathema to those interested in serious aesthetic expressions within the decorative arts. Recent academic work has tended to be equally critical, focusing on either commodity fetishism or structuralist arguments in which a "system of objects" is read as evidence of bourgeois false consciousness (Saisselin 1985; Richards 1991; Asendorf 1993; Baudrillard 1998; Maleuvre 1999; Stewart 1993). Most criticisms of this kind tend to focus on the class character of taste reflected in the ordering and display of the home, and little thought is given to its gender composition. The question remains: "Why did the Victorians design their parlors in the way that they did?"

The first and perhaps most famous commentator and critic of such displays of household taste was the American sociologist Veblen in his pioneering *The Theory of the Leisure Class* (1987 [1899]). Veblen developed an emulation theory of fashion and taste that argued that those with position and rank would initiate a taste and that others, lower down the social scale, would then try and emulate them in order to try and acquire some sense of elevated social status in the process. The aristocracy, he argued, were able to display their social position not only through their homes but through vicarious leisure—they didn't have to work for a living but could rely on income from land rents and so on. The emerging bourgeoisie, unable to emulate this leisured existence because they had to make their living through work, chose to display their rising status instead through vicarious or conspicuous consumption. Consumption, for Veblen, is seen as a conflict over status, rank, and reputation (1987). For Veblen, the possession and display of the trappings of wealth are how the "leisure class" maintains its social position. He indexes the much older tradition of potlatch as the model: gifts and feasts are laid on by one group for another in order to engage in the act of symbolic violence whereby they show that they are more powerful and have a higher status and wealth because they are able to be more wasteful (see Mauss 1990; Bataille 1991; also Bourdieu 1984). Veblen applies the same argument to displays of bourgeois taste through conspicuous consumption (1987, 47). The display of a large house with well-furnished rooms and many servants to do the work in maintaining it, as well as a leisured wife who looked after the home but who did not work herself, was the typical means through which a man could display his position within society. In Veblen's analysis, women become shoppers, they become the agents of consumption and status management. While Veblen's observations and criticisms of Victorian taste are expressed along sociological rather than aesthetic lines, his model is too simplistic and one-dimensional to fully account for the bourgeois culture he aims to describe. As various commentators have pointed out, fashions do not always trickle down from the wealthy to the poor (Campbell 1987; Lears 1989). Neither can consumption be reduced to status battles alone. This residual form of potlatch can indeed be seen within contemporary consumption practices such as in the purchase of things because of their exchange value rather than use value (pace Adorno too), or because of what a brand might signify, but this is not all that consumption is about. As Jackson Lears has pointed out, all culture is about display and to attack display for its agonistic elements, as Veblen does, is to attack culture in general and not just capitalist culture (1989, 75). Veblen's argument also sees the bourgeoisie embrace the marketplace and bring it into their homes through the practices of consumption, but this overlooks the considerable anxieties associated with the market and the strong desire to separate it from the space of the home. The furnished home also served as a retreat from the market as well as its embrace. It was a more paradoxical space than Veblen would allow for, and women were at the center of that uncertain space. While Veblen suggests that women are little more than an extension of the husband's property, his dismissal of consumption as display on the grounds that it can be defined in terms of status conflicts alone misses much of what was happening in the making of this social space. As Lears puts it:

> Participation in the market, given its associations with avarice and exotic sensuality, posed fundamental temptations. The moralists' nightmarish vision was that the self's moral and intellectual gyroscope would spin out of control as it entered the magnetic field of market relations, resulting in the pursuit of worldly goods that would lead to madness and death. (1989, 81)

Above all, the relationship between the marketplace and the home was not as simple as he assumes. Nor does conspicuous consumption alone explain the aims at totality, the desire to fill houses with stuff—some shop bought, some inherited, and some homemade. In some ways Veblen was writing about a home space in which this transition from a concern with character to personality was under way. It may well be that conspicuous consumption was an important characteristic of the process of transition but that it has become less significant since. While it has not gone away altogether, the more recent preoccupation with expressing one's identity through one's home rather than one's class position or status group is one that cannot rely on the practices of conspicuous consumption alone (see Bourdieu 1984).

While Veblen's analysis is still influential, more recent critiques of the Victorian interior have either followed the "bad taste" line of argument or a "commodity fetishism" one. What both have in common in particular is a critique of clutter and sentiment within the interior as indicative of the falsity of bourgeois culture, rather than seeing it as indicative of anything else. Remy Saisselin, for example, speaks of all the clutter and knickknacks that crowded the parlor as an example of the bibelotization of art in the bourgeois domestic sphere (1985). In part drawing on a rather simplistic reading of Benjamin's work, Saisselin says of this, "The bibelotization of art implies too much of anything from anywhere in the same space, and hence it is a bourgeois style, rather than a true style, namely, the creation of artists and architects, of mind-disciplining imagination, such as Louis XV, Louis XVI, or Directoire, the styles which suppose a harmony and unity" (1985, 68). In other words, the bourgeoisie have no style of their own; they simply copy from everywhere else and bring things together through bricolage. Such naïve stylistic imaginings, he suggests, are the work of aesthetic amateurs, women in particular (67ff.). The accumulation of things, along with shopping as a leisure activity, is, Saisselin suggests, a female response to the boredom of being confined in the private sphere and a vehicle of expressing one's desires, albeit in commodified form. In such arguments Saisselin manages to combine a high level of snobbish disdain for the poor taste of the bourgeoisie with a critique of their cultural susceptibility to the fetish character of the commodity. Women in particular are singled out as most susceptible to fetishism of this kind. While his argument clearly draws on Benjamin, it lacks the subtlety of the analysis of the latter and fails to offer an analysis of why rooms were decorated and displayed in such a way. It does not fully get to grips with the significance of interiority that lurks within the clutter.

More recently Didier Maleuvre has sought to offer us just such an interpretation largely based on a reading of Balzac's novels and his imaginary constructions and inventories of the bourgeois interior (1999). Again, he singles out the significance of an eclectic, cluttered style, of pastiche, and a taste for kitsch for critical disdain. In this case he reads the domestic interior as a commodified spectacle that borrows its analysis more from Debord or Adorno than Benjamin.

> The bourgeois observes his objects, he does not live with them: the home becomes a spectacle of itself. It is where the individual retires to contemplate "home" as an already distanced historical image of itself. This course has the effect of turning the interior inside out: home is no longer the ontological center of existence but one of the polarised and alienated objects of an already full-grown society of the spectacle. (1999, 119)

His argument is premised on the belief that there was once an authentic form of dwelling that has been alienated by capitalism through the culture of representation expressed through commodity fetishism with bourgeois interior as its outcome. In doing so he brings together Marxist analysis of the commodity with Heideggerian ideas about authenticity, dwelling, and belonging (Heidegger 1977a). Philosophically diverse as these two traditions of thought are, the one thing that they have in common is a notion of alienation of the essentials of human being under fabricated social-historical conditions or conditions of technology (Heidegger 1977b). For Maleuvre, the bourgeoisie become collectors and hoarders of things, producers of lists and compendium who measure themselves in the accumulation of things that surround them in their homes. They create a totalizing gaze on the world that creates a total world modeled as a mausoleum of history in which their subjectivity is mummified (1999, 144).

> The bourgeois interior's evasion of architecture bespeaks a crisis of dwelling for the modern inhabitant. Home becomes synonymous with its own avoidance, with the liquidation of ground and world.... The bourgeois interior is the place where one stages one's refusal to be somewhere. Anywhere out of the world: the interior dweller dwells in homelessness, outside the place-establishing frame of architecture. (1999, 151)

The interior in this analysis becomes the space of both the inauthentic and the fetish and the two are seen as tantamount to being the same thing. It becomes a dead space of the object, and of kitsch object and its expression of sentiment as a spectacle in particular.

While there is much of interest in Maleuvre's analysis, especially his discussion of the relationship between the interior and the museum (see my Chapter 7), he reproduces many of the same problems that we have seen with theories of commodity fetishism: it treats subjects as cultural dopes, it doesn't allow for the possibility for any dynamic relationship between subjective and objective world, and it bases its analysis on an idea of subjectivity associated solely with production rather than with consumption, only here that production is understood through Heideggerian ideas about building as an expression of authentic being rather than Marx's ideas about the realization of species being in productive labor. What they both share, of course, is Romanticism's nostalgia for a more authentic past where creativity could supposedly express itself fully through less mediated forms of craft. There is an implicit patriarchal position in play in such analysis too: man's authentic creative/laboring/building powers are being undermined by women's inauthentic consuming desires.

A much more fruitful approach to clutter and kitsch is offered by Celeste Olalquiaga in her Benjamin-influenced reading of the interior (1999). Drawing directly on Benjamin's development of the idea of dialectical images, she seeks to read kitsch items within the Victorian interior in a similar manner to Benjamin's own reading of artifacts in the arcades and other "dream house" spaces of the commodity. Rather than start from an aesthetic critique of kitsch, she reads the fascination with it in the Victorian home as a response to the loss of experience in modern capitalist society. Kitsch objects are defined by their associations with sentiments and memories rather than by their aesthetic qualities: nostalgia, memory, mourning, a delight in decayed nature, all suggest an engagement with the experience of loss and a desire for some kind of return when kitsch artifacts were put on display within the parlor. Kitsch objects symbolize in an indirect and allegorical manner. In this way holidays are turned into souvenir artifacts, nature is transformed into the aquarium, the fernery, the glass case full of stuffed animals, the fossil turned into an ashtray, and so on. When someone dies, photographs of the corpse or artifacts belonging to the dead person when they were alive are put on display in the parlor. In the high sentimentality of all this, Olalquiaga reads such artifacts as dialectical images that revealed the kinds of sentiments that preoccupied the bourgeoisie (a secure past, moral certainty, authenticity, the virtues of family life), but which were at the same time continually under threat as the shifting sands of the social relations within capitalism moved and changed and threatened a coherent sense of experience. Capitalism revolutionizes and erodes social life, Marx was certainly right about that. But it does so through consumption as much as through production. That is the key message that Benjamin gives us in his *Arcades Project* (see also Simmel 1990). The bourgeoisie are the principal beneficiaries of this condition, but that does not mean that they do not experience the fracturing of experiences or are not susceptible to the consequences of financial and social ruin that can come with changes in market conditions. Their homes were the spaces in which they responded to those changes and uncertainties. They were not merely spaces in which the market imposed a phantasmagoria of peace, stability, and security but where that had to be created in practice through the bricolage of ordering, displaying, arranging, collecting, and making sense of the material surroundings that were brought together within the space of the parlor. The things that they brought together expressed initially a concern with character and later on one with personality, and, in both cases, these cultural expressions reflect an attempt to take possession of things and give them a stable and ordered significance in a world where that appeared to be lacking.

Thad Logan has made similar arguments that stress the need for a social rather than an aesthetic reading of the artifacts found in the parlor in her recent work on the subject (2001). For Logan, we need to read the material culture of the parlor as a way in which the bourgeoisie and the bourgeois woman in particular sought to articulate and resolve social contradictions (2001, 106). The eclectic mix of things, not just kitsch items but also more upmarket objects such as furnishings, mirrors, paintings, and so on, filled this space, but Logan suggests that there were three main classes of artifact that were of key significance: "There are three specific classes of object found in the parlour that, I will argue, metaphorically negotiated major stress points of Victorian culture: things that cited or 'represented' nature, handcrafted articles produced and circulated within the domestic world of girls and women, and those things that came from 'away'—whether souvenirs of travel or other foreign objects" (2001, 140). The significance of these classes of objects, for Logan's structuralist reading of the interior (see also Stewart 1993), is that they are deployed in a series of binary oppositions that articulate key social tensions within bourgeois culture: nature/culture; mass-produced/handicraft, and domestic/foreign. For bourgeois culture the uncertainties and conflicts of urban life led to a romantic embrace of the rural and of nature. They filled their homes, Logan argues, with items that produced a fabricated nature (ferneries, aquarium, Wardian specimen cases, plants, birdcages, and so on) that expressed a nostalgia for a pre-urban past. Nature was also seen as more spiritual and more wholesome and a source of moral edification (2001, 145). In the case of the handmade, the tension that was addressed was the moral association with hard work by hand that had been lost with mass production and also the desire that women should fill their idleness with time spent doing useful work in the form of sewing, embroidery, lacework, dried flower arrangement, and so on. Handmade items were then put on display within the moral space of character that was the parlor. Logan's argument is weaker and less clear when she comes to the binary between domestic/foreign (182ff.), but it has to do with anxieties over the diversions of travel and the need to bring the fruits of one's excursions back home and a certain amount of anxiety about the character of empire (186).

In some ways Logan's reading is rather too simplistic in its reproduction of binary thinking. The social contradictions that this homemaking work set out to resolve are not always made apparent, nor is how these artifacts engage in the act of resolution actually spelled out. She is right to point to the significance of these classes of objects, however, and her emphasis on how the space that they are displayed within is made by its inhabitants rather than something that is already in existence as phantasmagoria is important. In a way, what Logan appears to get at is that these spaces are continually under threat within capitalism; a symbolic defense against that is achieved through the practice of bricolage by consuming subjects, and women are the key agents; and that commodity culture is part of this practice. The three classes of object certainly illustrate this kind of activity. Where Logan has less to say is on the relationship between the culture of the home and that of the capitalist market.

It is easy to dismiss, as writers such as Saisselin, Maleuvre, and others do, this phantasmagoric world as one merely of an alienated false consciousness. To do so requires some sense of belief that there was once an essentialist, authentic-producing subject who stood outside of social relations and that he (and it is invariably a he) as a producing subject has been alienated by capitalism and is now susceptible to the fetishistic effects of consumer culture. Benjamin's own approach, despite his omissions on issues of gender, is subtler than this. While he is equally scathing about the consequences that such phantasmagoria have for subjects, he is not so dismissive of their practice within such spaces. Figures like the flâneur, the collector, the gambler, and the cinemagoer are the figures who are constituted in the capitalist world of commodity fetishism (see also Kracauer 1995) and have their significance as distracted receivers of dialectical images. We might add the flâneuse and housewife to this list. Their fractured experience, their distracted mode of reception, dislocated from history and memory in a fabricated world of the interior, makes them most susceptible to the illusions of the phantasmagoric in his account. Yet it is these same figures who, for Benjamin, through their engagement with those worlds, through their belief in them, are the most likely agents of historical awakening, the most likely to experience the dialectical images that such spaces create. For Benjamin, the critique of capitalism and a rejection of the conditions it creates can only come through recognition of the impoverishment of experience rather than through the absolute bodily impoverishment that comes with destitution.

UNPORTABLE PROPERTY, WOMEN, AND INTERIORITY

In the Victorian interior, therefore, we see that social anxieties were worked out through the construction of meanings around the notion of interiority as character and latterly as personal expression. What we need to address is the relationship that this had with consumer activity. We know also that women were the key subjects of consumption in this space and that the constitution of their subjectivity was implicated in the process of establishing these senses of interiority. It was not, however, just issues of status and reputation that were at stake. The whole issue of property and the ambiguous relationship between the home and the marketplace was articulated through the practice of consuming within and for the home. In the previous chapter I drew on Lawrence Birken's argument (1988) that suggested that women's position as consumers in the nineteenth century challenged the prevailing productivist discourse of bourgeois culture and opened up the space for a consumer culture focused on shopping as more than a necessity but a cultural imperative in a world increasingly driven by capitalist market forces; this presented both opportunities and anxieties for the bourgeoisie. As they came to express themselves more and more through the trappings of consumption, ideas concerning moral character as a means of expressing social status came under threat, and over time a new discourse of personality emerged (Susman 2003). If the former conformed to a productivist understanding of this space, the latter can be related to a consumerist one. Women's positioning within the cultural space of the home became a focus for these opportunities and challenges. They were placed in the paradoxical position of being constituted as subjects of desire while that desire at the same time was seen as socially problematic and potentially undermining of the social fabric. Women's position within the home was much the same as in the department store, only here the patriarchal discourse of production (work) and character was even more strongly expressed than in new spaces of consumption like the department store.

The lesson of the department store is that it encourages people to express themselves as subjects through desire rather than work; indeed it defines modern experience in this way. In the space of character that was the early Victorian home, such cultural forces would inevitably have been seen as problematic and threatening. Women's paradoxical position within that space became a central focus. The great anxieties of bourgeois culture at this time were the loss of face (status and reputation) and the loss of property due to the uncertainties of the marketplace. Reputation at that time depended not so much on the consumables through which status was expressed but through the moral character of the artifacts on display and the sentiments they conveyed. These anxieties were expressed in a coded manner in the numerous domestic economy books of the time and in associated literature (see Chase and Levenson 2000). They were also to be found in some of the major novels of the era (notably by Charles Dickens; see Nunokawa 1994) and in the ordering and displaying of material culture within the home. In each case, the position of the wife was the central figure of contention. We know that central to the discourse of home at this time was that of an ordered and moral private space, a haven from the uncertainties of the outside world and a space in which the proper character of a man and his family could be displayed to others. The arrangement of houses, the functions of rooms, the ideology of domesticity, and the effective display of character through material culture were the central discursive preoccupations that constituted this space. Jeff Nunokawa's reading of the domestic interior in the Victorian novel, notably those of Dickens, illustrates some of these challenges in play at this time (1994).

Commodification was a shock to Victorian culture. It overturned and transformed everything, changing culture and bringing uncertainty and the risk of
financial ruin and prosperity in equal measure. The Victorian response was to create
in the home a space removed from these market forces, a haven of peace and de-
commodified tranquility. Yet this process is one that is always already compromised,
Nunokawa argues, because such a space is always implicated within the process
of commodification (rent, payment of servants, acquisition of commodities for the
home for both use and display, etc). The home is subject to the dictates of fashion,
to a concern with what others will think of one through what is on display there,
something that has to be maintained at a cost.

At the center of this paradoxical situation is the position of the wife. At the
same time, Nunokawa argues, she is the figure who comes to represent the de-
commodified ideological sense of the home removed from the marketplace, and
is expected to display an identity in keeping with such an ideal position. She has
to remove herself from all associations with the commodity and as housewife is
thereby contrasted discursively with the figure of the fallen woman or prostitute
who comes to be associated with the figure of the woman in the marketplace. She
must become all that this Othered figure is not if that sense of the home as removed
from the marketplace is to be sustained and its displaced meanings protected. In
effect, she attains a position of *de-commodified value*: value acquired through the
(marriage) market and then stripped of its market associations and their replace-
ment with moral ones instead within this paradoxical space of value transfiguration.
The anxiety that haunts Victorian culture, Nunokawa suggests, is that some kind of
catastrophe will befall a family such that they cannot sustain this fabricated position
and will therefore be exposed, and the amoral commodity nature of society under-
pinning bourgeois culture will be revealed. Such anxiety often centers not on the
actual practices of commerce as they invade the secure world of home but around
the figure of the wife more specifically. As Nunokawa puts it:

> [T]rauma ensues there when wives are called commodities, not because they
> are thus cast as property, but rather because such property is thus cast among
> the uncertainties of the marketplace. Trouble arises when women are cast as
> such property in the Victorian novel less because the proprietor's grasp goes
> too far when it reaches her than because that grasp is always loosened when the
> shadow of the commodity falls upon the object that it holds. (1994, 7)

There is a reason, Nunokawa argues, as to why the figure of the wife assumes such
importance. The bourgeois cannot stop the circulation of commodities through his
supposedly de-commodified and respectable home; he acquires wealth and loses it
depending on the whims of the marketplace, but his wife, symbolically and to some
extent legally his property, cannot be allowed to circulate in this way. She is both the
ultimate commodity and also the denial of the commodity at the same time—what

Nunokawa calls "unportable property" (1994, 11). In effect, the bourgeois ideal expressed through the gendered discourse of interiority is that a woman becomes a figure for *a form of property that is immune from loss*: she cannot be bought and sold, her exchange value is nil and unchanging. As a synecdoche, she becomes the commodity as virtue, the ideal commodity, stripped of all its uncertainty within the marketplace. The wife, figured in this way, allows for the home to be a space of possession and the circulation of commodities, but their association with her removes any sense that this involves the market in operation through the cash nexus. In such a manner the bourgeoisie's sense of subject-hood is protected. What the bourgeoisie fear most is anything that might unsettle this relationship: scandal, especially involving the wife and revealing her unvirtuous character; hard times that might require the wife to earn money; any suggestion that the wife could be a property owner or could engage in any form of market activity in her own right. The Victorian literature, from Dickens through to the popular penny novellas, were full of stories of the consequences of such effects, and it fascinated and horrified the bourgeois in equal measure (see also Chase and Levenson 2000). The ideology of domesticity is certainly about essentialized gender divisions but it is also about establishing a stable cultural understanding of consumption that culturally neutralizes its uncertain consequences. The woman is both a signifier of virtue through her proscribed conduct as a non-portable commodity and a meta-signifier of virtue itself in the context of a commodity society, allowing it under the correct conditions to be perceived as the basis for virtuous conduct. It is this double role that defines her cultural significance and her subjectivity. In being constituted in this dual way, she occupies a distinct and fluid figural position that allows for a transfiguring of value to take place.

The figure of the woman within the paradoxical space of the home is that of a blank figure (see Hetherington and Lee 2000). A particular form of signification, a blank figure is a underdetermined one, one that, like a joker in a pack of cards or a trickster within a particular culture (in the anthropological sense), can take on many signifying roles because it does not have a definite signifying value or position in its own right. It is both inside and outside of the space that it occupies—a topological figure in a topological space—not unknown altogether within that culture but an underdetermined figure nonetheless. This under-determination allows for it to place a role in ways that other figures cannot. She occupies a figural space in which she is both inside and outside the dominant representation of space—defined by them with little recourse to being able to change them (to figure) while at the same time being constituted as defining of that space in its totality. It is this role that, at a meta-level, establishes the paradoxical nature of such a space around this figure. Not only can we define women's position within spaces like the department store and the home in relation to different categories of signifying presence, but also more broadly by bringing into play the signifying roles of the categories of absence and presence that operate though such a form of figuring. Such a figure is at the same time absent (in the public realm) and all-defining within a space. In this case we are dealing with the commodified space of the home. Like the joker in a pack of cards, she has no signifying value in her own right in this context. Within patriarchal discourse she doesn't matter, she doesn't figure, she is nothing. And yet nothing can be much more than something; 0 is a far more powerful semiotic figure than 1 (see Rotman 1987; Hetherington and Lee 2000). She is a zero signifier in this respect, and the main quality that such a figure has is that it can not only be a signifier for nothing but also a meta-signifier for the whole system of ordering in which all figures are constituted.[9] The wife is the absent-presence of the marketplace within the home. She has the power to keep that hidden and for it be revealed. It is around such a figure and the homemaking practices associated with it that a certain kind of cultural work gets done; using the anthropologist McCracken's terms, this figure is at the center of the creation and maintenance of displaced meaning (1988).

With this term he is concerned with describing how we construct a culturally rich experience, through our engagement with artifacts, which is otherwise at some remove from our everyday lives. Different cultures are constructed around different ideals, myths, traditions, and customs that allow them to make sense and provide a feeling of belonging for their members and allow for a sense of self to emerge. In our everyday reality we do not encounter those intangible forms of cultural expression directly. What it is to be a person, a woman, a member of a particular class or status group, or of a particular family or community, is not always readily felt and expressed in our daily activities. What typically makes up our shared and communicable experience of belonging to a particular culture (*Erfahrung*) is not immediately apparent and realizable in the routines of daily life. In order to provide people with a sense of such a shared cultural experience, they invest signs and artifacts with meaning that allows them to connect with their cultural self-understanding and preserve that sense of subjectivity from the routines of life from which it might appear absent. This process McCracken calls "displaced meaning."

> Confronted with the recognition that reality is impervious to cultural ideals, a community may displace these ideals. It will remove them from daily life and transport them to another cultural universe, there to be kept within reach but out of danger. The displaced meaning strategy allows culture to remove its ideals from harm's way. (1988, 106)

In some contexts that is done through the construction of myths about ancestors, about a golden age that exists in the past or a utopian future or a broader sense of belonging within a harmonious community such as a nation, a religion, or a people. All such displaced meanings are expressed through artifacts that act as symbols of a broader intangible reality that is somewhere out there, safe and protected (religious icons, flags, and so on). In capitalist societies, where such an experience (*Erfahrung*) has been eroded and made increasingly uncertain through the process of individualization that is associated with this discourse of desire, new arenas (like the home) are needed for the construction of displaced meaning. Such ideals as belonging, authenticity, reality, community, security, stability—in a word, all the virtues once associated with experience as *Erfahrung* that are unattainable within capitalist society—are idealized and sought through less direct means of experience (through consumption in department stores and homemaking, for instance).

One of the most important ways in which they are sought is through an engagement with the material world—through artifacts—and in capitalist societies those artifacts are encountered as commodities. Consumption is, therefore, one of the most significant ways in which this is done, and some of its most important spaces—the department store, the home, and the museum—are the fetish-spaces in which this construction of displaced meaning is principally carried out. For McCracken, consumption is an important modern way for establishing cultural meaning (see also Douglas and Isherwood 1986). As he puts it, "[c]onsumption is one of the means by which a culture re-establishes access to the cultural meaning it has displaced" (1988, 104). A major addition to this argument is that in the broad context of consumption the artifact is the means through which this is achieved.

> To glimpse the role of goods in the recovery of displaced meaning is also to gain new insight into the systematic properties of consumption that are now dismissed as "irrational," "fantastic," or "escapist." When goods serve as bridges to displaced meaning they help perpetually to enlarge the individual's tastes and preferences and prevent the attainment of a "sufficiency" of goods. They are, to this extent, an essential part of the Western consumer system and the reluctance of this system ever to allow that "enough is enough." (1988, 105)

In other words, when we consume a thing we are not just buying it for its use, nor even as a sign, its sign value; rather, we are gaining access through it to cultural meanings that have been displaced. Displaced meaning is all about expressing a need through desire. Rather than a highly individualized act of self-expression, consumption is inherently an important way in which people access communitarian, displaced meanings in an individualized society. And it was women, because of their more paradoxical, blanks and uncertain social position within spaces like the department store or the parlor, who were best able to articulate this process in practice. The gendering of the male subject in the nineteenth century was still predominantly concerned with matters of production and need as key means of expression. Women, especially middle-class women who were largely removed from this realm of work, were better placed to be principally constituted as subjects of consumption.

McCracken suggests that there are four ways in which objects act as bridges to displaced meanings: (i) they act as concrete and enduring signs of mediation (1988, 113); (ii) they act synecdochically, as a small indicative instance of something bigger (114); (iii) their economic value can be readily translated into symbolic value (114); and (iv) they are plentiful and readily available to many.

> Goods serve so well in this capacity because they succeed in making abstract and disembodied meaning extant, plausible, possessable, and above all concrete. They represent displaced meaning by serving as synecdoches of this meaning. They represent this meaning by reproducing its value and scarcity through their own. Finally, they represent this meaning by creating a series of almost infinite expandable locations through finely articulated diversity. (1988, 115)

McCracken does not use the term fetish in his work but I would suggest that that is what he is describing here. It is not just goods that act as bridges in this way as he argues but commodified goods, goods as fetishes, which we are really talking about. The reason they are fetishes is because agency is attributed to them. They act in partnership with the person doing the consuming/bricolage, allowing access to an otherwise inaccessible, immaterial cultural realm of significance and meaning. This is the realm of experience (*Erfahrung*) and gaining access to it, as Benjamin knew well, is an inherently fetishistic process. But he was still too caught up in the productivist way of thinking about subjects and objects that has always preoccupied Marxism to fully realize the significance of the fetishistic character of the phantasmagoria that is displaced meaning.

If the department store is the space in Victorian society where desires are commodified and the consumer is constituted as a desiring subject (flâneuse), it is in her home that those commodities are truly possessed. This is done in the imaginary realm of the displaced meaning of interiority constituted beyond straightforward associations with functional use or exchange value alike—seemingly as a clutter of things that come to be seen as a reflection of the subject's taste and family's desire for respectability and status recognition. Yet the spirit of the commodity is not something that can ever fully be taken possession of; it always retains the fetish power to possess (haunt) its possessor—in the context of shopping through the promotion of desire and in the home through the context of displays of status and identity. The full meaning of "taking possession" of the commodity is at the heart of our capitalist culture of the fetish and the making of the subject as a consumer. Not something to be dismissed out of hand as illusion from the productivist high ground of alienation theory, I have argued instead that we need to grasp what it tells us about modern consumer societies as a set of often paradoxical, yet enduring, relations between subjective and objective worlds.

Things as commodities are addressed through the process of taking possession of them and thereby transfiguring them culturally. It is through acts of transfiguration that the bourgeoisie come to understand the world as a totality and itself within it as the center point. It is through taking possession of the commodity as artifact that the displaced meanings of interiority are expressed. Notwithstanding the importance of furnishings, art, and the trappings of a comfortable life, the wife is the main artifact within this process. Through her, all the aspirations and anxieties that shaped that bourgeois vision of interiority came to be articulated. She became the figure of value transfiguration and was both a source of cultural stability and anxiety in equal measure within this space. The main possessor of things within this space, she was also possessed by them.

Chapter Seven

Disposal and the Display Case

THE UNDERGROUND SPACE OF THE COMMODITY

Like the world exhibition, the department store, and the domestic interior, the museum is also one of Benjamin's highlighted phantasmagoric "dream houses" of fetishized commodity culture. Although he has less to say about the museum as a space than he does about these other sites, the general position he adopts in relation to these other spaces is also present in his thinking about the museum as well. There is nothing in either of the exposé to *The Arcades Project* on the museum, and only one of the convolutes, L, "Dream House, Museum, Spa," deals with the museum in any direct way. What he says is rather brief. Apart from a few references to wax museums, Benjamin only really makes two points about the museum as phantasmagoria. In the first instance he says:

> Museums unquestionably belong to the dream houses of the collective. In considering them, one would want to emphasize the dialectic by which they come into contact, one the one hand, with scientific research and, on the other hand, with "the dreamy tide of bad taste." (1999a, 406 [L1a,1])

He goes on, quoting Sigfried Gidion within his analysis:

> "Nearly every epoch would appear, by virtue of its inner disposition, to be chiefly engaged in unfolding a specific architectural problem: for the Gothic age, this is the cathedrals; for the Baroque, the palace; and for the early nineteenth century, with its regressive tendency to allow itself to be saturated with the past: the museum".... The thirst for the past forms something like the principal object of my analysis—in light of which the inside of the museum appears as an interior magnified on a giant scale. In the years 1850–1890, exhibitions take the place of museums. Comparison between the ideological bases of the two. (1999a: 406–7 [L1a,1])

In other words, Benjamin identifies the museum as a bourgeois space that is central to his analysis of the place of the past in capitalist society, yet he chooses to understand it by equating it with two other spaces: the bourgeois interior and the world exhibition. He does little more with this comment and does not develop his discussion of the museum, though he does have quite a lot more to say about one of the museum's chief functions: collecting, albeit more through an analysis of the figure of the collector than the museum as a collecting institution (1999a, 2002). A bit further on in this convolute, he makes one further observation:

> There are relations between department store and museum, and here the bazaar provides the link. The amassing of artworks in the museum brings them into communication with commodities which—where they offer themselves en masse to the passerby—awake in him the notion that some part of this should fall to him as well. (1999a, 415 [L5,5])

This is a wry comment, no doubt, but one that he does not develop further either. Indeed, more of this short convolute is taken up, counterintuitively at first glance, with an interest in the underground spaces of Paris (sewers, cemeteries, underground dwelling spaces, etc.) than it is with museums per se.[1]

Is it that the museum is only of secondary importance for him compared with these other spaces, its analysis already contained within his discussion of them? Or are we to make more of it? And what of this association, by juxtaposition at the very least, with a space preoccupied with collecting the past and those of the (infernal) underground in which the past as waste is normally disposed of that also appear in this convolute? Benjamin does not make his intentions clear here and, probably, given the paucity of information he provides on museums, it wasn't fully clear to him either; but I would suggest that this is an issue of note that concerns the relationship between disposal and the past within capitalist societies and that is something we should look at.

Even so, most recent cultural analysis of the museum has not taken its lead from Benjamin, probably because of the limited nature of this commentary on it both here and elsewhere in his writings. Instead, the museum has come to be understood as either an ordering and somewhat "panoptic" space of regulation, governmentality, and classification influenced by the work of Foucault (1977; see Hooper-Greenhill 1992; Bennett 1995, 2004; see also Markus 1993)[2] or as a space of taste formation and social reproduction derived largely from Bourdieu's analysis of social distinctions (1984; see in particular Fyfe 2000).[3] Those few works that do make use of Benjamin's analysis of the museum (Saisselin 1985; Asendorf 1993) largely do little more than replicate the associations between the museum and the department store and the interior (see also Harris 1990; Cummings and Lewandowska 2000).

Saisselin, for instance, in his work on the bibelotization of bourgeois culture, makes the connection between the museum and the department store, noting, in particular, their similar architecture, spatial arrangement, and ordering of goods. He also goes on to suggest that the chief difference between them is where they come in time within the life of the artifact as commodity: the department store at the outset and the museum at the end (1985, 42). He also goes on to suggest that they are in symbolic opposition around issues of value; the former concerned with exchange value and the latter with other cultural values. This easy separation is something that I want to question in this chapter; indeed, Saisselin himself later in his book does this himself to some degree when noting how important the issue of acquisition is to the institution of the museum (1985, 114ff.). In general, though, we can say that he is more interested in analyzing the department store rather than the museum, as was Benjamin.

Along with his discussion of the bourgeois interior, as discussed in the previous chapter, Maleuvre, however, does offer us a more in-depth critical analysis of the museum within bourgeois culture that makes use of Benjamin's insights (1999). As much influenced by Heidegger as Benjamin in a study largely based on a discussion of art museums (notably the Louvre), Maleuvre sees the museum as emblematic of a decadent (fetishistic) bourgeois culture through its construction of a particular sense of the past as memorial (see also Asendorf 1993, 52ff.). In a wide-ranging analysis, following a discussion of the philosophical and critical reception of the museum since the nineteenth century, the leading argument that Maleuvre makes that concerns us here is that in the idea of the museum the bourgeoisie sought to make their identity and culture appear eternal and timeless by constructing it as a space of monumental time (1999, 56ff.). In turning cultural artifacts into monuments to the past through their display in museums, those artifacts are removed from the lived present, he argues, and placed in an imagined time. This is an important observation but Maleuvre does not really do much to link it to the development of capitalist society, which is surely the context for it, nor with the kind of experience (*Erlebnis*) that Benjamin associates with that society. Although Maleuvre does not use the word *spectacle*, it is, in effect, a spectacle of the past that he is suggesting is constructed by the bourgeois museum. The Benjaminian theme that underpins this argument is that Maleuvre reads in this process of memorialization a form of cultural forgetting. The memorializing of the past, we might add, constitutes it as a ruin that can then be recovered as a fragment of civilization; constructing history as a fetishized eternal image beyond the fragmented experience of modernity. In effect, the past becomes a phantasmagoria for the bourgeoisie's sense of history and of an idealized *Erfahrung* in which, as a class, it is placed within that monumental time as its chief agent.[4] Significantly, though, what Maleuvre does do in a section of his chapter on the museum (1999, 56–63; see also Crimp 1997), is hint at the importance of the spaces of the underground/death/ruin that Benjamin associates with the museum for reading its cultural significance. It is these spaces more than world exhibitions, department stores, or domestic interiors that are important for him in understanding the function of the museum in that they too are often concerned with memorializing time.

Asendorf, too, makes a brief association between collecting and death (1993), using Balzac's writings as his touchstone. The collector, who he suggests is an economically passive character, recovers forgotten things and gives them a new life by ordering them and putting them on display in the new context of a collection. This collecting work is deeply imbricated, he believes, in the fetish character of the artifact that facilitates the fantastic transformation of things into stories that mean something to people (1993, 53ff.).

The key argument in Benjamin's analysis of the museum as a space associated with death and decay that lies behind such observations by Maleuvre and Asendorf comes in the first entry in convolute L of *The Arcades Project* where he make reference to the influence of the discovery of Herculaneum and Pompeii on bourgeois culture (1999a, 405 [L1,1]). While noting that this discovery took place and was the source of most fascination during the eighteenth century rather than the nineteenth century, and that references to this lost classical antiquity figured prominently as a reference in the French Revolution of 1789 and the culture and style of neoclassicism, it is the principle of responding to the past as fossilized memorial in bourgeois culture that persists into the nineteenth that is key for Benjamin.

> [I]n order to gauge the shudder of dread and exaltation that might have come over the idle visitor who stepped across this threshold, it must be remembered that the discovery of Pompeii and Herculaneum had taken place a generation earlier, and that the memory of the lava-death of these two cities was covertly but all the more intimately conjoined with the memory of the great Revolution. For when the sudden upheaval had put an end to the style of the ancien regime, what was here being exhumed was hastily adopted as the style of a glorious republic; and palm fronds, acanthus leaves, and meanders came to replace the rococo paintings and chinoiseries of the previous century. (1999a, 405 [L1,1])

There is more than an echo of Marx's opening passages in *The Eighteenth Brumaire of Louis Bonaparte* here: men making their own history but not as they please, the dead weighing on the brains of the living, and the most revolutionary periods dressing themselves in the style of the past and history repeating itself (1978, 9–10). But it is also more than this. This short, seemingly inconsequential passage in one of the briefest convolutes in the Arcades study perhaps reveals something key to its total ambition: Benjamin wanted to study Paris, then the epitome of a progressive capitalist culture in the nineteenth century, *as if it were already Pompeii*.[5] Not only did that Victorian/Second Empire culture submerge itself in the ruins of the past (the medieval and Gothic past in particular) and celebrate and memorialize death (through memorials and lavish cemeteries for example), but its continual move to change things, yet at the same time reproduce the same thing (the commodity form) as eternal recurrence, acted like lava overlaying a fossilizing and preserving sense of ruin on the past images of progress. Only by getting people to see Paris as if it were already Pompeii would the shock effect that he wanted as a source of cultural and political awakening be achieved. This juxtaposition of Pompeii/Paris is perhaps the central dialectical image of his entire work even if it is not suggested in either of the exposé.

We have already seen that Benjamin identified with Blanqui's view that the modern world was an infernal one (hence the interest in the underground) that presented a phantasmagoria of heaven that was actually hell (on images of the underground and their cultural reception, see Williams 1992). In this context, then, the bourgeois sense of interiority is more that of a tomb than a parlor.

> The dread of doors that won't close is something everyone knows from dreams. Stated more precisely: these doors that appear closed without being so. It was with heightened senses that I learned of this phenomenon in a dream in which, while I was in the company of a friend, a ghost appeared to me in the window of the ground floor of a house to our right. And as we walked on, the ghost accompanied us from inside all the houses. It passed through all the walls and always remained at the same height with us. I saw this, though I was blind. The path we travel through arcades is fundamentally just such a ghost walk, on which doors way and walls yield. (1999a, 409 [L2,7])

What underground spaces like tombs and sewers have in common with museums is that they are spaces of disposal and also of dread. In them the association of phantasmagoria with that of haunting is at its most literal. The former spaces elicited a mix of fascination and horror over the Victorian middle-class imagination for whom the discourses of sanitization and hygiene were significant in defining their class identity (Corbin 1986, 1995; Stallybrass and White 1986; Latour 1988). These were spaces that were perceived as ones of abject horror and cultural dread not simply because they were associated with pollution, disease, and decay but also because of their synecdochical association with a loss of control and uncertainty associated with the world of the capitalist marketplace (Douglas 1984; Stallybrass and White 1986; Nunokawa 1994). We dispose of human waste and human bodies through these underground spaces. They are seen as conduits to another world that can only be imagined. Less apparent, perhaps, but so too is the museum in Benjamin's reading of it. Not a conduit of waste and human bodies, nor even of artifacts as such, but of the commodity status of artifacts.

In this chapter I want to suggest that it is not just the association of the museum with the other spaces of the commodity that I have discussed in this book that is important, as these authors mentioned above have recognized, but also that with the idea of the underground spaces/archaic realm of waste and death that Benjamin sees as at the center of the allegorical nature of collecting activity. The issue of monumental time and the commodity are brought together through the issue of disposal. Rather than collecting or conserving, this should be key to our approach to the museum and, indeed, we might go as far as to say that because of this the museum is revealed, perhaps, as the key space for understanding our capitalist modernity and its consumer culture in general. In the interior, where things are not normally sold, the troubled relationship with the market we saw in Chapter 6 is there. That was resolved through the paradoxical and underdetermined signification of the "wife" as unportable property (see Nunokawa 1994). But is this the case in the museum too? I will contend that it is but that it is the thing itself rather than any person who performs this role. If we compare the museum solely with these other "dream houses" of consumption we would have to argue that the museum is indeed a different kind of space. However, the association with the function, if not the subject matter of what I will call the underground spaces of disposal, is central here. Benjamin does not offer us an explicit theory of disposal but there are traces of it in his work that we can bring out and develop alongside anthropological observations on the subject (Thompson 1979; Douglas 1984; Kopytoff 1986; Munro 1996, 1998, 2001; Lindroos 1998; Gordon 1997; Hetherington 2004). It is through an association with the issue of disposal and with what happens to value that the museum reveals itself, I will argue, to be at the center of any understanding of modern consumer culture. The spaces of the exhibition, shop, and home need to be complemented with the museum if we are to understand the full dynamics of consumer culture.

It would be wrong, however, when addressing the museum in relation to matters of disposal, to only consider its storage function and the spaces in which museums store artifacts that have no desire or no space to put on display. It is what is done on display in the glass cases and under the lights, as it was in the cases of the exhibition, department store, and interior that we have already looked at, that must concern us here. Disposal is something that is put on view rather than put away, and it has phantasmagoric qualities that we should wish to explore. The main issue here is one of the relationship among subjectivity, value, and history.

MODERNITY, MUSEUMS, AND THE VIEWED OBJECT[6]

While the museum has in recent years become a key space for thinking about the character of modernity, it has not so generally been discussed in the context of commodity culture (however, see Cummings and Lewandowska 2000). More typically the museum has been associated with the development of modern ways of seeing associated with the collecting, ordering, governing, and classifying roles that are central to museum scientific and display practices (Harris 1990; Hooper-Greenhill 1992; Bennett 1995; Maleuvre 1999; Fyfe 2000). The museum has typically been understood, therefore, as visual space of display, but it would be wrong to suggest that the museum has historically constituted a space for seeing in a way that has remained unchanged through the development of its history or one that has taken into account the development of capitalism. What the museum tries to achieve, it is often argued, is some form of ordered way of seeing that emerges from broader approaches to knowledge. The two issues, however, are not distinct. How things are put on display and how they are viewed, their regime of curiosity, cannot be separated in the modern context from that of commodity culture. Before we can turn to that matter we need to address the changing character of how museum displays were viewed in the past, as it reveals something of the status of both the subject and the object that we have already discussed in Chapter 3 in relation to the issues of viewing, fetishism, and phantasmagoria.

Museums have become all about seeing objects of one kind or another in an apparently clear manner and of being able to interpret them in the context of some broader display narrative. The spatial layout; display techniques; routing of visitors through the museum galleries; distinction between gallery spaces, stores, and study areas; and a sense of authenticity and naturalism in the display of things on view have all been important to this process (Vergo 1989; Pearce 1992; 1995; Duncan 1995; Greenberg et al. 1996; Phillips 1997; Macdonald 1999). However, this was not always the case. Such a museum is a recent product of modern society and its post-Kantian episteme of hermeneutics. In effect, we can suggest that the history of the "museum" moves through a number of regimes of curiosity/episteme over an extended period of time: from the princely palaces of the northern Italian Renaissance in the period from the fourteenth to the sixteenth century; to the seventeenth century classical/baroque spaces of the quasi-scientific cabinets of curiosity; to what we would call the modern museum based largely on an aesthetic experience that immerses the subject within the space of display and a desire for totality in representation in that space. It is the latter that came into full prominence during the nineteenth century, most notably in the "universal survey" museums such as the Louvre, Metropolitan, British Museum (Miller 1974; Duncan and Wallach 1980; Duncan 1995), geology and natural history museums (Bennett 2004), and in decorative arts museums like the South Kensington Museum (later Victoria and Albert Museum; Burton 1999). It is this modern museum that has the closest relationship to consumer culture. We can see how the subject is constituted with this space of display over time and the affinity that that has with changes within capitalist social relations.

If we begin with the Renaissance, we see a distinct and long-recognized relationship between the development of linear perspective in art and the epistemic intentions of palace collections of the time (those of the Medici, for example) that were often the places used to house it. The development of an abstract sense of space within the arrangements of linear perspective, as Panofsky went to some length to point out in the 1920s, was quite different from perceived space or what is actually seen by the eye (1991, 27–36). This abstraction of space in the relations of perspective created abstract relations between subjects and objects more generally. This was also reflected too in the palace "museum" collection of that period.

That perspectival understanding of space is based on a mathematical abstraction that simplifies perceived space and represents it without all of the actual distortions that are associated with seeing practices performed by the human eye. It performs a certain kind of arrangement that allows things to be seen clearly as if they were a representation of three-dimensional reality. Through this convention in painting, a two-dimensional surface becomes the medium through which three-dimensional space is depicted by leading the eye into the picture through a geometric arrangement of orthogonal lines around which the scene is arranged. What is most important in this arrangement is that linear perspective interpellates the viewer as a distinct subject through a relation with the picture while leaving his or her embodied experience of viewing it outside and separate from it (Bryson 1983). The viewing subject becomes a powerful, disembodied eye that is geometrically connected to the picture/object that it sees.

In this abstracted manner the Renaissance regime of curiosity was constituted as a way of seeing that came to be associated not just with looking at contemporary art but with looking at the past too (Hooper-Greenhill 1992, 32ff.). The rediscovery reevaluation of classical civilizations such as Greece and Rome from the fourteenth century onward was important here, and artifacts from that previous time as well as contemporary artworks that were influenced by the earlier styles were put on display in these palace collections. Princes and wealthy merchants began to establish collections of artifacts and to display them in their houses or in galleries within their houses (Holst 1976). They also often acted as patrons to artists, commissioning new works of art to display alongside their collections of antiquities. The objects were located in a private space largely away from the public gaze. The collections were only made available for viewing to invited guests. The audience was usually made up of other nobles, scholars, and artists who were deemed to be appreciative of such works and who might witness the relations of power exhibited therein. Nonetheless, the importance of a collection within a city and the collection it housed was often seen as an act of public patronage that promoted the interests and standing of the city.[7]

At this time, those objects on display were not treated as singular things to be judged solely in their own terms but were understood as signs that could be deciphered and read by the abstractly constituted outside viewer as part of a cosmological system of signs. Hooper-Greenhill has called this type of viewing a "calculating and measuring look" of the Renaissance subject (1992, 43). Following Foucault (1989), she suggests that the key feature of the Renaissance way of seeing that treated objects in this way was a belief that things could be understood through relationships of similitude that told a wider story only accessible to an educated few. This similitude was informed by a number of factors, including a belief in the animate nature of the universe, powers of the supernatural, a quickening sense of the present, a sense of history in which the present could be compared with the (classical) past, and the creation of a calculating and evaluative gaze by a distinct subject (1992, 23–46; see also Anderson 1983; Foucault 1989).

In this context viewing is established by the gaze of the subject through four particular forms of similitude: conventientia, aemulatio, analogy, and sympathy (Foucault 1989, 17–25; Hooper-Greenhill 1992, 14). The Renaissance world is a world of resemblances and circular relationships—what we would now call chains of signifiers—in which a wide array of artifacts are brought together and seen as distinct and yet they make secret connections. There is no representative narrative or fixity of meaning within these Renaissance collections. However, what gives them a unity is that they perform, as Hooper-Greenhill argues, the possibility of displaying abundance as a form of merchant power, prestige, and patronage.

In terms of their commodity status, these collections corresponded to the space and time of a nascent mercantile capitalism—they were treasure houses of accumulated and displayed wealth in which the value of rare things was expressed through money's similitude qualities (Rotman 1987). Money not only signifies (an amount) but also has meta-signifying properties as a universal signifier of value. It can be turned into anything. Importantly these collections became conspicuous displays of wealth, taste, and status (Jardine 1997). They came to reflect the glory of the prince who owned the collection. Filled with objects from classical antiquity, carved gems, and other items inscribed with magical powers, the order of contemporary paintings and art objects was not established through any form of classification but through correspondence. Through chains of signifiers, a seemingly endless ordering was constituted in these collections (Hooper-Greenhill 1992). What facilitated this and what made the similitude meaningful to the viewer was the objectivized and abstracted, moneyed subject (the prince and later the connoisseur, artist, and scholar) who stood outside as an appreciative, meta-signifying, and knowing eye. The Renaissance collection is an abstract space in which the subject/money can say that they see the multiplicity of their mercantile power and influence reflected in their collection. As a totality, the collection resembles the prince as subject and as money itself. The prince becomes the personification of money—his collection the anterior object world to which he is mirrored as subject. It is this external subject position that gives the collection a meaning as a whole rather than any ordering and classifying work that might get done within it. This was a world of mercantile power rather than commodity culture in the modern sense and the type of collection or proto-museum that existed then reflected this.

If we move forward about two centuries to the middle of the seventeenth century, to what Foucault has called the classical age (1989) (also often known as the Baroque), we see something of a challenge to the abstract and fixed geometry of linear perspective in Italian painting and Renaissance collecting. That challenge comes mainly from Dutch art, and alongside and corresponding to it we see the emergence of a new type of museum in Europe that reflects this change—the scientific collection or cabinet of curiosities (Alpers 1983; Bryson 1983; Impey and McGregor 1985; Rotman 1987; Saumarez Smith 1989; Hooper-Greenhill 1992; Law and Benschop 1997). Both Dutch art and the "cabinets of curiosity" have something in common; they are both engaged in the constitution of a new regime of curiosity and approach to the world of objects by the viewing subject.

The world was identifiable with the position of the objectivized subject during the Renaissance (the prince) and that identification was organized through similitude into an homology between a viewing subject and the multifarious object-world that made up "his" collection. Yet the classical age, as Foucault has shown, is all about the development away from this way of knowing through similitude to other ways of knowing through representation that constitute the subject in a different way (1989). While we might want to question the degree and the speed of this epistemic shift, representation as a way of knowing, as a form of gaze, comes to the fore through the separation of the subject from the world at this time.

If the prince already had something of this position before, its universalizing and abstraction to all humans—through the discourse of Man—takes place in this period. In this context, what Heidegger once called "the age of the world picture" (1977c),[8] the separate subject becomes fascinated with the infinity of creation and with its study and classification. Of particular interest are the freaks and anomalies that stand outside of known or established orders; they are figures that help define the boundaries and orders of knowledge. The work of Francis Bacon perhaps best exemplifies this (1974). He speaks directly of the importance of the anomalous and of the need to study it (view it) scientifically. Only by studying the anomalous and monstrous, the heteroclites, he argues, will we be able to discern the true natural history of the world. The heteroclite, as Foucault points out, is a major concern of the scientific community in the classical age of which Bacon was a prominent and influential member (1989). Heteroclites as oddities and exotic things also fascinated the "museum" collectors of the time as well, such as Elias Ashmole in Oxford, and became a prominent part of their collections (such things as corals, carved coconut shells, "unicorn" horns, "mermaid" tails, as well as artifacts from the New World of the Americas, are often juxtaposed in such collections side by side). It is through a recognition of the anomalous and freakish that the space of knowing that is constituted by the classical age, the two-dimensional classificatory table, comes into being. The former Renaissance regime of curiosity had constituted the world as a series of connected resemblances. These are seen to be broken by the heteroclite that stands outside as something that does not resemble anything else (Foucault 1989, xvii–xviii).

During the Renaissance we have seen that the princely subject, the one able to occupy the viewing point, became synonymous with the infinite collection. With Bacon, as indeed with artists like Velasquez and Vermeer who were his contemporaries (Alpers 1983) and with those scientific collectors who followed

Bacon's lead in establishing classificatory "museum" spaces in which to observe the heteroclites (Hooper-Greenhill 1992), the infinite variety of the world is laid out on a table to be viewed and classified by the viewer in the hope of attaining a position outside by viewing that world as a picture (Heidegger 1977c). For Foucault, the classical eye seeks to be able to describe the infinity of the world in a single table. This way of looking is reflected in the art of the time too. In the paintings of the Dutch artists of the seventeenth century, the subject ceases to be seen as objectivized reflection of what views but becomes a subject separate from the world who sees it from outside in an independent way and not from a fixed geometrically established point (Bryson 1983; Alpers 1983; Rotman 1993).

Separating the world as material stratum from the subject locates that subject outside of the picture altogether in an independent and abstract space previously seen as the preserve of God (the space of the God-eye). The viewing subject is no longer established through rigid geometrical relations with the picture/collection but through a more complex and fluid topological arrangement (Law and Benschop 1997). Foucault's well-known discussion of Velasquez's *Las Meninas* makes this point well (1989). The subject is not established as a mirrored viewing point as in linear perspective, and what is depicted is no longer understood through the conventions of similitude but through forms of abstracted representation. What this picture shows, and indeed is also shown in much of seventeenth century Dutch art (Alpers 1983; Bryson 1983), is the constitution of the subject at this time as something separate from and defined in relation to the world. The gaze of the subject is separate from the picture; he or she looks in on it from outside. The picture is laid out as a spectacle for the gaze of the detached subject. Whereas the relationship between the subject and object in linear perspective is a Euclidean one that allows for nothing but connection and correspondence, in the art of the seventeenth century (Alpers 1983; Bryson 1988), the relationship between subject and object is topologically more complex (Law and Benschop 1997).

So it is with wealth too. The collector is no longer defined as the mirror image of his collection but as a separate accumulator of things. One can stand in a multitude of different places and look in on a picture that has no distinct vanishing point. The assertion of the picture plane as an opaque surface for representing the multiplicity of the world allows for many particular subject positions but also a positioning of the subject as something apart from the world through his or her accumulation of things of interest.

Such was the case in the early "museums" of the time too. Many large houses had special, sometimes "secret" rooms used to house collections of exotic items, both natural and artistic, that could be subject to scrutiny by the collector or an invited guest, typically a gentleman-scientist. These cabinets of curiosities (or *Wunderkammer*, as they were called) took up Bacon's challenge that the scientist focus special attention on the heteroclites or anomalies that challenged the boundaries of knowledge. The aim of the cabinet of curiosities was an encyclo-pedic one; it sought to bring together in the same space all of the artifacts of the world and to order them so that the order of the world might be revealed (Hooper-Greenhill 1992). At the outset of this exercise, many collectors were still relying on the principles of similitude from the Renaissance—seeking hidden ciphers and codes to understanding in what they saw. Very soon, however, these cabinets began to undermine the principles of similitude they drew upon by creating sense of universal order and representation (Hooper-Greenhill 1992).⁹ The main task of the classical form of representation is that of comparison. Comparison, Foucault argues, takes two forms: measurement and order, what Foucault calls mathesis (1989, 53ff.). For something to resemble something else there has to be some form by which comparisons can be made to see if something does indeed resemble something else or not. For Foucault, this means that the world comes to be per-ceived as if it is laid out on a two-dimensional table, a principle that lay behind the cabinet of curiosities, so that comparisons could be made through the vision of the detached subject who looks on from outside. The table/cabinet of curiosities comes to represent an ordered system. What started out as ciphers that were connected through similitude became in their arrangement a classificatory mode of ordering that was a cipher for the idea of order itself.

This time also marks out the beginnings of the world of the commodity economy proper rather than just that of the market, and we see a transformation in the status of money that reflects these changes. Previously money had taken the form of bank money that was concerned with an interaction with a particular per-son (the prince/merchant, for example). Paper money took the form of a note that promised to pay a particular person a stated sum; in effect, it referred to a specific individual and took the form of an IOU. In this period, the seventeenth/early eigh-teenth century, money starts to change from this form of resemblance established by the signifying quality of money to one established through representation with money being seen as a sign for value in general. The development of paper money changes from a bank note referring to a particular named individual to an abstract, anonymous promissory note (Rotman 1987). In other words, money's similitude-signifying qualities give way to paper money's meta-signifying representational order within this regime of curiosity, which Rotman suggests develops in the sev-enteenth century and is reflected in the promissory qualities of paper money and its association with the un-located, de-spatialized bearer to whom it is addressed (1987, 46ff.): "[t]he scandal of paper money...is the loss of anteriority: paper money instead, of being a representation of some prior wealth, of some anterior pre-exist-ing quantity of real gold or silver specie becomes the creator, guarantor and sole evidence of this wealth" (1987, 49–50).¹⁰ In effect the subject/money in the classical episteme becomes self-referential rather than connected to an anterior state (the princely collection/gold). We look on paper money in the same way in which we look on the objects in a collection: they address us as disembodied, de-spatialized abstract subjects who order and are ordered by the infinity of the collection/commodity economy on which we gaze.

If, during the seventeenth century, the anomalous became of great interest, was accumulated, and was put on display, our modern society, by contrast, began to worry about the focus of such "disorderly" forms of understanding (Bauman 1987). We have already seen in Chapter 1 in the case of the Great Exhibition how much issues of classification and the idea of totality rather than accumulated infinity and the problem of the unclassifiable dominate the modern approach to thinking about order and how it is seen. The idea of eradicating rather than studying the heteroclite through the establishment of knowable forms of classification is an important part of the disciplinary project around which the idea of modernity is located. To order the world and make it knowable makes sense when these ideas are brought together and fit with the response to the totalizing experience of a developing consumer capitalist society. The museum plays a major part in this process. When talking about the seeing subject within modern society, we have to recognize that such subjectivity is no longer conceived as separated from the object world as previously (Foucault 1977; Crary 1990). During the Renaissance, subjectivity was objectified and connected to an anterior object world; during the Baroque it became separated from the anterior world of the objective in a desire to gain subjective mastery over it as a producing subject (Rotman 1987); in modernity, subjectivity becomes subjectivized within the world of things/consumption (Crary 1990). In particular, as we saw in Chapter 3, gazing at the outside world becomes a means not only to observation of it but to inner reflection as part of the Romantic idiom as well (see also Foucault 1977). This is nowhere better illustrated than in the "panoptic space" of the modern museum (Bennett 1995) and the type of regime of curiosity that it helps to establish. I have argued in the previous chapters that this should be reflected in a notion of the consuming rather than producing subject.

The modern museum facilitates this reflective way of looking as consuming just as the carceral institution does for the deviant subject. Modern museums were established from the latter half of the eighteenth century as public sites for the conservation, investigation, interpretation, and display of artifacts to an exclusive and often invited audience. Their role increasingly became that of conserving and representing high cultural forms and of educating the public into an appreciation of their aesthetic and moral worth as individuals (Bennett 1995). The ordering of objects, their spatial arrangements, were generally Euclidean in character, allowing the relationships between objects, their grouping, and their order to make sense and form a narrative, often a narrative about seriality in one form or another: sequence, evolution, development, and so forth—in each a sense of improvement or progress was typically expressed through the display.

Rather than an infinite classifying table as was the case with the cabinet of curiosities, the modern museum is a totality, an enclosed space ordered into departments, separate rooms, distinct displays, well-organized cabinets, or, in the case of smaller museums, into some form of narrative in which artifacts become indexes to help tell a particular developmental story. One is immersed in that space as a surrounding, part of the story but also a reader who makes sense of oneself through the interpretive acts that such stories encourage in a reflexive viewing subject. The modern museum is not just about order and classification; it is also about experience and how one measures up to the indexes of culture and taste that are found there on display. Above all, it is about the reflexive process of self-understanding through education. The didactic mission of most museums in the nineteenth century was to educate their visitors not only about the things that they saw but also about matters of culture and order in general (Miller 1974). This project of governance (Bennett 1995) has no equal in the earlier museums. The museum was contrasted to the unruly spaces of spectacle, such as the fair and the entertainment, as order was to disorder in what Bennett has described as the exhibitionary complex (1995), seeking to turn the crowd into an audience some decades before cinema took on this role (Schwartz 1999). But education is just a part of this role that the museum plays; more broadly it addresses the issue of experience. Self-reflexive education is one of the chief means to that experience.

At the heart of this modern institution of the museum is a concern with the question of experience (*Erfahrung*). Modernity alters the character of experience fundamentally. As we have seen already with Benjamin, modern capitalism, with its de-traditionalizing effects, forces a breakdown of experience as a totality (*Erfahrung*) grounded in the topos of memory, custom, and epic narrative and sees the emergence of a more fractured and fragmentary set of experiences where the present is seen as a series of events whose lived character resists understanding and easy communication (*Erlebnis*; Benjamin 1973c 1999a). That this corresponds with both the birth of the museum (Bennett 1995) and the birth of consumer culture (McKendrick et al. 1982; Campbell 1987) is also evident. But the museum is not simply an institution concerned with governance of subjects—though I agree that it is that—it is also a response to the uncertainties of capitalism.

Through its presentation of stories about art, culture, and taste in material cultural form, the museum is a space that tries to develop within modern society a fabricated feeling of *Erfahrung*. Museums often have the aim, through the objects they collect, their display regimes, their narratives, pedagogic aims, and ordering logics, to give people a sense of ordered totality grounded in historical narrative and imagined community in which they belong (Anderson 1983; Koselleck 2004). In other words, they seek to provide people with a sense that they are living in a world where an uncertain and complex set of experiences that mark out capitalism make sense and have coherence. Museums seek to place us in an historical topos that appears natural. The emphasis on epic narrative around such themes as Civilization, Empire, evolution, and so on bring to the fore this panoramic, totalizing quality. Indeed, as Maleuvre points out, it is a place that monumentalizes history as something fixed, knowable, and eternal. Of course, museums are not all the same. They range from the universal survey museums like the Louvre, Metropolitan, and British Museum through to art collections, specialist collections, collections associated with particular places, crafts, technologies, or design fields, and so on; each tells a different kind of story. In the British Museum, for example, the story was one of Britain's singular position in the world as the center of Empire, a prosperous and scientific nation with strong political traditions associated with liberty and tolerance in the context of the capitalist market (Miller 1974). In France, the revolutionary situation produced a somewhat different museum space in the Louvre. This was one that shifted from being a princely collection to one that came to represent a bourgeois nation more in political than economic terms (Duncan 1995). But it is the question of the character of experience and attempt to place it in a singular narrative space of history that often informs both their collecting and displaying epistemologies nonetheless. In the varied fields of art, of historical narrative, in the placing of civilizations in context with one another, in addressing a sense of belonging to a shared space of locality or community through the display of artifacts, museums seek to articulate narratives of experience and identity and to make sense of the relationship between time and space in a modern world where they are thrown continually into doubt by the vicissitudes of the commodity economy. If that marketplace is the epitome of the flow and uncertainty of commodified time, the museum seeks to represent itself as a timeless space outside of the flow of the everyday.

If the space of the Renaissance "museum" was a palace and in the Baroque age it was a classifying table, in the modern age, as Benjamin was keenly aware, it is a bourgeois space, a "display case" for the phantasmagoria of experience as *Erfahrung* in which the uncertainties of market-shaped social relations reflected in the commodity status of artifacts are seemingly magically erased. This is above all a space that presents itself as the antithesis of the marketplace. The main process through which this is achieved has been called *singularization* by the anthropologist Igor Kopytoff (1986). It is through this process, which is one of de-commodification, that the construction of monumental time is achieved and that those vicissitudes of capitalism—addressed and displaced meanings such as stability, permanence, order, progress, and eternity—are constructed as an alternative.

Artifacts travel and they are motile as well as mobile. Arjun Appadurai has suggested that artifacts as commodities not only have social lives that give them their significance, they also follow varying "diversionary paths" (1986, 26ff.). Things once bought do not sit in a stable place on the mantelpiece forever. Sometimes they get moved, stored, transferred, lost, stolen, or damaged. On other occasions they need to be re-sold in order to raise money for something else. The museum seeks to put a stop to that flow by giving a permanent home to the things that its trained curators, and supposedly society more broadly, values. These processes are often associated with the changing social status of artifacts and that too is not always a stable and predictable thing. In spaces like the Great Exhibition, we have seen that the commodity status of the artifacts on display was overtly denied but it managed to leak out nonetheless. In the domestic interior the anxiety over economic security informed the spatial practice of that site, deploying the paradoxical signifying position of the wife as a neutralizing force against uncertain market conditions. The museum plays this supposedly stabilizing role for capitalist society in more general terms.

For Kopytoff, similarly, commoditization is a fluid and uncertain process and not a stable condition, but it is one where people often try to achieve a stable state as an ideal. Objects, he suggests, have a cultural biography. As they move in society (from shop to home to auction to museum, for example), their recontextualization often helps to redefine the artifact as it travels. Much of the time that redefinition relates not so much to its use value (though that can change—a useful pot can become an ornamental vase over time, etc.) but to the exchange value of the item as well (availability, desirability, rarity, disposability, and so on). The de-commodification of an artifact is a part of this process. In Western societies, at least, de-commodification confers a particular status on something: specialness, uniqueness, apartness, aura, and so on (1986, 69) or it confers the status of rubbish, worthlessness (Thompson 1979). In both instances items become "priceless." Both the museum and the rubbish heap are sites of disposal, yet what goes into each is often, though not always, quite different. In the context of rising status, de-commodified artifacts are singular, Kopytoff argues, whereas commodities are common. Many singular objects start out as commodities but because of their culturally defined specialness they come to be valued in ways that require them to transcend that status and be put apart—spatially as well as in terms of their status. The museum is a key institution that performs this role. To singularize something is to remove it from its commodity status and flow of things in the market and to only allow other values of specialness to be associated with it. Paintings, rare jewels, sacred objects, heirlooms, and so on are the sorts of things that Kopytoff has in mind but it can be much more than this. The particular role that singularization plays, he suggests, is to introduce the conditions of stasis into the world of flow and movement that characterizes the commodity market (1986, 82). Each allows for a vantage point to be seen on the other. By bringing the flow of things in the market to a stop reveals that flow as a process, just as the stop looks different from the flow. In modern society the museum is a place of such a stop—an indefinite pause—it is the place where things stop being traded as commodities and are singularized as "treasures," "great works of civilization," or "iconic examples" of one kind or another (on the stop, see Appelbaum 1995). While this is most apparent with one-off artifacts like paintings, it is true but in different ways with other things, where an example is placed in a museum while other examples of that thing continue to circulate as commodities.

Central to Kopytoff's argument is the principle of movement and flow. He acknowledges that there are no eternal commodities (things ultimately decay or get destroyed) and no eternal singularized artifacts (even items in the possession of a museum or a church might eventually find their way back into the market and be re-commodified). But there is another issue at work here in this interrelationship between movement and stasis that he hints at but does not fully develop, and that is the issue of disposal. Museums are not just spaces of the singularization of things but also of the disposal of their commodity status; indeed, we might suggest that they are significant conduits of disposal in this respect. This is a theme that I wish to consider further because it is perhaps central to understanding the modern museum and its relationship to consumer culture. It also takes us back to the theme of the spaces of the infernal underground that Benjamin hints at in his brief discussion of the museum.

COMMODITIES, DISPOSAL, AND THE MUSEUM[11]

Common sense knowledge would suggest that disposal is all about waste or getting rid of something absolutely. However, there is an anthropological literature on "waste" that suggests a principle of circulation is at work within the idea of disposal that challenges this view. In work on the gift and potlatch (Mauss 1990; Titmuss 1970), burial rites (Hertz 1960), pollution (Douglas 1984), and sacrifice we see how getting rid of things is a mobile and uncertain process, integral to the performance of social relations, kinship networks, and ritual knowledge and activity (Hubert and Mauss 1964; Girard 1979). Indeed, there have been serious attempts to understand consumption using some of these categories (Sahlins 1972; Douglas and Isherwood 1986; Bataille 1991, Miller 1998). This idea of circularity and movement fits better with the processes associated with the museum than the idea that disposal be treated simply as a synonym for waste. What we might add to this is the idea that disposal be seen as a continual, recursive practice of engaging with making and holding things in a state of absence, and of understanding how something can be in a state of abeyance and be "at your disposal" at the same time. That is the central paradox at work in the space of the museum and it relates to the commodity status of artifacts. If we are to understand what disposal means in relation to consumption and to the museum, we would do well to analyze it as such. When we dispose of something to hand, a material form of some kind, we do not necessarily get rid of its significance, and the effects that are generated can linger and continue to have significant effects.

When discussing disposal, I argue that we should begin with the position that challenges from the outset the idea of disposal as a final state of getting rid of something. Social relations, such as those enacted by museums, are not only performed around what is there but also around the *presence* of what is not. What is there in a museum is a host of artifacts; what is absent *but as a presence* is a host of commodities. Given the social rather than individual basis of consumption acts (Douglas and Isherwood 1986), this has implications not only for what we do to things but also for how those things (and their absence) are implicated in how we *do* social relations more broadly in consumer society. Disposal, then, is fundamentally implicated in the making of modes of representational order—it helps to make value in a consumer society make sense.

The recent writing that exists on disposal is small but useful, though as yet undeveloped, and still often takes the limited "problem" of waste as its central theme (Munro 1995, 1998; Chappells and Shove 1999; O'Brien 1999; Strathern 1999; Hawkins 2000). In addressing the relationship between consumption—the associated acts of acquiring, possessing, valuing, exchanging, and using an object, good, or service of some kind—and disposal, we can find some guidance from earlier work on the relationship between consumption and production. First discussed by Marx in the *Grundrisse* and repeated many times since (1973), we find the argument that there is never an altogether clear-cut distinction between production and consumption, nor a simple temporal sequence to these processes (Lury 1996). We may buy something from a shop that has been produced and can, in acquiring and using it, or in attributing some significance to that object, be said to be consuming it. However, in so doing, productive work may still be required of us. Production and consumption are entangled together in these and other cases. Production does not always come before consumption; it may also come after in the sequence of events. Likewise, to produce something itself requires prior acts of consumption before it can be made ready for consumption. We should consider disposal in the same light as these other entanglements. It is not just the last act in a sequence that runs from production to consumption to disposal in a straightforward linear manner, but is recursively implicated in the ordering of the whole sequence of events.

How societies make things absent and the role that that plays in creating social classifications, boundaries, and orders have for a long time been a theme of significance within anthropology. Beginning with Hubert and Mauss's work on sacrifice (1964) and Mauss's analysis of the gift, especially his discussion of potlatch (1990), we see that getting rid of something is profoundly implicated in the maintenance of a recognizable state of social order as a form of presence. The destructive waste of a life or of precious goods is seen as a conduit for the ongoing maintenance of a sense of social stability. Even the most extreme destructive or violent acts against persons or things can have effects that make sense within the social order that members of that society understand. In this sense, disposal, expressed through its material forms, is part of the accomplishment of the ordering work that goes into making a society (Bataille 1991; Girard 1979). The object as gift, the scapegoat, and the sacrificial victim are all made as agents of order through their disposability in a cycle of ongoing ritual practices. In engaging in such acts, members of a society can be seen to get rid of the unwanted and thereby stabilize social categories of membership and belonging around their removal. In making something absent, either through death or destruction, a representation of social order is apparently secured, though never for all time. Such ritual acts often need to continue in an endless processional sequence in order to help continually reaffirm a sense of social order as a stable thing. *In the museum it is the commodity that is visibly sacrificed, thereby reaffirming the values of a consumer society as something fixed and eternal.*

To develop this point about disposal, we can look to a series of recent papers in which Rolland Munro has begun to open up our understanding of this theme of disposal (1995, 1998, 2001). Munro suggests that dirt or pollution can never be fully disposed of. What we do as consumers will not simply depend on the choices we make in deciding what to consume but also through an acknowledgement in advance of the "conduits for disposal" (1995, 313) that are available to us through which we can dispose of the meaning of the goods we consume. We put things in a supposedly stable context—dispose of them—so that we do not have to deal with their implications in a direct way. We do not just produce such implications when we acquire goods, we also dispose of them too by keeping certain things outside. An implication of this analysis is that the disposal outcome is not one of rubbishing but of placing, acknowledging that sometimes we cannot get rid of the consequences of our actions but that they hold us accountable by translating our actions into other forms that are "out of control." Disposal is a means, therefore, of managing our accountability and our debt to such transfiguring effects.

Disposal in this approach often becomes a question of accounting and of the way in which we use or deal with gaps with the unfinished disposal within our otherwise seamless representations.

> Gaps in our knowledge, whatever else they are, are also places in which the unspeakability of the Other can reenter. Where gaps are closed through exclusion, they are also fissures through which the Other can leak back in. (Munro 1998, 145)

Munro recognizes that representational stability, associated with acts of disposal, is never ultimately achieved as a form of closure. The idea that societies develop conduits of disposal that are themselves fluid and uncertain is a useful one here. Yet rather than see the rubbish bin as the archetypal conduit of disposal, I suggest the door is a better example. Not only do doors allow traffic in both directions when open, they can also be closed to keep things outside/inside, present/absent, at least temporarily and provisionally. Figuratively, the door better captures the role of the museum as a conduit of disposal within consumption. Conduits of disposal are not just implicated in changes of value of particular materials, but the fluidity of such conduits are also implicated in the establishment of social relations like those associated with stability, provenance, and trustworthiness. And some conduits are better at this than others because they are more readily implicated in established relations of trust. Disposal as a fluid practice is implicated in the ordering processes associated with representational stability. What it shows, though, is that change and transformation are a part of that process; indeed, one cannot always predict in advance what will remain in the category of rubbish and what will return highly valued. If we are, then, to fully understand the significance of disposal in relation to consumption and the place of the museum in relation to it, we need to open up our understanding of the fluid character of value. Certainly, disposal can be about binning something, but it can also be about forgetfulness (sometimes deliberate); it can even be about maintaining something in such a state of abeyance so that it does not become rubbish, not only in the home but in the institutions of public culture.

Consuming subjects of all kinds engage in acts of disposal with things that they have. But the erasure of an object is never complete. There is always a trace effect that is passed on by its absence. The question is not specifically about how an object gets placed but what happens to the ordering effects of that object within that placing. All acts of arrangement and ordering involve moving representations in order to stabilize them; but that sense of order, stillness, is rarely achieved in practice. Above all, then, disposal is about the mobilization of absence in the making of ordering processes through placing activity. Indeed, getting into the terrain of definitions, we might go a little further and say that disposal is about the mobilization, ordering, and arrangement of the *agency* of the absent.

Museums engage in the act of disposal principally through the process of singularization, and the narratives that they then tell though their displays around such singularized artifacts. To singularize an artifact is to dispose of its exchange value. But such an act of singularization translates that disposed value into other cultural values such as rarity, aura, importance, and so on. It is all about displaced cultural meanings. This may, of course, also have the unintended effect of promoting the monetary worth of a similar artifact elsewhere. Putting something in a museum confers a certain status on it and similar things not in the museum might therefore go up in value as a consequence. However, what really matters is that it is the disposal of exchange value that is at the center of the phantasmagoric story that the museum tells about monumental historical time (Maleuvre 1999).

While Benjamin is rather brief in what he says about museums in *The Arcades Project*, he has much more to say about collecting with convolute H dedicated to the theme and the figure of the collector that is useful here. Benjamin was himself an avid collector, notably of books, and *Arcades* is, above all, the work of a collector as much as a writer—a collection of forgotten fragments brought back into view in a new, if convoluted and allegorical, ordering, which aims to reveal new meaning through their re-contextualization. Convolute H on the collector is perhaps, then, the most autobiographical section of Benjamin's Arcades study. In it he begins to build up something of a picture of the collector as a type. As with the flâneur, Benjamin is ambiguous in his valuation of this character, seeing in him or her both the archetypal consuming subject possessed by his or her fetish possessions and also best able to see through the fetish status of the commodity that veils the object underneath because he or she is unconcerned with its exchange value.

The collector, Benjamin argues, engages in the act of removing things from their functional context (use value) and places them somewhere else in an imaginary and allegorical ream of constructed meaning (or what I have called in the previous chapter, following McCracken [1988], displaced meaning). While modern collecting is all about creating order and homology within a sense of a totality (a collection), collectors also construct convoluted stories through their collections. Indeed, Benjamin describes the collector as an allegorist who sees in a collection hidden knowledge about the past (1999a, 206 [H2,1]). Through this act of storytelling the collector is able to gain access to an archaic past that is resembled in the object and in so doing the collector takes on the role of refusing the commodity status of the object. Instead, the collector goes in search of the archaic status of the object (1999a, 210–11[H4,4; H4a,1]). Benjamin associates the collector with the imaginary construction of the past (as with the museum in the later convolute) through ideas about the discovery of a hidden archaic realm in the acts of accumulating, ordering, and storytelling associated with collections—and with experience as *Erfahrung*. Such a mode of apprehending the past is one that constructs a way of seeing that is counter to that of consumer society even if it is not fully removed from its logic.

Collecting is a form of singularization. Singularization is all about trying to produce a stop or pause in the biography of an artifact and to transfigure its value by telling another story around it and its companion artifacts. It is about trying to fix the artifact within the flow of value and allow it to hold a position of significance. In effect, it is about trying to establish the qualities of eternity and of memorialized history on things that are transient and will eventually pass away. What Benjamin and Maleuvre after him see in the museum is a dead static history of eternal recurrence that is fetishized as real and universal for the bourgeois subject. They argue that lived history disappears in such a space. Objects are decontextualized, but not in the sense of removing them from a sacred context and placing them in a secular one, but of removing them from the flow of time by placing them in a space of History.

CONCLUSION

In perhaps one of the most famous passages of all from Benjamin's work, the much quoted and analyzed passage on the angel of history from his enigmatic *Theses on the Philosophy of History* (1973b), he says:

> A Klee painting named "Angelus Novus" shows an angel looking as though he is about to move away from something he is fixedly contemplating. His eyes are staring, his mouth is open, his wings are spread. This is how one pictures the angel of history. His face is turned toward the past. Where we perceive a chain of events, he sees a single catastrophe which keeps piling wreckage upon wreckage and hurls it in front of his feet. The angel would like to stay, awaken the dead, and make whole what has been smashed. But a storm is blowing from Paradise; it has got caught in his wings with such violence that the angel can no longer close them. The storm irresistibly propels him into the future to which his back is turned, while the pile of debris before him grows skyward. The storm is what we call progress. (1973b, 249)

In the context of modernity, what is it, precisely, that the angel is looking at? Kia Lindroos in her close reading of this figure has suggested that the angel figure tries to bring the flow of progressive time to a standstill because that time is in fact one of hell (1998). In Benjamin's terms what the angel sees in the rubbish before it is a museum. The museum is a space of disposal. In disposing of the commodity through the singularization of the artifact it creates a static, ossified sense of history as monument. It seeks to deny the possibility of the uncertain flow of time that is the reality of the capitalist market. But disposal is double edged. What is gotten rid of (the commodity) remains as an absent-presence, something that Benjamin's dialectical images seek to reveal.

Perhaps the most useful account we have of disposal comes not from the study of museums or commodities but from the disposal of the dead in Robert Hertz's account of the practices of first and second burial within funeral rites (1960). Through a comparative study of funeral rites, Hertz was able to show the two-stage nature that those rites take in many cultures. Once a person has died, his or her family or community becomes responsible not only for the disposal of the bodily remains but also the soul. The act of disposal often involves an initial and provisional "burial," which may last from a few days to a number of years, depending on the particular culture in question. After that burial the remains are still available to the community. Subsequently, a second and more final burial will take place when the remains of the person disposed of finally will assume a form of closure once the soul is assumed to have passed on, often into the company of other souls.

It is what happens in the gap between these two burials that is of particular interest for Hertz and for us in considering the fluid composition of disposal and the museum. In part, this gap is a space for preparing the soul for its final place of rest and, in part, it involves the living honoring a debt they feel they have to the departed—a space for the construction of displaced meanings where the annihilating significance of death is held at bay. The ritual is, of course, in part about ordering and controlling possible sources of pollution and the unmanaged return of unsettled and maligned spirits, but it is also about the use that is made of absence within presence. The gap between first and second burial has both a temporal and a spatial dimension: interval in the first instance and segregation in the second. Disposal is an act of double take. Disposal of the body allows preparation for the soul before the final disposal of the body allows the soul to move on. The body is disposed of and then brought back before being finally disposed of. The gap—the time-space between the two funerals—is concerned with the motility of presence and absence and their enfolded state in a seemingly valueless/valuable set of material remains. It is a space of abeyance in which living persons (re)construct their identities through an extension of themselves beyond their own bodies in the realm of these material bodily remains. Remains are put at a distance representationally while remaining close physically in first burial, and then brought back as representationally close but physically distant after second burial. Through such rites of the double take, a debt is honored, the person and the soul of the departed reaches a settled state, and the person doing the honoring establishes a sense of who he or she is through a closure to the act of disposing.

The museum is such a space of the gap, a space where the commodity comes to rest, is stripped of its commodity status through singularization, and transfigured into something else that is seen as an instance of some aspect of the displaced meanings of bourgeois culture (memorialized history in general). In this respect the museum, like the arcade, is the door or portal to the buried space beneath the commodity logic while also being a part of that commodity logic too. More overtly than the arcade, it addresses the bourgeois conception of the past, of experience, and of the death and rebirth of the commodity. In that sense it is a space of the underground.

It is not the artifact itself that is disposed of in the museum—quite the contrary, in fact—but its associations with exchange value. It is the commodity status of the artifact that is seemingly disposed of through the conduit of the museum into some imaginary realm beyond, preserving instead a pristine memory of the artifact as culture rather than a product of the capitalist marketplace. At least, that is the overriding cultural intention of the museum as a space of singularization whereby commodities are returned to their status as "priceless" artifacts and works of art. As with other spaces of the fetish/phantasmagoria, its role is more creative and more ambiguous than the theory of commodity fetishism might suggest. The museum both affirms and denies consumer society in equal measure, and the bourgeois sense of monumental time is constructed out of the wreckage.

Afterword
Taking Possession

To take possession of the commodity is to possess it and to be possessed by it at the same time. That, perhaps, is the main point that I have argued in this book in contrast to most theories of commodity fetishism, which stress the latter sense and do not allow any scope for the former. Jeff Nunokawa makes a similar point in passing reference to this issue of taking possession of the commodity in the space of the home in his work on property in the domestic space, suggesting that it be seen as a tautology: "to possess is to take possession" (1994, 20). However, he does not situate this remark in its full phantasmagoric context. It is Benjamin's equally fleeting use of the term "taking possession" in relation to the figure of the collector in the 1935 exposé to *The Arcades Project* (1999b, 9) that further suggests this. Like many of his suggestive remarks, he does not develop them in detail. He repeats this theme of taking possession in the 1939 exposé too, albeit in a slightly different form, and that is noteworthy. What he says is in 1935 is:

> The interior is the asylum of art. The collector is the true resident of the interior. He makes his concern the transfiguration of things. To him falls the Sisyphean task of divesting things of their commodity character by taking possession of them. But he bestows on them only connoisseur value, rather than use value. The collector dreams his way not only into a distant or bygone world but also into a better one—one in which, to be sure, human beings are no better provided with what they need than in the everyday world, but in which things are freed from the drudgery of being useful. (1999b, 9)

In 1939, he says:

> The interior is the asylum where art takes refuge. The collector proves to be the true resident of the interior. He makes his concern the idealization of objects. To him falls the Sisyphean task of divesting things of their commodity character by taking possession of them. But he can bestow on them only connoisseur value, rather than use value. The collector delights in evoking a world that is not

just distant and long gone but also better—a world in which, to be sure, human
beings are no better provided with what they need than in the real world, but in
which things are freed from the drudgery of being useful. (1999c, 19)

The changes are subtle rather than dramatic. The main difference being that the early
reference to dreaming has been replaced by evoking—a more purposeful and con-
trolled act. In the former we might say that in its susceptibility to dreams, wishes,
and desires Benjamin is struggling toward a consumption view of the subject around
this figure of the collector—it might equally be of the consumer in general. However, after Adorno's criticisms of this piece, he draws back from that and returns to a
more familiar production view of the subject, one more recognizable from within the
Marxist tradition in the 1939 version. Yet that earlier interest is still there as a ghost in
The Arcades Project and can bee seen in Benjamin's other writings on surrealism, the
city, experience, time, and the distracted reception of cinematic works. The producing
subject is possessed by the ghosts in the phantasmagoria, by commodity fetishism.
The consuming subjects are too, but they also take possession of those ghosts in their
imaginations, their wishes, their dreams, and their consumer practices as well, and
in so doing transfigure them in practice, into displaced meanings, into stories about
themselves (identities) and the social relations that they inhabit. They are not so readily held in thrall, not so readily haunted/alienated/manipulated as a consequence of
this.

    This issue of the fetish has proven to be problematic in Marxism ever since
Marx first adopted the term through the trope of the phantasmagoria. Above all,
what has proved most problematic to Western understandings of the fetish is that
the fetish might be premised on figural rather than discursive knowledge and to
suggest that that might have validity in relation to the constitution of the subject. To
reevaluate figural forms of knowledge and practice (engaging with things, constructing displaced meanings, believing in the mythic stories that commodities tell) is not
to assert the salience of mythical, irrational, primitive, or religious understanding
against that of a rational scientific one, but it is to suggest that there are other ways
of knowing that are largely overlooked by the "realism" of this Marxist tradition,
common ways of knowing that are shown through the culturally expressed ways
in how people deal with objects within their lives. To argue this is to recognize
fetishism as a resource for knowledge practices and culturally established regimes of
curiosity rather than simply as the preeminent figure of unreason (see also Strathern
1988; Latour 1999, 2002; Howes 2003). As Latour puts it:

    Yet somehow the fetish gains in strength in the hands of the anti-fetishists. The
    more you want it to be nothing, the more action springs back from it. (1999,
    270)

This is the alternative position, a détourned one, to that offered by Marx and his followers, one that still recognizes the importance of the fetish within social relations but that does not resort to a fetishistic form of analysis when addressing it (see Latour 1999). It is a view that begins with the idea of subjectivity and of the subject as actively constituted through consumption and not just production; creative in the world of things and signs that is also the world of social relations. This is a subject that lives in a world of the fetish and finds ways of incorporating it into its life. The idea of culture, under whatever conditions we might attribute to it, is always already an idea of fetishistic mediation. The objective conditions of life draw things, including representations of things, into their constitution. That mediation will have a role in shaping what we call society and that society may be unjust, unequal, or may be said to be experienced as uncertain or contradictory, but that does not amount to a totality of manipulated consciousness through spectacle. Such a term does not account for the multiple ways and forms that the fetish might mediate social relations.

The spaces that I have looked at here can be better understood as surroundings, in the same way that the original phantasmagoria shows were a surrounding rather than just a projected image on a screen. In this respect the regime of curiosity of the modern phantasmagoria is different to that of the Medici palace or Baroque classifying table. Relations between subjects and objects and the effects they have in constituting each other have altered across this time. This is something that the theory of commodity fetishism has yet to account for. Each in its way is a form of spectacle, suggesting this complex term requires understanding as a historical specificity rather than a totalizing concept that mirrors a capitalist logic, or code of understanding.

In these modern surroundings, panoramic totalities that have a start in spaces like the Great Exhibition, that constitute the subject as a distracted participant unable to grasp the whole from any outside point of recognition, fetishes are not simply alienated ghostly products of once-creative labor that stand as separate from people; they are incorporated into what Mauss called the habitus that we learn through our practice. Our social life is constituted through extensions into this mediated world (McLuhan 1987; Strathern 1991; Munro 1996). This is not a product of capitalism per se; it is not even a condition peculiar to humans, although the idea of the human is inseparable from the idea of a mediated sociality (see Latour 2002). It is, however, where we might start in developing a consumption view of the subject. When the Portuguese and later Dutch traders first encountered the fetish as they traveled down the cost of West Africa, they were troubled by its significance— its multivalent and figural significance in particular—and sought to understand it in (Christian) discursive terms. Around that discourse over the succeeding centuries developed a view of the subject who produced and mastered the external world through rational knowledge and action as a subject of skilled vision; anyone who appeared himself to be mastered by that world, through his attribution of powers to the things around him, through his wants rather than needs, through his dreams, passions, and desires, to be consumed by him, came to be seen as primitive or fetishistic in this outlook. That ghost is still to be found in much of the post-Marxist writing on consumer culture that wishes to judge it in a critical light. It does this because for the most part it wants to start with an understanding of the subject as producer rather than consumer.

The direction that Benjamin points us in, even if he ultimately does not travel the full road, is to open up for us, under the sign of the phantasmagoria, a different way of thinking about the subject: someone who is constituted through consumption rather than through production. In this respect, that subject occupies the paradoxical space of possession—in exhibitions, shops, homes, museums, and no doubt in other spaces of consumption in ways that allow for a more complex and contested way of thinking about consumer practices within a capitalist society. These spaces of acquisition, use, and disposal are spaces of *both/and* rather than *either/or* composition; spaces of bewilderment, fantasy, manipulation, fragmented experience, mythical displaced meanings, and social membership. Like the first fetishists, but not like their succession of critics, we know as consumers how to treat commodities in multiple ways, know how to engage in the act of transfiguring their value through the allegorical, folded, détourned meanings we construct around them. It is in that place that the analysis of consumption should begin.

Notes

CHAPTER 1

1. Quoted in Henry Cole (1884, 197).
2. There is now an extensive literature on the history of consumption and urban culture that draws on the theme of spectacle with varying degrees of success (for instance, Clark 1984; Bowlby 1985; Richards 1991). I discuss this work in some detail in Chapter 2, where I analyze Debord's development of the term (1977).
3. The recently redeveloped British galleries in the Victoria and Albert Museum provide a gallery with some of the original exhibits on display and offer a commentary that reflects on these criticisms.
4. The 1889 Paris exhibition is also remembered but not for the exhibition as a whole—only for one building: the Eiffel Tower.
5. A number of books on the great exhibition were published in 1951 (see Luckhurst 1951; Fay 1951).
6. Although commentators such as Charles Babbage (1851) criticized the organizers for not taking up his suggestion that mechanical devices should be incorporated into turnstiles at the entrance to count the number of people entering the Palace, some fairly accurate figures are available on attendance that give not only absolute numbers but also some indication of social class composition of the visitors, through the fact that prices varied on different days to attract both the wealthy and those of humbler means. A full account of number and weekly takings can be found in John Timbs's *The Year-Book of Facts in the Great Exhibition of 1851* (1851, 337–342).
7. The British Library has a copy of a visitor survey style postcard "Industrial Exhibition Remembranced" that was given out to visitors to the Great Exhibition. They were asked to post it back with their comments. Visitors were asked to comment on their expenditure, the number of visits made, and the items of interest that they saw.
8. On the provincial reception of the exhibition, see Morris 1970.
9. This issue of character is one that I discuss in more detail in Chapter 6 on the domestic interior.
10. On the issue of improvement in general, see Briggs (1959) and Hetherington (2001).
11. For a clear illustration of this, see Robert Plot's survey of Staffordshire (1686).
12. See, for example, the opening lines of Adam Smith's *The Wealth of Nations*: "The greatest improvement in the productive powers of labour, and the greatest part of the skill, dexterity, and judgement with which it is anywhere directed or applied seems to have been the effects of the division of labour" (1922, 5).

13. Numerous poems and sermons were published about the exhibition too. There were also commemorative souvenirs, china, medals, and other ephemera available. Prints were also on sale: daguerreotype, mezzotints, and lithographs (some took photographs—still a very novel technique at the time). These were made available either as individual pictures or in the form of expensive plate books illustrated with steel engravings.

14. Henry Cole (1884) was perhaps the exception.

15. Marx and Engels, *Collected Works*, vol. 38, 1975, 348.

16. Marx and Engels in *Neue Rheinische Zeitung Revue*. http://www.marxists.org/archive/marx/works/1850/11/01.htm (accessed March 3, 2004).

17. I am grateful to John Urry for discussions on the importance of developments in the 1840s to the capitalist economy.

18. I discuss this term in more detail in Chapter 2.

19. In this panoptic spatial arrangement, much attention has been given to the central watchtower but not enough to the backlit cell. To focus on the watchtower alone within the panoptic arrangement is to reintroduce a subject-object set of relations that approximate the camera obscura, only placing an absent subject at the center rather than an image. To recognize that the technology of the panopticon involves all elements, including the cells, is to recognize the immersion of subject formation within the materiality of the object world. It is this latter view that I wish to follow here.

20. I discuss Crary's argument in more detail in Chapter 3.

21. On proximal understandings and their relationship to distal approaches, see Cooper and Law (1995).

22. The term surface of emergence that I use here comes from Foucault's *Archaeology of Knowledge* (1974, 41) and refers to that part of the rules of formation whereby an object comes to be discursively constituted, that is, concerned with the spatio-temporal configuration of formerly individual statements into a recognized discursive object that can be put into operation as such. The term is associated with the practices of enunciation amongst different groups around a particular discursive object. It is concerned above all with how some new object comes into being, and Foucault deploys it in order to challenge foundationalist understandings of origin or singular beginning, recognizing that surfaces of emergence of particular discourses will vary in time and space for different societies. I am concerned in this book, therefore, not with the origins of consumer society but with the surface of emergence of some of its key discursive objects. Methodologically the four spaces that I consider here—the Great Exhibition and, in later chapters, department stores, parlors, and museums—are, therefore, important as sites in which we see a surface of emergence of some aspect of the discourse of modern consumption as something new and recognizable. This aim should not be confused, therefore, with any sort of quest for origins.

23. On the processes of de-territorialization and re-territorialization, see Deleuze and Guattari (1988).

24. What this means will become apparent when I discuss the technique of détournment in Chapter 2.

CHAPTER 2

1. It might seem at first as if sociology in its beginnings in the late nineteenth century missed this moment of consumer culture. Consumption is not emphasized in the twentieth-century reception of early sociology. Certainly it is something diminished by Parson's mid-century establishment of the sociological canon (1937). Rather, it is

often seen to be 1950s America that is taken as the beginning for the study of consumer culture within sociology (Riesman 1950; Packard 1961). However, as Williams has shown, consumption was a major source of social scientific anxiety in France in the latter years of the nineteenth century. Many of the sociologists at the time, not least Durkheim and Tarde, were centrally concerned with the effects of consumption upon social solidarity (Williams 1982). Likewise, German sociologists such as Simmel and Sombart, among others, are centrally concerned with consumption. Indeed, even Weber's classic study of the origins of modern, acquisitive capitalism in the Protestant Reformation is premised on the denial of hedonistic, consumer pleasures (1985), at least until the eighteenth century (see Campbell 1987). Later too, Elias's figurational sociology of the civilizing process and of court society is centrally concerned with issues of consumption (1978, 1983).

2. For a discussion of Clark's involvement with the Situationists, see Gray (1974) and Clark and Nicholson-Smith (1997).

3. Sadie Plant makes the argument that Raoul Vaniegem, particularly in his book *The Revolution of Everyday Life* (1983), deserves to be treated as equally important to Debord's *Society of the Spectacle*. The argument is unconvincing. While Vaniegem may well have had some influence among followers of the Situationists in the anarchist milieu of the 1970s and 1980s, his writings have had little impact elsewhere. Certainly the culture of playful protest that he advocates remains an important part of radical protest—its latest manifestation being the anticapitalist protests of the 1990s—but this tradition of theater and joissance within protest predates Vaniegem's analysis.

4. Debord quotes this passage from Feuerbach at the beginning of Chapter 1 of *The Society of the Spectacle* (1977). Contrary to Debray's (1995) accusation of plagiarism against Debord, he is in fact engaging in a form of détournement and not plagiarism throughout that book as well as in much of his other writings. While there are some useful observations in Debray's critique, his analysis is rather marred by his drift into a rather facile character assassination. For a critique of Debray, equally bad in its penchant for critique by character assassination, see Clark and Nicholson-Smith (1997).

5. Baudrillard's early work (which emerged from much the same radical milieu as Debord) has considerable similarities with Debord, notably *The System of Objects* (1996 [1968]) and *The Consumer Society* (1998 [1970]). It is still present in later work on simulation and hyperreality (1983). Baudrillard was to undergo something of a similar transformation in reception in Anglo-American academic work during the 1980s as Debord; the early publication of a couple of his books by the critical theory journal *Telos* in the 1970s (1975, 1981) was to give way to a flood of books and essays in the past decade as well as to a plethora of secondary analysis thereafter.

6. In the film script, written in 1961, for *Critique of Separation*, Debord is quite clear in his use of the cinema as illustrating the condition of separation and stasis that exists in capitalist society. The cinema is seen as a passive and immobilizing form of theatricality in which the dead time of the spectacle is presented through forms of mobile pseudo-adventure that are separated from communal life and a lived theatricality. In the cinema, as in the city, we find again an example of an argument against the spatialization of time (see Levin 1989). The audience is assumed to be passive, immobile, and isolated (clearly there was little actual ethnographic work on cinema audiences behind this observation).

Yet, like earlier avant-garde groups, the Situationists saw the potential for cinema as a potential medium for understanding the world but one that had been colonized by capitalism early on, and that now used it to its own ends in providing simple forms of spectacular entertainment. The dismissal of mainstream cinema (and indeed avant-garde cinema too—Godard is given the full treatment) on these grounds is reminiscent of Adorno, and Horkheimer adds little to their critique of Hollywood (Adorno and Horkheimer 1979). Where Debord differs from Adorno, though, is that he actually made films himself, seven in all between 1952 and 1992. As in the critique of urbanism, where a psychogeographical alternative was offered to planning, in cinema too, Debord sought to offer an alternative form of cinema that would serve as a critique of the capitalist spectacle in this arena. His first film was *Hurlements en faveur de Sade* (1952). This consisted of a film made up of a series of totally black and totally white screens with a disconnected voice-over (five voices) made up of a series of détournements from avant-garde texts, literature, and popular expressions (see Levin 1989). The last twenty minutes are totally silent and the screen is completely blank (only the sounds from the auditorium can be discerned). The film caused a minor riot when it was first shown in Paris and angry protests from the audience when shown at the ICA in London in 1960 (Levin 1989, 82). Debord sought to turn the showing of the film itself into an event—a situation (he succeeded)—rather than its content, which is basically about nothing except the banality of sitting for over an hour watching nothing while thinking one is going to see something juicy from de Sade at some point. The point is clear and today seems rather facile, although it probably needed to be made. Later films such as *Sur le Passage de Quelque Personnes a Travers une Assez Courte Unite de Temps* (On the Passage of a Few People through a Rather Brief Moment in Time); a film version of *The Society of the Spectacle* (Debord 1992); *Critique de la Separation*; and *In Girum Imus Nocte et Conmumimur Igni* (a palindrome that means "we go round in circles in the night and are consumed by fire") (Debord 1991) all continue to use the practice of détourned images, words, and text but are often constructed around a story of the activity of the Situationists themselves as well as of the Paris they felt was disappearing. All aim to convey the theory of the spectacle and to use cinema as a critique of cinema as a form of spectacle. As Levin puts it, the films seek to challenge the false coherence offered by a capitalist cinema through a détournement of its techniques, use of narrative, and spectacular images (1989).

There is little written on Debord's films, in large part because he stopped them from being shown when, in 1984, sections of the French press tried to implicate him in the murder of his publisher and friend Gerard Lebovice. But the texts that we do have are of a piece with Situationist writing, its early use of détourned artworks, and continual practice of détourning images such as advertisements. The practice of détournement, like the dérive within the city, is concerned with the establishment of a rupture, a punctum, in the spatializing of time and the pseudo-history provided by the city planners and by film directors in their different media. As a source of intervention, it seeks to bring movement into what it sees as a condition of stasis that encourages isolation, separation, and passivity in its audiences. Above all, though, it was through the idea of the event—the situation—that the Situationists sought to develop their critique of the spectacle into a form of praxis.

7. I discuss Benjamin's approach to commodity fetishism, including issues of eternal recurrence, in detail in Chapter 4.

8. Cornelius Castoriadis and Jean-Francois Lyotard were both at one time members of the group (Gombin 1978; Plant 1992). It is notable for its concern not only with the development of capitalism but also with the increasing pervasiveness of bureaucracy within a technocratic society. The Marxist two-class model of capitalists and proletariat, central to nineteenth-century industrial capitalism, was, this group argued, being transformed into a bureaucratic service economy of order givers and order takers, where managerialism had replaced ownership as the central question of capitalist

power relations. Along with Lefebvre's critique of everyday life in capitalist societies, this group was to have some considerable influence on Debord's understanding of spectacular society.

9. Debord later suggests that the spectacle, as he describes it in the *Society of the Spectacle* (where no date for its origin is given), begins in the late 1920s (1990; see also Crary 1997). He goes on to suggest in this later work that we have seen a shift from the earlier diffused form of spectacle to one that has subsequently become integrated. All forms of resistance to the latter are apparently futile—indeed, seen as the product of the spectacle itself, "The society whose modernization has reached the stage of integrated spectacle is characterized by the combined effect of five principle features: incessant technological renewal; integration of state and economy; generalized secrecy; unanswerable lies; an eternal present" (1990, 11–12).

10. For over two centuries Paris has been understood as a city of movement, of mobilization, and of activism in particular. From the crowds that mingled, assembled, and organized in the gardens of the Palais Royal in the 1780s (Hetherington 1997), to the social revolutions on the street in 1832 and especially 1848, to the commune of 1871 (Ross 1988), the modernity of Paris is a modernity of the street, the barricade, and of the mobile body of the crowd. In the periodic tumult of Paris between 1789 and 1871 it would be easy to see a contrast between the lived reality of the street, bohemia, and the barricade on the one hand and that of the spectacle of the arcade, the boulevard, and the department store on the other: a contrast between action and passivity in particular. Yet as Benjamin shows us, things are perhaps not that simple (1973a). But wind forward to the 1950s. After the experiences of war, occupation, and then liberation, France began to open itself up to modernization again. City planners were brought in to zone the city, and ramshackle old slum quartiers were demolished to be replaced by buildings in a functionalist, modernist architectural style (Sadler 1999). As in Britain, consumer culture came late but rather rapidly to France from the mid-1950s after a period of postwar restructuring. Premised on consumer durables and on the car, this was to have an influence on the character of urban life—reasserting the values of the nuclear family and the culture of privatism associated with it. And while the processes of suburbanization might not have been as strong in France as they were in America or Britain, it was clear that the French city was changing in a similar direction.

The Situationists (and their forerunners the Lettrists) were among the first to notice and to critique these processes of transformation. In many respects, they were as significant in scope as the much more commented upon changes to Paris in the 1860s. The Situationists' critique was of the spread of the capitalist relations of production into areas beyond production—consumption and social reproduction—and that critique was expressed through a nostalgia for the activism and community of the street and quartier of earlier times (several years before Jane Jacobs was to say similar things about street life and the American city, 1961). The Situationists were themselves based in the area of the St. Germain de Prés, just as many of the avant-garde of the 1920s and 30s had been also. From that vantage point they looked on in dismay at a disappearing city.

The Surrealists had already noticed the ruins of the capitalist city in the 1920s. Breton's *Nadja* (1960 [1928]) and Aragon's *Le Paysan de Paris* (1987 [1924–26]) found a source of imaginative wonder in the ruins of the arcades, gardens, and run-down flea markets of Paris (Nadeau 1987 [1944]). But for them this was a source of wonderment rather than critique. They continued the tradition of flânerie, strolling through the city searching for chance encounters, imaginative inspiration, and the uncanny just as Rimbaud and Lautréamont in the 1870s, Baudelaire in the 1860s, Restif de la Bretonne in the 1790s, and Rousseau in the 1760s had done before them in their own ways. But those writers up to the Surrealists were fascinated by the modernity of the new; for the Surrealists, it was the juxtaposition of the old with the new that was more a source of fascination. In the Situationists, that fascination turned into nostalgia, critique, and a potential form of revolutionary activity in equal measure.

11. I discuss Lukacs's analysis of reification in more detail in Chapter 4.

CHAPTER 3

1. While there have been attempts to apply Freudian (or, more specifically, Lacanian) ideas about the sexual fetish to a more general inquiry about commodity fetishism (notably Zizek 1989), most recent debate surrounding Freudian approaches to the fetish have come from feminists seeking to challenge the idea that fetishism is the sole preserve of men and rare in women. The importance of fetishism for women, and within lesbian culture in particular, is in the making of identities and in challenging the gender binarism and heterosexism associated with the Freudian legacy (see, for example, Apter 1991; Apter and Pietz 1993; Grosz 1995, 1995; McCallum 1999). In this context, a recognition of the inter-cultural origins of the fetish, and its implicit challenge to the idea that cultures encounter one another separately rather than within a paradoxical space of mingling, is applied as a demonstration of "intersex" or "intergender" position that challenges the Western constructions of sex and gender and its essentialist thinking (Butler 1990, 1993).

2. I am grateful to Bob Jessop for discussion of *Capital* in German.

3. See http://www.marxists.org/archive/marx/ (accessed March 3, 2004).

4. This is something that was recognized, above all, by Walter Benjamin in his *Arcades Project* (1999a), and the term was to become influential in the development of Western Marxism in the twentieth century. I discuss this in detail in Chapter 4.

5. Interestingly, the Palais Royal was also the site of the first spaces of modern consumer culture, the Arcades, (Geist 1985) which, as we shall see in the next chapter, have taken on the figurative significance of an origin for consumer culture (Benjamin 1999a).

6. I discuss this issue in more detail in relation to the development of the museum in Chapter 7.

7. Surprisingly, Crary does not make this point. His discussion of the phantasmagoria is brief and one that relegates it to a position of marginal significance in his otherwise important narrative (1990, 132–33).

CHAPTER 4

1. From the philosophical preface to Benjamin's Trauerspiel study (1985c, 56).

2. As is well known, Marx's 1844 manuscripts were not published until the 1930s. His earlier work on alienation, therefore, was not available to Marxist scholars until that time. Instead, a new theory of alienation was developed prior to this, initially in a non-Marxist context, by Georg Simmel in his 1900 *The Philosophy of Money* (1990). This text influenced Lukacs, a one-time student of Simmel, who sought to develop a Marxist theory of alienation by going back to Hegel's discussion of the theme of subject-object identification (see Avineri 1968; Feenberg 1981; Jay 1984).

3. This was certainly true until the 1960s when the adoption of Lacanian structuralism and an antihumanist argument into Marxism offered an alternative strand to Western Marxism than that offered by those in the Lukacsian tradition (see Althusser 1969, 1971).

4. Strictly speaking, Debord is not "post-Marxist." Rather, his work can be seen as a return to Lukacs through a critical reception of the work of Marxist writers on everyday life like Lefebvre, influences from 1920s council-communism, and the surrealist avant-garde tradition and its postwar successors (see Plant 1992).

5. Benjamin is the one, albeit ambiguous, exception here in that he retains a focus on the materiality of the commodity and of commodity culture in general.

6. This thing/image reversal is taken to its totalizing conclusion in Debord in 1967, exactly one hundred years after Marx published *Capital*.

7. The writer who later goes on to develop this argument to its fullest extent is Henri Lefebvre in his analysis of capitalist spatiality, notably through his conception of representational spaces (1991).

8. There is a short essay by Lukacs on the relationship between theatre and popular cinema (2001) that sees theater as the site of serious metaphysical reflection being debased by popular theatrical entertainments. For Lukacs, the cinema will come to take the place of popular theater, leaving theater once again as the space for serious reflection on the conditions of existence. However, this essay was written in 1913, some ten years before *History and Class Consciousness* and therefore cannot be seen as a reflection of his Marxist approach to reification and alienation that only begins after his turn to Marxism in 1918.

9. For an early and influential argument along these lines, see Alan Swingewood's *The Myth of Mass Culture* (1977). Simply dismissing Adorno's criticisms of the culture industry on grounds that he had elite tastes in art and music, and that elitism is automatically a bad undemocratic thing, has become commonplace within cultural studies in recent years with its celebration of audience reception as a skilled practice. His position is often counterposed to that in Benjamin's essay "The Work of Art in the Age of Mechanical Reproduction" (1973a). While there are criticisms to be made of Adorno's argument, this is one of the weakest and least useful. As he recognized, the issue was not one of taste (1991a) but of the subject's position in relation to the cultural object and of the extension of exchange value into the realm of use value. It is his argument around these subject-object relations that should be subject to critique, not his liking for difficult bourgeois art. Similarly, Benjamin's argument is not as populist and uncritical of audience reception of some of his supporters like to assume.

10. Phantasmagoria is just one area of critical analysis that Adorno gives us of Wagner. The others include gesture, motif, sonority, musical color, drama, myth, and chimera (1981). A critique of the theme of illusory effect as a presentation of reality is central throughout.

11. Neither Aragon nor Benjamin considers the possibility that rubbish might help reproduce exchange value by becoming desirable in its own right. Luxuries don't just turn into rubbish; quite often they can turn back into desirable and collectable luxuries again at a later point. On the dynamics of rubbish in the making of exchange value and the reputation of certain forms of material culture, see Thompson's *Rubbish Theory* (1979); on issues of consumption and disposal as a recursive process, see Hetherington (2004). While in the twenty-first century there are still many provincial arcades that have closed down or retain the seediness that Benjamin describes, others have gone upmarket again. Likewise, the glass-roofed space of the arcade became an important architectural reference for many glass atriums that were a part of the design of 1980s shopping malls. While Benjamin is right to challenge the linear myth of progress, he

still sees "disposal as end point" in rather too linear a fashion. While the myth of progress is still with us, so too are the myths of "heritage" and "nostalgia" that capitalist enterprises have made much use of (see Huyssen 1995, 2003).

12. Although Benjamin never makes the point, the phantasmagoria shows are the arcades' direct contemporary—becoming popular at the same time (and beginning in the same place—the Palais Royal) and going into decline at the same time (in the case of the phantasmagoria, as developments in photography became more sophisticated and the techniques of concealment more widely known).

13. Marx/phantasmagoria perhaps? Given that Marx did spend some time in Paris in the 1840s.

14. For Adorno's overview of Benjamin's work, see his essay on him in his book *Prisms* (1967, 229–41).

15. Adorno's full name was Theodor Wiesengrund Adorno.

16. Ironically, perhaps, the camera obscura is an important device in the history of the mechanical reproduction of images.

17. Siegfried Kracauer offers a similar argument in his discussion of distraction at the cinema (1995).

CHAPTER 5

1. Rappaport makes use of Rose's (1993) argument about paradoxical space in the creation of the shopping West End in London in the later Victorian–Edwardian period (2000). Her main concern is to see this space as a space of female hedonism. There are, however, a number of other paradoxes that we can associate with this space, which I discuss below.

2. It goes without saying that consumer culture did not begin with women shopping in department stores after 1860 (on the history of shopping, see Aldburgham 1964). By talking about a start, I am choosing my words carefully. I am not trying to tell a foundational story about origins/beginnings, just as I am not trying to ignore the significance of consumption in earlier times that we call "modern" (Sombart 1967; McKendrick et al. 1982; Campbell 1987; Weatherill 1988; Brewer and Porter 1993), nor the place that women played in the significance that consuming had in defining it (Kowaleski-Wallace 1997). Rather, a start refers to a surface of emergence (Foucault 1974), a time-space where a particular configuration of both discursive and nondiscursive practices come to challenge what went before and to define what is to come, thereby naturalizing it.

3. This chapter looks at the issues of desire and acquisition. The two that follow do so through a linear narrative that addresses issues of use (home) and disposal (museum). In practice, this linear story does not exist, as these three sets of practices are implicated and folded into one another in complex ways. I will return to this issue in the conclusion. Another way of looking at it is that I treat the department store as a space for the making of the subject, the home for subject-object connections, and the museum as a space for the making of the object in consumer society. Again the narrative device belies the complexity of the issues involved and I return to that in the conclusion too. It should start to become apparent that the reason why I began this book with an illustrative chapter on the Great Exhibition is because it condenses all of these issues into one space. It was, in effect, a model for the department store, the domestic interior, and the museum, all rolled into one, with all the messiness that such complexity would inevitably produce.

4. For studies of other stores, see, for instance (for UK department stores), Mass Observation's study of Browns in Chester (1947), Corina's study of Debenhams (1978), Honeycombe's study of Selfridges (1984), and Rappaport's study of the development of the shopping West End in London focused on Whiteley's (2000). For a general study of U.S. department stores, see Hendrickson (1979), Leach (1993); for particular studies, see Kogan and Wendt's study of Marshall Fields (1952).

5. Burlington Arcade in London with its leather travel goods, cashmeres, antique pens, jewelry, and handmade shoes comes to mind.

6. Looking through the Harrods catalog for 1895 is much like looking at the catalogs for the Great Exhibition in their overwhelming scale. The differences are that the Harrods catalog's classification is easier to follow and prices are listed.

7. Earlier versions of this consumption thesis can be found in Sombart's work on the importance of luxury as an impetus for fashion and taste among the elites in the European courts of the early-modern period (1967), and Bataille's emphasis on dealing with issues of expenditure, profligacy, and waste in the ordering of social relations (1991); both, in their very different ways, place consumption rather than production at the center of thinking about what drives societies to develop and change. This is quite in contrast to the productivism found in the work of the political economists of the Enlightenment, which culminates in Marx's theories of capitalist society (1938; see Baudrillard 1975).

8. There were some exceptions, such as Liberty of London, which was an important outlet after 1870 for promoting the artifacts of the arts and crafts movement that, inspired by William Morris and others, established itself on making handmade, quality designed, and craft production principles (such as truth to materials and revealed construction) in opposition to the kind of mass production found in most department stores of the day (Calloway 1992).

9. Some department stores are still ordered like this. For example, if one goes to Libertys on Regent Street in London, one finds the sale items and end-of-line goods in the basement; departments are then arranged on different succeeding floors, culminating in the top floor, which is given over to expensive antiques, many of which reflect the types of goods sold originally in that store during the period from about 1870–1920 (arts and crafts influenced) as well as modern designer pieces.

10. The theater was also an important influence (Miller 1981, 186).

11. There are notable exceptions. Miller's study of the Bon Marché adopts a Weberian argument that focuses on issues of rationalization and paternalism within bourgeois culture (1981), and Lancaster's account of British department stores is critical of much recent theorizing, preferring to offer instead an empiricist historical account (1995).

12. Williams suggests, though she does not fully develop the argument, that a commodity fetishized/reified way of seeing is a stage within the ongoing civilizing process (1982, 148ff.). Elias's developmental model of the internal passification of desires and the development of a more rational subject, which itself applies Freud's analysis in *Civilization and its Discontents* (1985) to a historical study of a thousand years of European history (Elias 1978, 1983), is used by Williams to suggest that fetishized ways of seeing are primitive and in the process of being developed over time into something more rational. Her argument looks at the development of the department store in France from the 1860s and the concerns over the impact of consumption on social solidarity among leading French social theorists of the late nineteenth century, of whom Durkheim is most prominent (1964). Their concerns seem to echo the reasons versus passions debates among Enlightenment thinkers of the previous century (Hirschman 1977) but set the tone in French thought for an anticonsumerist stance (Debord 1977; Baudrillard 1981, 1983, 1990).

13. Recent feminist analysis of the department store and middle-class women's life in the city in general has begun more in this direction (Wilson 1991; Walkowitz 1992; Rappaport 2000; Parsons 2003). I discuss this analysis in this chapter.

14. Benjamin is as much influenced here by Simmel's treatment of the modern city (1971a) as a space of strangers who are bombarded by stimuli and must experience the world in a new way and develop ways of coping with the shocks and uncertainties that modern life creates (Benjamin 1973a, 38).

15. This essay was originally published in 1985.

16. I discuss this issue of woman as a blank figure in more detail in the next chapter on the space of the domestic interior.

17. For a similar line of argument but from a quite different approach (a Hegelian one), Daniel Miller has argued that we see the housewife as the vanguard of history and the bringer of change (1995).

18. I will explore the paradoxical situation of the object in my chapter on the museum (Chapter 7).

19. On the cultural shift from character to personality in the nineteenth century, see Susman (2003) and Sennett (1977). Again, this is something I discuss in more detail in the next chapter.

CHAPTER 6

1. For a discussion of the cultural significance of the practice of bricolage, see Levi-Strauss's *The Savage Mind* (1966). The term was taken up and adopted as a key concept for understanding the cultural practices of youth subcultures in the postwar years, notably by Dick Hebdige and other members of the Birmingham school for cultural studies during the 1970s (Hall and Jefferson 1976; Hebdige 1979).

2. For an exception that draws on Benjamin, see Remy Saisselin's *Bricabracomania* (1985).

3. Susman's research was carried out in the United States and while some elements of this discourse are particular to that country the general tenor of this discourse can also be applied to European nations as well, providing that we note that there are subtle variations based on the different cultural histories of each particular society. Republican virtues such as those associated with the ideals of democracy were never as strong in Britain or France, for instance.

4. In the eighteenth century, character was forged in exclusive spaces within the public sphere such as the club or Masonic lodge. In the nineteenth century, it is the home that becomes central (Sennett 1977; Hetherington 1997, chapter 5).

5. On the legislative rather than interpretive role of experts at this time, see Bauman's *Legislators and Interpreters* (1987).

6. Norbert Elias has looked at how similar processes worked in the aristocratic courts of earlier times, not just in manners books but also in the proper use and display of material culture (1978, 1983).

7. One of the key features that I identified in Chapter 5 was the distinction between character and personality in the two models. I did not discuss it in relation to the department store but intend to do so here in relation to the home interior, where its characteristics are more apparent.

8. A succession of subsequent "culture and personality" writers during the 1970s, including Susman, took up these issues and sought to use them to understand the direction that American consumer society was going in after the 1960s and the impact that it was having on individuals and dominant personality types. Daniel Bell (1974), Richard

Sennett (1977), John Carroll (1977), and Christopher Lasch (1979) all sought to identify the defining personality type of the time and sit in moral judgment upon it. The model that emerged and that has stuck is that of a typically insecure narcissistic personality that is in constant need of both gratification and recognition by others. This is seen to develop variously as the result of (i) cultural trends that developed out of the privatism of the nineteenth-century bourgeois interior (Sennett), with the fragmenting of bourgeois public culture beginning with modernism in the 1920s (Bell), or (ii) with the impact of 1960s counterculture and its erosion of traditional patriarchal cultural values (Lasch). I do not intend to discuss all of this work in detail here, as much of it is interested in a later time beyond the scope of this book (for my discussion of this work, see Hethering- ton 1998, chapter 2). Clearly, though, along with Susman's argument, which has been taken up in discussions of the Victorian interior (Bronner 1989; Agnew 1989; Halttunen 1989), Sennett's highly influential *The Fall of Public Man* (1977) is directly relevant here. Sennett discusses the rise of personality in the private sphere of the Victorian home and the undermining of an earlier public personality that existed in the eighteenth century as the bourgeoisie retreated from the public to the private sphere. For him, the privatized, narcissistic emphasis on the cultivation of personality that defines our time begins here and then becomes increasingly pervasive and increasingly public during the subsequent century. His argument might be read as a historical elaboration of Susman's thesis about the shift from character to personality after about 1880.

9. For a summary of the role of the zero signifier, see the paper I wrote with Nick Lee (Hetherington and Lee 2000). For a broader study of the cultural history of the number zero and its signifying role, see Brian Rotman's *Signifying Nothing* (1987). The person who has done most to develop a philosophical understanding of the idea of the blank figure and its role in the performance of social orders is Michel Serres (1982, 1991).

CHAPTER 7

1. Susan Buck-Morss (1989) does not make any reference to the museum in her influen- tial study of Benjamin's *Arcades Project*.

2. I draw on this earlier piece of my own in this chapter (1999). In that earlier analysis, I was interested in using the history of the museum to study the history of a key trope in actor-network theory: heterogeneity. Here, I am more concerned with how the museum has shaped how subjects see and the relationship of that to the question of the disposal of the commodity.

3. This observation on the two key influences of Foucault and Bourdieu is made by Chia- Ling Lai in her unpublished doctoral thesis, "Museums in Motion" (2004).

4. A similar argument has been developed recently by Andreas Huyssen in his broader analysis of the urban-based heritage industry in the late twentieth century (1995, 2003). Here, too, the regeneration of cities through conserving the past and "museu- mification" is seen as a form of forgetting, where the past's lived reality is transformed into a fetishized idea of the past. It is as if the nineteenth-century phantasmagoria of progress has been replaced with a twentieth-century one of heritage.

5. On the nonlinear layering of cities in time, see also Michel Serres's *Rome* (1991).

6. This section draws on a chapter I published in the *Sociological Review Monograph*, "Actor-Network Theory and After." I am grateful to the publishers for allowing me to reproduce sections of it here.

7. The significance of museums in aiding the development of the symbolic economy of a city (see Zukin 1995) is not a new one.
8. For an interesting discussion of the influence of this work by Heidegger on Foucault (1989), see Stuart Elden's *Mapping the Present* (2001).
9. The ancient art of memory was a mnemonic device used in classical times by political orators as part of the skill of rhetoric. A speaker, living in a time before printing, had to devise a method of remembering a speech and delivering it in such a way as to try and convince the audience of the validity of the argument. This was done by associating parts of the speech with parts of a remembered building and the objects contained within it. The speaker learned the skill of being able to travel through the building in his mind's eye, in his memory, looking at its architectural features and the objects within it—its materiality—associating each of those features with a part of his speech. A distinct route was followed and, in so doing, the speaker was able to remember each part of his speech faultlessly and, in some cases, was able to deliver an oration fluently for hours without need for any other prompt. This art of memory was rediscovered during the classical age and given a new meaning. Philosophers like Giordino Bruno adapted this memory skill into a hermetic skill used in the attempted discovery of secret and lost knowledge that was believed to be encoded in the symbolism of the architectural features of buildings (Rykwert 1980; Yates 1992). Buildings, architectural features, and gardens were believed to contain symbols and ciphers that, if the similitude of correspondences could be correctly interpreted, would reveal secret or forgotten knowledge, known only to the ancients, and to the skilled interpreter.
10. The scandal referred to here is that associated with the introduction of paper money in Scotland in the late seventeenth century (Rotman 1987, 48–49), where people lost their wealth by buying into the paper money system.
11. This section is in part based on a previously published paper on disposal (Hetherington 2004).

Bibliography

Abelson, E. 1989. *When Ladies Go A-Thieving: Middle-Class Shoplifters in the Victorian Department Store*. New York: Oxford University Press.

Adburgham, A. 1964. *Shops and Shopping, 1800–1914*. London: George Allen and Unwin.

Adorno, T. 1967. *Prisms*. London: Spearman.

Adorno, T. 1981. *In Search of Wagner*. London: Verso.

Adorno, T. 1991a. On the fetish character in music and the regression of listening. In *The Culture Industry: Selected Essays on Mass Culture*, 26–52. London: Routledge.

Adorno, T. 1991b. Culture industry reconsidered. In *The Culture Industry: Selected Essays on Mass Culture*, 85–92. London: Routledge.

Adorno, T. 2002. Letters to Walter Benjamin. In *Aesthetics and Politics: The Key Texts of the Classic Debate Within German Marxism*, T. Adorno, W. Benjamin, E. Bloch, B. Brecht, G. Lukacs, 110–133. London: Verso.

Adorno T., W. Benjamin, E. Bloch, B. Brecht, and G. Lukacs. 2002. *Aesthetics and Politics: The Key Texts of the Classic Debate within German Marxism*. London: Verso.

Adorno, T. and M. Horkheimer. 1979. *The Dialectic of Enlightenment*. London: Verso.

Agamben, G. 1993. *Infancy and History: On the Destruction of Experience*. London: Verso.

Agnew, J-C. 1986. *Worlds Apart: The Market and the Theatre in Anglo-American Thought, 1550–1750*. Cambridge, UK: Cambridge University Press.

Agnew, J-C. 1989. A house of fiction: Domestic interiors and the commodity aesthetic. In *Consuming Visions: Accumulation and Display of Goods in America, 1880–1920*, ed. S. Bronner, 133–155. New York: Norton.

Aldburgham, A. 1964. *Shops and Shopping, 1800–1914*. London: George Allen and Unwin.

Alpers, S. 1983. *The Art of Describing: Dutch Art in the Seventeenth Century*. London: Penguin.

Althusser, L. 1969. *For Marx*. Harmondsworth, UK: Penguin.

Althusser, L. 1971. *Lenin and Philosophy*. London: New Left Books.

Altick, R. 1978. *The Shows of London*. Cambridge, MA: Belknap Press of Harvard University Press.

Amato, J. 2001. *Dust: A History of the Small and the Invisible*. Berkeley: University of California Press.

Anderson, B. 1983. *Imagined Communities: Reflections on the Origins and Spread of Nationalism*. London: Verso.

Anonymous. 1989. Detournement as negation and prelude. In *The Situationist International Anthology*, ed. K. Knabb, 55–56. Berkeley CA: Bureau of Public Secrets.

Appadurai, A. 1986. Introduction: Commodities and the politics of value. In *The Social Life of Things: Commodities in Cultural Perspective*, ed. A. Appadurai, 3–63. Cambridge, UK: Cambridge University Press.

Appelbaum, D. 1995. *The Stop*. New York: SUNY.

Apter, E. 1991. *Feminizing the Fetish: Psychoanalysis and Narrative Obsession in Turn-of-the-Century France*. Ithaca, NY: Cornell University Press.

Apter, E. and W. Pietz, eds. 1993. *Fetishism as Cultural Discourse*. Ithaca, NY: Cornell University Press.

Aragon, L. 1987. *Paris Peasant*. London: Picador.

Arato, A. and P. Breines. 1979. *The Young Likacs and the Origins of Western Marxism*. London: Pluto Press.

Arnold, M. 1960. *Culture and Anarchy*. Cambridge, UK: Cambridge University Press.

The Art Journal Illustrated Catalogue of the Industry of All Nations: 1851. 1851. London: George Virtue.

Asendorf, C. 1993. *Batteries of Life: On the History of Things and Their Perception in Modernity*. Berkeley: University of California Press.

Atkins, G. 1978. *Asger Jorn: The Crucial Years*. London: Lund Humphreys.

Auerbach, J. 1999. *The Great Exhibition of 1851: A Nation on Display*. New Haven, CT: Yale University Press.

Avineri, S. 1968. *The Social and Political Thought of Karl Marx*. Cambridge, UK: Cambridge University Press.

Babbage, C. 1851. *The Exposition of 1851; Or, The Views of the Industry, the Science, and the Government of England*. London: John Murray.

Bachelard, G. 1969. *The Poetics of Space*. Boston: Beacon Press.

Bacon, F. 1974. *The Advancement of Learning*. Oxford, UK: Clarendon Press.

Bakhtin, M. 1984. *Rabelais and His World*. Bloomington: Indiana University Press.

Bann, S. 1995. Shrines, curiosities, and the rhetoric of display. In *Visual Display: Culture Beyond Appearances,* eds. L. Cooke and P. Wollen, 14–29. Seattle, WA: Bay Press.

Barnouw, E. 1981. *The Magician and the Cinema*. New York: Oxford University Press.

Barrows, S. 1981. *Distorting Mirrors: Visions of the Crowd in Late Nineteenth-Century France*. New Haven, CT: Yale University Press.

Barthes, R. 1973. *Mythologies*. London: Paladin.

Bataille, G. 1991. *The Accursed Share*. New York: Zone Books.

Baudelaire, C. 1964. The painter of modern life. In *The Painter of Modern Life and Other Essays*, 1–40. New York: Da Capo Press of Phaidon Press.

Baudelaire, C. 1970. *Paris Spleen*. New York: New Directions.

Baudrillard, J. 1975. *The Mirror of Production*. St. Louis, MO: Telos Press.

Baudrillard, J. 1981. *For a Critique of the Political Economy of the Sign*. St. Louis, MO: Telos Press.

Baudrillard, J. 1983. *Simulations*. New York: Semiotexte.

Baudrillard, J. 1988. *America*. London: Verso.

Baudrillard, J. 1996. *The System of Objects*. London: Verso.

Baudrillard, J. 1998. *The Consumer Society*. London: Sage/TCS.

Bauman, Z. 1987. *Legislators and Interpreters*. Cambridge, UK: Polity Press.

Bauman, Z. 1991. *Intimations of Postmodernity*. London: Routledge.

Beard, Mayall, et al. 1852. *Tallis's History and Description of the Crystal Palace and the Exhibition of the Worlds Industry in 1851*, 2 vols. London: John Tallis.

Beeton, I. 1968. *The Book of Household Management*. London: Johnathan Cape.

Bell, D. 1979. *The Cultural Contradictions of Capitalism*, 2nd ed. London: Hutchinson.

Benjamin, W. 1973a. The work of art in the age of mechanical reproduction. In *Illuminations*, 211–244. London: Fontana.

Benjamin, W. 1973b. Theses on the philosophy of history. In *Illuminations*, 245–255. London: Fontana.

Benjamin, W. 1973c. *Charles Baudelaire: A Lyric Poet in the Era of High Capitalism*. London: Verso.

Benjamin, W. 1985a. Surrealism. In *One Way Street and Other Writings*, 225–239. London: Verso.

Benjamin, W. 1985b. A Berlin chronicle. In *One Way Street and Other Writings*, 293–346. London: Verso.

Benjamin, W. 1985c. *On the Origins of German Tragic Drama*. London: Verso.

Benjamin, W. 1999a. *The Arcades Project*. Cambridge, MA: Belknap Press of Harvard University Press.

Benjamin, W. 1999b. Paris, the capital of the nineteenth century [Exposé of 1935]. In *The Arcades Project*, 3–13. Cambridge, MA: Belknap Press of Harvard University Press.

Benjamin, W. 1999c. Paris, the capital of the nineteenth century [Exposé of 1939]. In *The Arcades Project*, 14–26. Cambridge, MA: Belknap Press of Harvard University Press.

Benjamin, W. 2002. Eduard Fuchs, collector and historian. In *Walter Benjamin, Selected Writings, Volume 3, 1935–1938*, 260–302. Cambridge, MA: Belknap Press of Harvard University Press.

Bennett, T. 1995. *The Birth of the Museum: History, Theory, Politics*. London: Routledge.

Bennett, T. 2004. *Pasts Beyond Memory: Evolution, Museums, Colonialism*. London: Routledge.

Benson, J. 1994. *The Rise of Consumer Society in Britain, 1880–1980*. London: Longman.

Beresford Chancellor, E. 1925. *The Pleasure Haunts of London*. London: Constable.

Berger, J. 1972. *Ways of Seeing*. Harmondsworth: Penguin.

Berlyn P. 1851. *A Popular Narrative of the Origins, History, Progress and Prospects of the Great Industrial Exhibition, 1851*. London: James Gilbert.

Berman, W. 1982. *All That Is Solid Melts into Air*. London: Verso.

Birken, L. 1988. *Consuming Desire: Sexual Science and the Emergence of Culture of Abundance, 1871–1914*. Ithaca, NY: Cornell University Press.

Bonnett, A. 1989. Situationism, geography and poststructuralism. *Environment and Planning D: Society and Space* 7: 131–146.

Bosman, W. 1967. *A New and Accurate Description of the Coast of Guinea*. London: Cass.

Bourdieu, P. 1984. *Distinction: A Social Critique of the Judgment of Taste*. London: Routledge & Kegan Paul.

Bowlby, R. 1985. *Just Looking: Consumer Culture in Dreiser, Gissing and Zola*. New York: Methuen.

Bracken, L. 1997. *Guy Debord—Revolutionary*. Venice, CA: Feral House.

Braidotti, R. 1991. *Patterns of Dissonance: A Study of Women in Contemporary Philosophy*. Cambridge, UK: Polity Press.

Brendon, P. 1991. *Thomas Cook: 150 Years of Popular Tourism*. London: Secker and Warburg.

Breton, A. 1960. *Nadja*. New York: Grove Press.

Brewer, J. and R. Porter. 1993. *Consumption and the World of Goods*. London: Routledge.

Briggs, A. 1959. *The Age of Improvement, 1783–1867*. London: Longman.

Briggs, A. 1990. *Victorian Things*. Harmondsworth, UK: Penguin.

Bronner, S., ed. 1989. *Consuming Visions: Accumulation and Display of Goods in America, 1880–1920*. New York: Norton.

Bryden, I. and J. Floyd, eds. 1999. *Domestic Space: reading the Nineteenth-Century Interior.* Manchester, UK: Manchester University Press.

Bryson, N. 1981. *Word and Image: French Painting of the Ancient Regime.* New York: Cambridge University Press.

Bryson, N. 1983. *Vision and Painting: The Logic of the Gaze.* Basingstoke, UK: Macmillan.

Bryson, N., ed. 1988. *Calligram: Essays in New Art History from France.* Cambridge, UK: Cambridge University Press.

Buck-Morss, S. 1989. *The Dialectics of Seeing: Walter Benjamin and the Arcades Project.* Cambridge, MA: MIT Press.

Burton, A. 1999. *Vision and Accident: The Story of the Victoria and Albert Museum.* London: V&A Publications.

Butler, J. 1990. *Gender Trouble: Feminism and the Subversion of Identity.* New York: Routledge.

Butler, J. 1993. *Bodies that Matter: On the Discursive Limits of "Sex."* New York: Routledge.

Butsch, R. 2000. *The Making of American Audiences: From Stage to Television, 1750–1990.* Cambridge, UK: Cambridge University Press.

Calder, J. 1977. *The Victorian Home.* London: Book Club Associates.

Calloway, S. 1992. *Liberty of London: Masters of Style and Decoration.* Boston: Bullfinch Press.

Campbell, C. 1987. *The Romantic Ethic and the Spirit of Modern Consumerism.* Oxford, UK: Basil Blackwell.

Carlyle, T. 2000. *Sartor Resartus.* Berkeley: University of California Press.

Carroll, J. 1977. *Puritan, Paranoid, Remissive: A Sociology of Modern Culture.* London: RKP.

Castle, T. 1995. *The Female Thermometer: 18th Century Culture and the Invention of the Uncanny.* Oxford, UK: Oxford University Press.

Chadwick, G. 1961. *The Works of Sir Joseph Paxton.* London: Architectural Press.

Chaney, D. 1983. The department store as cultural form. *Theory, Culture and Society* 13: 22–31.

Chappells, H. and E. Shove. 1999. The dustbin: A study of domestic waste, household practices and utility services. *International Planning Studies* 4: 267–280.

Chase, K. and M. Levenson. 2000. *The Spectacle of Intimacy: A Public Life for the Victorian Family.* Princeton, NJ: Princeton University Press.

Chia-Ling, L. 2004. Museums in motion. PhD diss., Lancaster University.

Chtchegelov, I. 1989. Formulary for a new urbanism. In *The Situationist International Anthology,* , ed. K. Knabb, 1–4. Berkeley, CA: Bureau of Public Secrets.

Clark, K. 1962. *The Gothic Revival: An Essay in the History of Taste,* 3rd ed. London: John Murray.

Clark, T. J. 1984. *The Painting of Modern Life: Paris in the Art of Manet and His Followers.* London: Thames and Hudson.

Clark T. J. and D. Nicholson-Smith. 1997. Why art can't kill the Situationist International. *October* 79: 15–31.

Cohen, G. 1978. *Karl Marx's Theory of History: A Defence.* Princeton, NJ: Princeton University Press.

Cohen, M. 1989. Walter Benjamin's phantasmagoria. *New German Critique* 48: 87–107.

Cohen, M. 1995. *Profane Illumination: Walter Benjamin and the Paris of the Surrealist Revolution.* Berkeley: University of California Press.

Cole, H. 1884. *Fifty Years of Public Works of Sir Henry Cole,* 2 vols. London: George Bell and Sons.

Comment, B. 1999. *The Panorama.* London: Reaktion Books.

Cooper, R. and J. Law. 1995. Organization: Distal and proximal views. *Research in the Sociology of Organizations* 13: 237–274.

Corbin, A. 1986. *The Foul and the Fragrant: Odor and the French Social Imagination*. Cambridge, MA: Harvard University Press.

Corbin, A. 1995. *Time, Desire and Horror: Towards a History of the Senses*. Cambridge, UK: Polity Press.

Corina, M. 1978. *Fine Silks and Oak Counters: Debenhams, 1778–1978*. London: Hutchinson Benham.

Coverley, M. 2006. *Psychogeography*. Harpenden, UK: Pocket Essentials.

Crary, J. 1984. Eclipse of the spectacle. In *Art After Modernism*, eds. B. Wallis and M. Tucker, 283–294. New York: New Museum of Contemporary Art/David Godine Inc.

Crary, J. 1990. *Techniques of the Observer: On Vision and Modernity in the Nineteenth Century*. Cambridge, MA: MIT Press.

Crary, J. 1997. Spectacle, attention, counter-memory. *October* 79: 97–107.

Crary, J. 1999. *Suspensions of Perception: Attention, Spectacle, and Modern Culture*. Cambridge, MA: MIT Press.

Crimp, D. 1997. *On the Museums Ruins*. Cambridge, MA: MIT Press.

Crossick, G. and S. Jaumain, eds. 1999. *Cathedrals of Consumption: The European Department Store, 1850–1939*. Aldershot, UK: Ashgate.

Cummings, N. and M. Lewandowska. 2000. *The Value of Things*. Basel, Switzerland: Birkhauser.

Davidoff, L. and C. Hall. 1987. *Family Fortunes: Men and Women of the English Middle Class, 1780–1850*. London: Routledge.

Davis, J. 1999. *The Great Exhibition*. Stroud, UK: Sutton Publishing.

Debord, G. 1977. *Society of the Spectacle*. Detroit, MI: Black and Red.

Debord, G. 1989a. Introduction to a critique of urban geography. In *The Situationist International Anthology*, ed. K. Knabb, 5–8. Berkeley, CA: Bureau of Public Secrets.

Debord, G. 1989b. Report on the construction of situations and on the International Situationist tendency's conditions of organization and action. In *The Situationist International Anthology*, , ed. K. Knabb, 17–25. Berkeley, CA: Bureau of Public Secrets.

Debord, G. 1989c. Situationist theses on traffic. In *The Situationist International Anthology*, , ed. K. Knabb, 56–58. Berkeley, CA: Bureau of Public Secrets.

Debord, G. 1989d. Perspectives for conscious alterations in everyday life. In *The Situationist International Anthology*, ed. K. Knabb, 68–75. Berkeley, CA: Bureau of Public Secrets.

Debord, G. 1990. *Comments on the Society of the Spectacle*. London: Verso.

Debord, G. 1991. *In Girum Imus Nocte Et Consumimur Igni*. London: Pelegian Press.

Debord, G. 1992. *The Society of the Spectacle and Other Films*. London: Rebel Press.

Debord, G. 1995. *Society of the Spectacle*, trans. D. Nicholson-Smith. New York: Zone Books.

Debord, G. and G. Sanguinetti. 1990. *The Veritable Split in the International*. London: Chronos Publications.

Debray, R. 1995. Remarks on the spectacle. *New Left Review* 214: 134–141.

De Certeau, M. 1984. *The Practice of Everyday Life*, vol. 1. Berkeley: University of California Press.

Defoe, D. 1971. *A Tour through the Whole Island of Great Britain*. Harmondsworth, UK: Penguin.

Deleuze, G. and F. Guattari. 1988. *A Thousand Plateaus: Capitalism and Schizophrenia*. London: Athlone.

Derrida, J. 1994. *Spectres of Marx: The State of the Debt, the Work of Mourning, and the New International*. New York: Routledge.

Donald, M. 1999. Tranquil havens? Critiquing the idea of home as the middle-class sanctuary. In *Domestic Space: Reading the Nineteenth-Century Interior*, eds. I. Bryden and J. Floyd, 103–120. Manchester, UK: Manchester University Press.

Douglas, M. 1984. *Purity and Danger*. London: Ark/Routledge.

Douglas, M. and B. Isherwood. 1986. *The World of Goods: Towards an Anthropology of Consumption*. London: Routledge.

Du Gay, P. and M. Pryke, eds. 2003. *Cultural Economy: Cultural Analysis and Commercial Life*. London: Sage.

Duncan, C. 1995. *Civilizing Rituals: Inside Public Art Museums*. London: Routledge.

Duncan, C. and A. Wallach. 1980. The universal survey museum. *Art History* 3: 447–469.

During, S. 2002. *Modern Enchantments: The Cultural Power of Secular Magic*. Cambridge, MA: Harvard University Press.

Durkheim, E. 1964. *The Division of Labour in Society*. New York: Free Press.

Durkheim, E. 1971. *The Elementary Forms of Religious Life*. London: Allen and Unwin.

Eastlake, C. 1969. *Hints on Household Taste in Furniture, Upholstery and Other Details*. New York: Dover Publications.

Elden, S. 2001. *Mapping the Present: Heidegger, Foucault and the Project of a Spatial History*. London: Continuum.

Elias, N. 1978. *The Civilizing Process*. Oxford, UK: Blackwell.

Elias, N. 1983. *The Court Society*. Oxford, UK: Blackwell.

Ellen, R. 1988. Fetishism. *Man* (N.S.) 23: 213–235.

Fay, C. 1951. *Palace of Industry, 1851. A Study of the Great Exhibition and its Fruits*. Cambridge, UK: Cambridge University Press.

Featherstone, M. 1991. *Consumer Culture and Postmodernism*. London: Sage/TCS.

Feenberg, 1981. *Lukacs, Marx and the Sources of Critical Theory*. Oxford, UK: Robertson.

Ferguson, A. 1966. *An Essay on the History of Civil Society*, Edinburgh. UK: Edinburgh University Press.

Ferry, J. 1960. *A History of the Department Store*. London: Macmillan.

Feuerbach, L. 1881. *The Essence of Christianity*, 2nd ed.: Trubner.

Fiennes, C. 1949. *The Journeys of Celia Fiennes*. London: Cresset Press.

Fiske, J. 1989. *Understanding Popular Culture*. Boston: Unwin Hyman.

Flanders, J. 2004. *The Victorian House: Domestic Life from Childbirth to Deathbed*. London: Harper Perennial.

Flint, K. 2000. *The Victorians and the Visual Imagination*. Cambridge, UK: Cambridge University Press.

Foucault, M. 1974. *The Archaeology of Knowledge*. London: Tavistock.

Foucault, M. 1977. *Discipline and Punish: The Birth of the Prison*. Harmondsworth, UK: Penguin.

Foucault, M. 1983. *This Is Not a Pipe*. Berkeley: University of California Press.

Foucault, M. 1989. *The Order of Things*. London: Tavistock/Routledge.

Freud, S. 1958. The uncanny. In *The Standard Edition of the Complete Psychological Works of Sigmund Freud*, vol. 17, ed. J. Strachey, 218–252. London: Hogarth Press.

Freud, S. 1977a. Three essays on the theory of sexuality. In *On Sexuality: Three Essays on the Theory of Sexuality and Other Works*, 33–169. Harmondsworth, UK: Penguin.

Freud, S. 1977b. Fetishism. In *On Sexuality: Three Essays on the Theory of Sexuality and Other Works*, 345–357. Harmondsworth, UK: Penguin.

Freud, S. 1985. Civilization and its discontents. In *Civilization, Society and Religion: Group Psychology, Civilization and Its Discontents and Other Works*, 243–340. Harmondsworth, UK: Penguin.

Fried, M. 1980. *Absorption and Theatricality: Painting and the Beholder in the Age of Diderot*. Chicago: University of Chicago Press.

Friedberg, A. 1993. *Window Shopping: Cinema and the Postmodern*. Berkeley: University of California Press.

Frisby, D. 1981. *Sociological Impressionism*. London: Heinemann.

Frisby, D. 1985. *Fragments of Modernity: Theories of Modernity in the Work of Simmel, Kracauer and Benjamin*. Cambridge, UK: Polity Press.

Frisby, D. 1994. The flâneur in social theory. In *The Flâneur*, ed. K. Tester, 81–110. London: Routledge.

Fritzsche, P. 1999. *Reading Berlin 1900*. Cambridge, MA: Harvard University Press.

Fyfe, G. 2000. *Art, Power and Modernity: English Art Institutions, 1750–1950*. London: Leicester University Press.

Gabel, J. 1975. *False Consciousness*. Oxford, UK: Blackwell.

Gadamer, H. 1975. *Truth and Method*. New York: Seabury Press.

Geist, J. 1985. *Arcades: The History of a Building Type*. Cambridge, MA: MIT Press.

Gibson, J. 1986. *The Ecological Approach to Visual Perception*. London: Erlbaum.

Giedion, S. 1941. *Space, Time and Architecture: The Growth of a New Tradition*, 4th ed. Cambridge, MA: Harvard University Press.

Gilloch, G. 1995. *Myth and Metropolis: Walter Benjamin and the City*. Cambridge, UK: Polity Press.

Girard, R. 1979. *Violence and the Sacred*. Baltimore, MD: Johns Hopkins University Press.

Gluck, M. 2003. The flâneur and the aesthetic appropriation of urban culture in mid-19th-century Paris. *Theory, Culture and Society* 205: 53–80.

Gombin, R. 1978. *The Origins of Modern Leftism*. Harmondsworth, UK: Penguin.

Gordon, A. 1997. *Ghostly Matters: Haunting and the Sociological Imagination*. Minneapolis: University of Minnesota Press.

Gouldner, A. 1973. *The Coming Crisis of Western Sociology*. London: Heinemann.

Gray, C. 1974. *Leaving the Twentieth Century: The Incomplete Work of the Situationist International*. London: Free Fall.

Greeley, H. 1851. *Glances at Europe: In a Series of Letters from Great Britain, France, Italy, Switzerland, etc. during the Summer of 1851: Including Notices of the Great Exhibition, or World's Fair*. New York: Dewitt and Davenport.

Greenberg, R., B. Ferguson, and S. Nairne, eds. 1996. *Thinking About Exhibitions*. London: Routledge.

Greenhalgh, P. 1988. *Ephemeral Vistas: The Expositions Universelles, Great Exhibitions and World's Fairs, 1851–1939*. Manchester, UK: Manchester University Press.

Greysmith, B. 1976. *Wallpaper*. London: Studio Vista.

Grosz, E. 1995. *Space, Time and Perversion: Essays on the Politics of Bodies*. London: Routledge.

Gruber Garvey, E. 1996. *The Adman in the Parlor: Magazines and the Gendering of Consumer Culture, 1880s to 1910s*. New York: Oxford University Press.

Habermas, J. 1989. *The Structural Transformation of the Public Sphere*. Cambridge, MA: MIT Press.

Hall, C. 1992. *White, Male and Middle Class: Exploration in Feminism and History*. Cambridge, UK: Polity Press.

Hall, S. 1992. Encoding, decoding. In *The Cultural Studies Reader*, ed. S. During, 90–103. London: Routledge.

Hall, S. and R. Jefferson. 1976. *Resistance through Rituals: Youth Subcultures in Post-War Britain*. London: Hutchinson.

Halttunen, K. 1989. From parlor to living room: Domestic space, interior decoration, and the culture of personality. In *Consuming Visions: Accumulation and Display of Goods in America, 1880–1920*, ed. S. Bronner, 157–189. New York: Norton.

Haraway, D. 1991. Situated knowledges: The science question in feminism and the privilege of partial perspective. In *Simians, Cyborgs and Women: The Reinvention of Nature*, 183–202. London: Free Association Books.

Harris, N. 1990. *Cultural Excursions: Marketing Appetites and Cultural Tastes in Modern America*. Chicago: University of Chicago Press.

Harrods. 1972. *Victorian Shopping: Harrods Catalogue, 1895*. Trowbridge: David and Charles.

Harvey, D. 1985. *Consciousness and the Urban Experience*. Oxford, UK: Blackwell.

Harvey, D. 2003. *Paris, Capital of Modernity*. New York: Routledge.

Hawkins, G. 2000. Plastic bags: Living with rubbish. *International Journal of Cultural Studies* 4: 5–23.

Hayden, D. 1981. *The Grand Domestic Revolution: A History of Feminist Designs for American Homes, Neighborhoods, and Cities*. Cambridge, MA: MIT Press.

Heard, M. 1996. Paul de Philipsthal and the phantasmagoria in England, Scotland and Ireland, part 1. *The New Magic Lantern Journal* 81: 2–7.

Hebdige, D. 1979. *Subculture: The Meaning of Style*. London: Routledge.

Hegel, G. 1956. *The Philosophy of History*. New York: Dover Publications.

Heidegger, M. 1977a. Building, dwelling, thinking. In *The Question Concerning Technology and Other Essays*, New York: Harper.

Heidegger, M. 1977b. The question concerning technology. In *The Question Concerning Technology and Other Essays*, 3–35. New York: Harper.

Heidegger, M. 1977c. The age of the world picture. In *The Question Concerning Technology and Other Essays*, 115–154. New York: Harper.

Hendrickson, R. 1979. *The Grand Emporiums: The Illustrated History of America's Great Department Stores*. New York: Stein and Day.

Hertz, R. 1960. *Death and the Right Hand*. London: Cohen and West.

Hetherington, K. 1997. *The Badlands of Modernity: Heterotopia and Social Ordering*. London: Routledge.

Hetherington, K. 1998. *Expressions of Identity: Space, Performance, Politics*. London: Sage/TCS.

Hetherington, K. 1999. From blindness to blindness: Museums, heterogeneity and the subject. In *Actor-Network Theory and After*, J. Law and J. Hassard, eds., 51–73. Oxford, UK: Blackwell.

Hetherington, K. 2001. Moderns as ancients: Time, space and the discourse of improvement. In *Timespace: Geographies of Temporality*, eds. J. May and N. Thrift, 49–72. London: Routledge.

Hetherington, K. 2004. Secondhandedness: Consumption, disposal and absent presence. *Environment and Planning D: Society and Space* 22: 157–173.

Hetherington, K. and N. Lee. 2000. Social order and the blank figure. *Environment and Planning D: Society and Space* 18: 169–184.

Hirschman, A. 1977. *The Passions and the Interests*. Princeton, NJ: Princeton University Press.

Holst, N. 1976. *Creators, Collectors and Connoisseurs: An Anatomy of Artistic Taste from Antiquity to the Present*. London: Book Club Associates.

Home, S. 1988. *Assault on Culture: From Lettrisme to Class War*. London: Aporia Books.

Honeycombe, G. 1984. *Selfridges: Seventy Five Years, The Store of Stores, 1909–1984*. London: Selfridges.

Hooper-Greenhill, E. 1992. *Museums and the Construction of Knowledge*. Leicester, UK: Leicester University Press.

Howes, D. 2003. *Sensual Relations: Engaging the Senses in Culture and Social Theory*. Ann Arbor: University of Michigan Press.

Hubert, H. and M. Mauss. 1964. *Sacrifice: Its Nature and Function*. Chicago: University of Chicago Press.

Hunt, R. 1851. *Hunt's Handbook to the Official Catalogues: An Explanatory Guide to the Natural Productions and Manufactures of the Great Exhibition of the Industry of All Nations, 1851*, 2 vols. London: Spicer Brothers.

Huyssen, A. 1995. *Twilight Memories: Marking Time in a Culture of Amnesia*. New York: Routledge.

Huyssen, A. 2003. *Present Pasts: Urban Palimpsests and the Politics of Memory*. Stanford, CA: Stanford University Press.

The Illustrated Exhibitor. 1851. London: Cassell.

The Illustrated London News Collection of Great Exhibition Articles and Supplements. 1851. London, n.p.

Impey, O. and A. McGregor, eds. 1985. *The Origins of Museums: The Cabinet of Curiosities in Sixteenth and Seventeenth Century Europe*. Oxford, UK: Oxford University Press.

Ivins, W. 1953. *Prints and Visual Communication*. London: Routledge & Kegan Paul.

Jacobs, J. 1961. *Death and Life of Great American Cities*. Harmondsworth, UK: Penguin.

Jameson, F. 1991. *Postmodernism, or the Cultural Logic of Late Capitalism*. London: Verso.

Jappe, A. 1999. *Guy Debord*. Berkeley: University of California Press.

Jardine, L. 1997. *Worldly Goods: A New History of the Renaissance*. London: Papermac.

Jay, M. 1978. *Marxism and Totality*. Cambridge, UK: Polity Press.

Jay, M. 1994. *Downcast Eyes*. Berkeley: University of California Press.

Kant, I. 1952. *Critique of Judgement*. Oxford, UK: Clarendon Press.

Keenan, T. 1993. The point is to (ex)change it: Reading capital, rhetorically. In *Fetishism as Cultural Discourse*, eds E. Apter and W. Pietz, 152–185, Ithaca: Cornell University Press.

Kellum, R. 1996. *Capitalism and the Eye*, 2 vols. Unpublished PhD thesis, State University of New York at Binghamton.

Kenseth, J., ed. 1991. *The Age of the Marvelous*. Hanover, NH: Hood Museum of Art/Dartmouth College.

Kern, S. 1983. *The Culture of Time and Space, 1880–1918*. Cambridge, MA: Harvard University Press.

Klein, N. 2001. *No Logo*. London: Flamingo.

Knabb, K., ed. 1989. *The Situationist International Anthology*. Berkeley, CA: Bureau of Public Secrets.

Kogan, H. and L. Wendt. 1952. *Give the Lady What She Wants! The Story of Marshall Field and Company*. Chicago: Rand McNally.

Kolakowski, L. 1981. *Main Currents of Marxism*, 3 vols. Oxford, UK: Oxford University Press.

Kopytoff, I. 1986. The cultural biography of things: Commoditization as process. In *The Social Life of Things: Commodities in Cultural Perspective*, ed. A. Appadurai, 64–91, Cambridge, UK: Cambridge University Press.

Koselleck, R. 2004. *Futures Past: On the Semantics of Historical Time*. New York: Columbia University Press.

Kotanyi, A. and R. Vaniegem. 1961. Elementary program of the Bureau of Unitary Urbanism. In *The Situationist International Anthology*, 1989, ed K. Knabb, 65–67. Berkeley, CA: Bureau of Public Secrets.

Kowaleski-Wallace, E. 1997. *Consuming Subjects: Women, Shopping, and Business in the Eighteenth Century*. New York: Columbia University Press.

Kracauer, S. 1995. The little shopgirls go to the movies. In *The Mass Ornament: Weimar Essays*, 291–304. Cambridge, MA: Harvard University Press.

Krafft-Ebing, R. 1965. *Psychopathia Sexualis: A Medico Forensic Study*. New York: Stein and Day.

Kumar, K. 1978 *Prophesy and Progress*. Harmondsworth, UK: Penguin.

Kusamitsu, T. 1980. Great exhibitions before 1851. *History Workshop* 9: 70–89.

Lancaster, B. 1995. *The Department Store: A Social History*. London: Leicester University Press.

Langland, E. 1995. *Nobody's Angels: Middle-Class Women and Domestic Ideology in Victorian Culture*. Ithaca, NY: Cornell University Press.

Lasch, C. 1979. *The Culture of Narcissism: American Life in the Age of Diminished Expectations*. New York: Warner Books.

Latour, B. 1988. *The Pasteurization of France*. Cambridge, MA: Harvard University Press.

Latour, B. 1993. *We Have Never Been Modern*. London: Harvester Wheatsheaf.

Latour, B. 1999. *Pandora's Hope: Essays on the Reality of Science Studies*. Cambridge, MA: Harvard University Press.

Latour, B. 2002. Morality and technology: The end of the means. *Theory, Culture and Society* 195–96: 247–260.

Law, J. 2004. *After Method: Mess in Social Science Research*. London: Routledge.

Law, J. and R. Benschop. 1997. Resisting pictures: Representation, distribution and ontological politics. In *Ideas of Difference: Social Spaces and the Labour of Division*, eds. K. Hetherington and R. Munro, 158–182. Oxford, UK: Blackwell.

Leach, W. 1993. *Land of Desire: Merchants, Power, and the Rise of the New American Culture*. New York: Random House/Vintage.

Leapman, M. 2001. *The World for a Shilling: How the Great Exhibition of 1851 Shaped a Nation*. London: Headline Book Publishing.

Lears, J. 1989. Beyond Veblen: Rethinking consumer culture in America. In *Consuming Visions: Accumulation and Display of Goods in America, 1880–1920*, ed. S. Bronner, 73–97. New York: Norton.

Lefebvre, H. 1971. *Everyday Life in the Modern World*. New York: Harper & Row.

Lefebvre, H. 1991. *The Production of Space*. Oxford, UK: Blackwell.

Levin, T. 1989. Dismantling the spectacle: The cinema of Guy Debord. In *On the Passage of a Few People through a Brief Moment in Time*, ed. E. Sussman, 72–123. Cambridge, MA: MIT Press.

Levi-Strauss, C. 1966. *The Savage Mind*. London: Wiedenfeld and Nicholson.

Lichtheim, G. 1961. *Marxism: A Historical and Cultural Study*. London: Routledge & Kegan Paul.

Lindberg, D. 1976. *Theories of Vision from Al-Kindi to Kepler*. Chicago: University of Chicago Press.

Lindroos, K. 1998. *Now-Time/Image-Space: Temporalization of Politics in Walter Benjamin's Philosophy of History and Art*. Jyvaskyla: SoPhi/University of Jyvaskyla.

Lindroos, K. 2001. Scattering Community: Benjamin on experience, narrative and history. *Philosophy and Social Criticism* 276: 19–41.

Loeb, L. 1994. *Consuming Angels: Advertising and Victorian Women*. New York: Oxford University Press.

Logan, T. 2001. *The Victorian Parlour: A Cultural Study.* Cambridge, UK: Cambridge University Press.

Lowe, D. 1982. *History of Bourgeois Perception.* Brighton, UK: Harvester Press.

Luckhurst, K. 1951. *The Story of Exhibitions.* London: Studio Publications.

Lukacs, G. 1971. *History and Class Consciousness.* London: Merlin Press.

Lukacs, G. 2001. Thoughts toward an aesthetic of cinema. *Polygraph* 13: 13–18.

Lunn, E. 1982. *Marxism and Modernism: A Historical Study of Lukacs, Brecht, Benjamin and Adorno.* Chicago: University of Chicago Press.

Lury, C. 1996. *Consumer Culture.* Cambridge, UK: Polity.

Lury, C. 1998. *Prosthetic Culture.* London: Routledge.

Lyotard, J-F. 1984. *Driftworks.* New York: Semiotexte.

McCallum, E. 1999. *Object Lessons: How to Do Things With Fetishism.* New York: State University of New York Press.

McCracken, G. 1988. *Culture and Consumption: New Approaches to the Symbolic Character of Consumer Goods and Activities.* Bloomington: Indiana University Press.

McKean, J. 1994. *Crystal Palace: Joseph Paxton and Charles Fox.* London: Phaidon.

McKendrick, N., J. Brewer, and J. Plumb, eds. 1982. *The Birth of Consumer Society: The Commercialization of Eighteenth-Century England.* Bloomington: Indiana University Press.

McLuhan, M. 1987. *Understanding Media: The Extension of Man.* London: Ark.

McNair Wright, J. 1884. *The Complete Home: An Encyclopaedia of Domestic Life and Affairs.* Brantford, Ontario: Bradley, Garretson & Co.

Macdonald, S., ed. 1999. *The Politics of Display: Museums, Science, Culture.* London: Routledge.

Maleuvre, D. 1999. *Museum Memories: History, Technology, Art.* Stanford, CA: Stanford University Press.

Malraux, A. 1978. *Voices of Silence.* St. Albans, UK: Paladin.

Marcus, G. 1989. *Lipstick Traces: A Secret History of the Twentieth Century.* London: Secker and Warburg.

Marcuse, H. 1968. *One-Dimensional Man.* London: Sphere.

Markus, T. 1993. *Buildings and Power: Freedom and Control in the Origin of Modern Building.* London: Routledge.

Marx, K. 1938. *Capital,* vol. 1. London: George Allen and Unwin.

Marx, K. 1973. *Grundrisse.* Harmondsworth, UK: Penguin.

Marx, K. 1975a. The leading article in no. 179 of the Kolnische Zeitung. In *Collected Works,* vol. 1, 184–202. London: Lawrence and Wishart.

Marx, K. 1975b. Economic and philosophical manuscripts. In *Marx: Early Writings,* 279–400. Harmondsworth, UK: Penguin.

Marx, K. 1978. *The Eighteenth Brumaire of Louis Bonaparte.* Peking, China: Foreign Language Press.

Marx, K. and F. Engels. 1970. *The German Ideology.* London: Lawrence Wishart.

Marx, K. and F. Engels. 1975. *Collected Works, Volume 38.* London: Lawrence Wishart.

Mass Observation. 1947. *Browns and Chester: A Portrait of a Shop.* London: Lindsay Drummond.

Mauss, M. 1978. Body techniques. In *Sociology and Psychology: Essays,* 95–123. London: Routledge & Kegan Paul.

Mauss, M. 1990. *The Gift.* London: Routledge.

Mészáros, I. 1970. *Marx's Theory of Alienation.* London: Merlin Press.

Miller, A. 1995. *Novels Behind Glass: Commodity Culture and Victorian Narrative.* Cambridge, UK: Cambridge University Press.

Miller, D. 1995. Consumption as the vanguard of history. In *Acknowledging Consumption: A Review of New Studies*, ed. D. Miller, 1–57. London: Routledge.

Miller, D. 1998. *A Theory of Shopping*. Cambridge, UK: Polity Press.

Miller, E. 1974. *That Noble Cabinet: A History of the British Museum*. Athens: Ohio University Press.

Miller, M. 1981. *The Bon Marché: Bourgeois Culture and the Department Store, 1869–1920*. London: George Allen and Unwin.

Morris, R. 1970. Leeds and the Crystal Palace. *Victorian Studies* 133: 283–300.

Morrison, K. 2003. *English Shops and Shopping*. New Haven, CT: Yale University Press.

Motherwell, R. ed. 1989. *The Dada Painters and Poets*. Cambridge, MA.: Harvard University Press.

Mulvey, L. 1996. *Fetishism and Curiosity*. Bloomington: Indiana University Press.

Munro, R. 1995. The disposal of the meal. In *Food Choices*, ed. D. Marshall, 313–326. London: Blackie Academic Publishers.

Munro, R. 1996. The consumption view of self: Extension, exchange and identity. In *Consumption Matters: The Production and Experience of Consumption*, eds. S. Edgell, K. Hetherington, and A. Warde, 248–273. Oxford, UK: Blackwell.

Munro, R. 1998. Disposal of the x gap: The production and consumption of accounting research and practical accounting systems. *Advances in Public Accounting* 7: 139–159.

Munro, R. 2001. Disposal of the body: Upending postmodernism. *Ephemera: Critical Dialogues Organization* 12: 108–130.

Nadeau, M. 1987. *The History of Surrealism*. London: Plantin.

Nava, M. 1997. Women, the city and the department store. In *The Shopping Experience*, eds. P. Falk and C. Campbell, 56–91. London: Sage/TCS.

Nead, L. 2000. *Victorian Babylon: People, Streets and Images in Nineteenth-Century London*. New Haven, CT: Yale University Press.

Nesci, C. 2001. Flora Tristan's urban odyssey: Notes on the missing flâneuse and her city. *Journal of Urban History* 276: 709–722.

Newton, C. 1999. *Victorian Designs for the Home*. London: V&A Publications.

Nietzsche, F. 1961. *Thus Spake Zarathustra*. Harmondsworth, UK: Penguin.

Nunokawa, J. 1994. *The Afterlife of Property: Domestic Security and the Victorian Novel*. Princeton, NJ: Princeton University Press.

Oakley, A. 1974. *Housewife*. London: Allen Lane.

O'Brien, M. 1999. Rubbish power: Toward a sociology of the rubbish society. In *Consuming Cultures*, eds. J. Hearn and S. Roseneil, 262–277. Basingstoke, UK: Macmillan.

October. 1997. Special Issue on Guy Debord, vol. 79.

Official, Descriptive and Illustrated Catalogue of the Great Exhibition of the Works of Industry of All Nations, 1851. 1851. London: Spicer Brothers.

Olalquiaga, C. 1999. *The Artificial Kingdom: A Treasury of the Kitsch Experience*. London: Bloomsbury.

Ollman, B. 1979. *Social and Sexual Revolution*. London: Pluto Press.

Ozouf, M. 1987. *Festivals and the French Revolution*. Cambridge, MA: Harvard University Press.

Packard, V. 1961. *The Hidden Persuaders*. Harmondsworth, UK: Penguin.

Panofsky, E. 1991. *Perspective as Symbolic Form*. New York: Zone Books.

Parkhurst Ferguson, P. 1994. The flâneur on and off the streets of Paris. In *The Flâneur*, ed. K. Tester, 22–42. London: Routledge.

Parsons, D. 1999. Flâneur or flâneuse? Mythologies of modernity. *New Formations* 38: 91–100.

Parsons, D. 2003. *Streetwalking the Metropolis: Women, the City and Modernity*. Oxford, UK: Oxford University Press.

Parsons, T. 1937. *Structure of Social Action*. New York: Free Press.

Pearce, S. 1992. *Museums, Objects and Collections: A Cultural Study*. Washington, DC: Smithsonian Institution Press.

Pearce, S. 1995. *On Collecting: An Investigation into Collecting in the European Tradition*. London: Routledge.

Pels, D., K. Hetherington, and F. Vandenberghe. 2002. The status of the object: Performances, mediations, and techniques. *Theory, Culture and Society* 195–96: 1–22.

Pevsner, N. 1936. *Pioneers of Modern Design: From William Morris to Walter Gropius*. London: Faber and Faber.

Pevsner, N. 1951. *High Victorian Design; A Study of the Exhibits of 1851*. London: Architectural Press.

Phillips, D. 1997. *Exhibiting Authenticity*. Manchester, UK: Manchester University Press.

Pietz, W. 1985. The problem of the fetish I. *Res* 9: 5–17.

Pietz, W. 1987. The problem of the fetish II. *Res* 13: 23–45.

Pietz, W. 1988. The problem of the fetish III. *Res* 16: 105–23.

Pietz, W. 1993. Fetishism and materialism: The limits of theory in Marx. In *Fetishism as Cultural Discourse*, eds. E. Apter and W. Pietz, 119–151. London: Cornell University Press.

Plant, S. 1992. *Most Radical Gesture*. London: Routledge.

Plot, R. 1686. *The Natural History of Staffordshire*. Oxford, n.p.

Poe, E. 1938. The man of the crowd. In *The Complete Tales and Poems of Edgar Allen Poe*, 475–481. New York: Modern Library.

Pollock, G. 1988. *Vision and Difference: Femininity, Feminism and Histories of Art*. London: Routledge.

Porter Benson, S. 1979. Palace of consumption and machine for selling: The American department store, 1880–1940. *Radical History Review* 21: 201–221.

Porter Benson, S. 1988. *Counter Cultures: Saleswomen, Managers and Customers in American Department Stores, 1890–1940*. Urbana: University of Illinois Press.

Prendergast, C. 1995. *Paris and the Nineteenth Century*. Oxford, UK: Blackwell.

Quigley, M. 1948. *Magic Shadows: The Story of the Origin of Motion Pictures*. Washington, DC: Georgetown University Press.

Ranciere, J. and P. Vauday. 1988. Going to the expo: The worker, his wife and machines. In *Voices of the People: The Social Life of La Sociale at the End of the Second Empire*, eds. A. Rifkin and R. Thomas, 23–44. London: Routledge & Kegan Paul.

Rappaport, E. 1996. "A husband and his wife's dresses": Consumer credit and the debt to family in England, 1864–1914. In *The Sex of Things: Gender and Consumption in Historical Perspective*, eds. V. de Grazia and E. Furlough, 163–187. Berkeley: University of California Press.

Rappaport, E. 2000. *Shopping for Pleasure: Women in the Making of London's West End*. Princeton, NJ: Princeton University Press.

Redding, C. 1851. *The Stranger in London; or Visitors Companion to the Metropolis and its Environs, with an Historical and Descriptive Sketch of the Great Exhibition*. London: Henry Bohn.

Richards, T. 1991. *The Commodity Culture of Victorian England: Advertising and Spectacle, 1851–1914*. London: Verso.

Riesman, D. 1950. *The Lonely Crowd*. New York: Doubleday Books.

Rose, G. 1978. *The Melancholy Science: An Introduction to the Thought of Theodor W. Adorno*. New York: Columbia University Press.

Rose, G. 1993. *Feminism and Geography: The Limits of Geographical Knowledge.* Cambridge, UK: Polity Press.

Ross, K. 1988. *Emergence of Social Space.* Basingstoke, UK: Macmillan.

Ross, K. and H. Lefebvre. 1997. Lefebvre on the Situationists: An interview. *October* 79: 69–83.

Rotman, B. 1987. *Signifying Nothing: The Semiotics of Zero.* Stanford, CA: Stanford University Press.

Rotman, B. 1993. *Ad Infinitum.* Stanford, CA: Stanford University Press.

Ruskin, J. 1854. *The Opening of the Crystal Palace, Considered in Some of its Relations to the Prospects of Art.* London: Smith, Elder and Co.

Ryan, J. 1994. Women, modernity and the city. *Theory, Culture and Society* 114: 35–63.

Rykwert, J. 1980. *First Moderns: The Architects of the Eighteenth Century.* Cambridge, MA: MIT Press.

Sadler, S. 1999. *The Situationist City.* Cambridge, MA: MIT Press.

Sahlins, M. 1972. *Stone Age Economics.* New York: Hawthorne.

Said, E. 1979. *Orientalism.* New York: Vintage Books.

Saisselin, R. 1985. *Bricabracomania: The Bourgeois and the Bibelot.* London: Thames and Hudson.

Saumarez Smith, C. 1989. Museums, artifacts and meanings. In *The New Museology*, ed. P. Vergo, 6–21. London: Reaktion Books.

Saunders, G. 2001. *Wallpaper in Interior Decoration.* London: Victoria and Albert Museum.

Schacht, R. 1971. *Alienation.* London: Allen & Unwin.

Schivelbusch, W. 1986. *The Railway Journey: The Industrialization of Time and Space in the Nineteenth Century.* Berkeley: University of California Press.

Schivelbusch. W. 1988. *Disenchanted Night: The Industrialization of Light in the Nineteenth Century.* Berkeley: University of California Press.

Scholem, G. 1954. *Major Trends in Jewish Mysticism.* New York: Schocken Books.

Schor, N. 1987. *Reading in Detail: Aesthetics and the Feminine.* New York: Methuen.

Schwartz, V. 1999. *Spectacular Realities: Early Mass Culture in Fin-De-Siecle Paris.* Berkeley: University of California Press.

Schwartz Cowan, R. 1983. *More Work for Mother: The Ironies of Household Technology from the Open Hearth to the Microwave.* New York: Basic Books.

Sennett, R. 1977. *The Fall of Public Man.* London: Faber and Faber.

Sennett, R. 1987. Plate glass. *Raritan* 64: 1–15.

Serres, M. 1982. *The Parasite.* Baltimore, MD: John Hopkins University Press.

Serres, M. 1991. *Rome: The Book of Foundations.* Stanford, CA: Stanford University Press.

Shields, R. 1989. Social spatialization and the built environment: The West Edmonton Mall. *Environment and Planning D: Society and Space* 7: 147–164.

Shields, R., ed. 1992. *Lifestyle Shopping.* London: Routledge.

Shields, R. 1999. *Lefebvre, Love and Struggle.* London: Routledge.

Short, A. 1966. Workers under glass in 1851. *Victorian Studies* 102: 193–202.

Simmel, G. 1971a. The stranger. In *On Individuality and Social Forms*, ed. D. Levine, 143–149. Chicago: University of Chicago Press.

Simmel, G. 1971b. The metropolis and mental life. In *On Individuality and Social Forms*, ed. D. Levine, 324–339. Chicago: University of Chicago Press.

Simmel, G. 1971c. `Fashion. In *On Individuality and Social Forms*, ed D. Levine, 294–323. Chicago: University of Chicago Press.

Simmel, G. 1990. *The Philosophy of Money.* London: Routledge.

Smiles, S. 1986. *Self-Help.* Harmondsworth, UK: Penguin.

Smith, A. 1922. *The Wealth of Nations.* London: Methuen.

Sombart, W. 1967. *Luxury and Capitalism.* Ann Arbor: University of Michigan Press.

Spadafora, D. 1990. *The Idea of Progress in Eighteenth-Century Britain*. New Haven, CT: Yale University Press.

Sparke, P. 1995. *As Long as It's Pink: The Sexual Politics of Taste*. London: Pandora Press.

Spyer, P., ed. 1998. *Border Fetishisms: Material Objects in Unstable Spaces*. New York: Routledge.

Stallybrass, P. and A. White. 1986. *The Politics and Poetics of Transgression*. London: Methuen.

Steegman, J. 1987. *Victorian Taste: A Study of the Arts and Architecture from 1830 to 1870*. London: Century Hutchinson.

Stephenson, R. 1851. *The Great Exhibition, Its Palace and Its Principle Contents*. London: George Routledge and Co.

Stewart, S. 1993. *On Longing: Narratives of the Miniature, the Gigantic, the Souvenir, the Collection*. Durham, NC: Duke University Press.

Strasser, S. 1999. *Waste and Want: A Social History of Trash*. New York: Henry Holt/Owl Books.

Strathern, M. 1991. *Partial Connections*. Savage, MA: Rowan & Littlefield.

Strathern, M. 1999. The aesthetics of substance. In *Property, Substance and Affect*, 45–64. London: Athlone.

Susman, W. 2003. *Culture as History: The Transformation of American Society in the Twentieth Century*. Washington, DC: Smithsonian Books.

Swingewood, A. 1977. *The Myth of Mass Culture*. Basingstoke, UK: Macmillan.

Taussig, M. 1980. *The Devil and Commodity Fetishism in South America*. Chapel Hill: University of North Carolina Press.

Taussig, M. 1992. *Mimesis and Alterity: A Particular History of the Senses*. New York: Routledge.

Tester, K., ed. 1994. *The Flaneur*. London: Routledge.

Thompson, E. P. 1968. *The Making of the English Working Class*. Harmondsworth, UK: Penguin.

Thompson, F. M. L. 1988. *The Rise of Respectable Society: A Social History of Victorian Britain*. London: Fontana.

Thompson, M. 1979. *Rubbish Theory: The Creation and Destruction of Value*. Oxford, UK: Oxford University Press.

Thompson, Z. 1852. *Journal of a Trip to London, Paris and the Great Exhibition in 1851*. Burlington, VT: Nichols and Warren.

Tiedemann, R. 1999. Dialectics at a standstill. In *The Arcades Project*. W. Benjamin, 929–945. Cambridge, MA: Belknap Press of Harvard University Press.

Timbs, J. 1851. *The Year-Book of Facts in the Great Exhibition of 1851*. London: David Bogue.

Titmuss, R. 1970. *Gift Relationships*. London: George Allen and Unwin.

Vaniegem, R. 1983. *The Revolution of Everyday Life*. London: Rebel Press.

Vaniegem, R. 1990. *The Book of Pleasures*. London: Pending Press.

Veblen, T. 1987. *The Theory of the Leisure Class*. New York: Dover Publications.

Vergo, P., ed. 1989. *The New Museology*. London: Reaktion Books.

Vickery, A. 1998. *The Gentleman's Daughter: Women's Lives in Georgian England*. New Haven, CT: Yale University Press.

Vienet, R. 1990. *The Enrages and Situationists in the Occupation Movement, France, May 68*. London: Rebel Press.

Walkowitz, J. 1992. *City of Dreadful Delight: Narratives of Sexual Danger in Late-Victorian London*. London: Virago Press.

Walsh, J. 1874. *A Manual of Domestic Economy Suited to Families Spending From £150 to £1500 a Year*, rev. ed. London: George Routledge and Sons.

Watson, R. 1897. *The Art of the House*. London: George Bell and Son.

Weatherill, L. 1988. *Consumer Behaviour and Material Culture in Britain, 1660–1760*. London: Routledge.

Weber, M. 1978. *Economy and Society: An Outline of Interpretive Sociology, Volume 1*. Berkeley: University of California Press.

Weber, M. 1985. *The Protestant Ethic and the Spirit of Capitalism*. London: Counterpoint/Unwin.

Whewell, W. 1851. The general bearing of the Great Exhibition on the progress of art and science. Inaugural Lecture to the Society of Arts, 26 November 1851.

Whimster, S. and S. Lash. 1987. *Max Weber: Rationality and Modernity*. London: George Allen and Unwin.

Williams, R. 1982. *Dream Worlds: Mass Consumption in Late Nineteenth-Century France*. Berkeley: University of California Press.

Williams, R. 1992. *Notes on the Underground: An Essay on Technology, Society and the Imagination*. Cambridge, MA: MIT Press.

Willis, P. 1991. *Common Culture: Symbolic Work and Play in the Everyday Cultures of the Young*. Milton Keynes, UK: Open University Press.

Wilson, E. 1991. *The Sphinx in the City: Urban Life, the Control of Disorder and Women*. London: Virago Press.

Wilson, E. 2001. *The Contradictions of Culture: Cities, Culture, Women*. London: Sage/TCS.

Winckelmann, J. 1972. *Winckelmann: Writings on Art*. London: Phaidon.

Wolff, J. 1990. The invisible flaneuse: Women and the literature of modernity. In *Feminine Sentences: Essays on Women and Culture*, 34–50. Cambridge, UK: Polity Press.

Wolin, P. 1982. *Walter Benjamin*. New York: Columbia University Press.

Wolin, P. 1989a. Bitter victory: The art and politics of the Situationist International. In *On the Passage of a Few People through a Brief Moment in Time*, ed. E. Sussman, 20–61. Cambridge, MA: MIT Press.

Wolin, P. 1989b. Experience and materialism in Benjamin's Passagenwerk. In *Benjamin: Philosophy, Aesthetics, History*, ed. G. Smith, 210–227. Chicago: University of Chicago Press.

Yates, F. 1992. *The Art of Memory*. London: Pimlico.

Yeo, E. and S. Yeo, eds. 1981. *Popular Culture and Class Conflict, 1590–1914*. Brighton, UK: Harvester.

Young, H. 1999. *English Porcelain: Its Makers, Design, Marketing and Consumption*. London: Victoria and Albert Museum.

Ziarek, K. 2001. *The Historicity of Experience: Modernity, the Avant-Garde and the Event*. Evanston, IL: Northwestern University Press.

Zizek, S. 1989. *The Sublime Object of Ideology*. London: Verso.

Zukin, S. 1988. *Loft Living: Culture and Capital in Urban Change*. London: Radius.

Zukin, S. 1995. *The Cultures of Cities*. Oxford, UK: Blackwell.

Index